American Restaurant Design
アメリカのレストランデザイン

CONTENTS

NEW YORK NEW YORK HOTEL & CASINO < Las Vegas > 7
   IL FORNAIO CUCINA ITARIANA/10, IL FORNAIO PANETTERIA/14
   CHIN CHIN/16, RESTAURANT AMERICA/20, GALLAGHER'S STEAKHOUSE/24
   HAMILTON'S/26, CONEY ISLAND FOOD PAVILION/28

THE ORLEANS < Las Vegas > 30
   CANAL STREET GRILL/32, COURTYARD CAFE/34, VITO'S ITARIAN RESTAURANT/36
   DON MIGUEL'S/38, FRENCH MARKET BUFFET/40

MONTE CARLO RESORT & CASINO < Las Vegas > 42
   BUFFET/44, CAFE/46, DRAGON NOODLE COMPANY/48,
   MONACO GARDENS FOOD COURT/49, MARKET CITY CAFFE/50,
   MONTE CARLO PUB & BREWERY/52

THIRSTY BEAR < San Francisco > 56
HAWTHORNE LANE < San Francisco > 60
ROSE PISTOLA < San Francisco > 64
BABALOO < San Francisco > 68
VERTIGO RESTAURANT & BAR < San Francisco > 72
GRAND CAFE < San Francisco > 76
MONSOON CAFE < Santa Monica > 80
2424 PICO < Santa Monica > 84
WOLFGANG PUCK CAFE < Santa Monica > 88
OBACHINE < Beverly Hills > 92
LE COLONIAL < West Hollywood > 96
MONDRIAN HOTEL < Los Angeles > 100
   The Lobby Dinner/101, Coco Pazzo/102, The Pool Bar/105

JIRAFFE < Santa Monica > 106
FENIX < West Hollywood > 110
NICOLA < Los Angeles > 114
CAFE PINOT < Los Angeles > 118
ECLIPSE < West Hollywood > 122
THE ORIGINAL SONORA CAFE < Los Angeles > 126
BARNEY GREENGRASS < Beverly Hills > 130
CAVA < Los Angeles > 134
DAILY GRILL < Los Angeles > 138
TWIN PALMS < Pasadena > 142
IL FORNAIO CUCINA ITALIANA < Pasadena > 146
CHART HOUSE < Malibu > 150
RIVIERA < Redondo Beach > 154
CHIMAYO GRILL < Newport Beach > 158
ROUTE 66 < Pasadena > 162
THUNDER ROADHOUSE CAFE < West Hollywood > 166
DIVE < Los Angeles > 170
THE STINKING ROSE < Los Angeles > 176

INDEX 182

目　次

ニューヨーク・ニューヨーク・ホテル＆カジノ〈ラスベガス〉 …………………………… 7
　　イル・フォーナイオ・クチナ・イタリアーナ／10，イル・フォーナイオ・パネッテリア／14
　　チン・チン／16，レストラン・アメリカ／20，ガラガーズ・ステーキハウス．／24
　　ハミルトンズ／26，コニー・アイランド・フード・パビリオン／28

ジ・オーリンズ〈ラスベガス〉 ……………………………………………………………… 30
　　カナル・ストリート・グリル／32，コートヤード・カフェ／34，ヴィトス・イタリアン・レストラン／36，
　　ドン・ミゲルス／38，フレンチ・マーケット・ビュッフェ／40

モンテ・カルロ・リゾート＆カジノ〈ラスベガス〉 ……………………………………… 42
　　ビュッフェ／44，カフェ／46，ドラゴン・ヌードル・カンパニー／48，
　　モナコ・ガーデンズ・フードコート／49，マーケット・シティ・カフェ／50，
　　モンテカルロ・パブ＆ブリュワリー／52

サースティ・ベアー〈サンフランシスコ〉 ………………………………………………… 56
ホーソーン・レーン〈サンフランシスコ〉 ………………………………………………… 60
ローズ・ピストーラ〈サンフランシスコ〉 ………………………………………………… 64
ババルー〈サンフランシスコ〉 ……………………………………………………………… 68
バータゴウ・レストラン＆バー〈サンフランシスコ〉 …………………………………… 72
グランド・カフェ〈サンフランシスコ〉 …………………………………………………… 76
モンスーン・カフェ〈サンタモニカ〉 ……………………………………………………… 80
２４２４・ピコ〈サンタモニカ〉 …………………………………………………………… 84
ウルフガング・パック・カフェ〈サンタモニカ〉 ………………………………………… 88
オバシン〈ビバリーヒルズ〉 ………………………………………………………………… 92
ル・コロニアル〈ウエストハリウッド〉 …………………………………………………… 96
モンドリアン・ホテル〈ロサンゼルス〉 ……………………………………………………100
　　ザ・ロビー・ダイナー／101，ココ・パッツォ／102，ザ・プール・バー／105
ジラフ〈サンタモニカ〉 ………………………………………………………………………106
フェニックス〈ウエストハリウッド〉 ………………………………………………………110
ニコラ〈ロサンゼルス〉 ………………………………………………………………………114
カフェ・ピノ〈ロサンゼルス〉 ………………………………………………………………118
イクリプス〈ウエストハリウッド〉 …………………………………………………………122
ジ・オリジナル・ソノラ・カフェ〈ロサンゼルス〉 ………………………………………126
バーニィ・グリーングラス〈ビバリーヒルズ〉 ……………………………………………130
カバ〈ロサンゼルス〉 …………………………………………………………………………134
デイリー・グリル〈ロサンゼルス〉 …………………………………………………………138
ツイン・パームス〈パサデナ〉 ………………………………………………………………142
イル・フォーナイオ・クチナ・イタリアーナ〈パサデナ〉 ………………………………146
チャート・ハウス〈マリブ〉 …………………………………………………………………150
リビエラ〈レドンド・ビーチ〉 ………………………………………………………………154
チマヨ・グリル〈ニューポート・ビーチ〉 …………………………………………………158
ルート・６６〈パサデナ〉 ……………………………………………………………………162
サンダー・ロードハウス・カフェ〈ウエスト・ハリウッド〉 ……………………………166
ダイブ〈ロサンゼルス〉 ………………………………………………………………………170
ザ・スティンキング・ローズ〈ロサンゼルス〉 ……………………………………………176

索引 ……………………………………………………………………………………………182

Preface
Gen T. Saito

As I noticed during my long time on the scene, the American restaurant industry was drastically segmented as well as diversified in the 1970's and 1980's. Various dietary concepts, fads and trends influenced the eating habits of the American people as well as the food service industry in general. In particular, during the 1980's, a diversified "American food" was developed. Subsequently, international gourmets accepted the American cuisine even though it took as long as 200 years to gain that recognition.

Fast food and family restaurants have dominated the food service industry by creating manuals or standardizing design systems and improving productivity and efficiency on their premises. Innovative creators have always adopted new ideas and produced restaurants with various specialties and managerial styles, such as ethnic, trendy, casual, healthy, gourmet, and upscale restaurants, among others.

Restaurant types can be divided into several categories: the fast food/ family restaurant for adults as well as for children; the dinner restaurant, mainly for adults, with full menu and luxury premises; the fine dining restaurant, the most upscale; the theme restaurant with a clearly defined theme or atmosphere; and the casual restaurant with entertainment and an informal setting, popular with young adults. However, for all these restaurants, the dividing boundaries are becoming more and more vague as economic cycles and life styles change.

In particular, the American restaurant industry changed dramatically after the recession. High-class and expensive restaurants closed one after the other, and substantial new investment was temporarily halted. Instead, a sense of value, quality, health, and entertainment was pursued. As discussed in "American Restaurant Design," recent restaurant designs and menus reflect the owners' concepts and ideas, with a strong emphasis on originality.

Since people come from all over the world to live in "the melting pot" of America, various ethnic restaurants, such as Italian, French, Mexican, Thai, Chinese, and Vietnamese, are naturally popular in the United States. Here, after having adopted Pan-Asian, Caribbean, and Mediterranean cuisine, restaurants can now offer specialties from almost all countries of the world. Further, trendy menus can also be observed in restaurants. Some premises are now equipped with open kitchens, mesquite grills, wood burning ovens, and display counters, creating impressive visual images as well as adopting a wide range of cooking procedures.

As far as restaurant design is concerned, there are many trends: contemporary designs using high technology; designs emphasizing natural tastes and materials; designs with original art works; designs adopting foreign cultures and regional characters; and characteristic designs with automobiles, motorcycles, submarines, and breweries, for instance.

"American Restaurant Design" introduces not only popular restaurants in Los Angeles and San Francisco, whose residents are presumably as trend-conseious as New Yorkers, but also more recent hotel restaurants in Las Vegas. Reference information for the restaurants as well as photographs of their specialties are listed in the index.

September, 1997

序文
斎藤 武

米国のレストラン業界を長年取材していると、1970～80年代は業態の区分化や多様化が顕著に行なわれた時代であった。斬新なコンセプトの出現、トレンドや一時的流行が外食様式と食習慣に影響を及ぼし続けた。特に、1980年代はフード革命の中にあって、多様化した"アメリカ料理"が美味しく、素晴らしいということを認識した時期とも云える。そして、世界の美食家たちも漸くアメリカ料理を認めるようになったわけであるが、それまでには実に200年以上もかかっている。

レストラン業界はシステム、生産性、効率、店舗デザインの統一などを追求してマニュアル化し、発展してきたファーストフードやファミリーレストラン業界に学ぶものも多かった。さらに、革新的コンセプトのクリエイターたちは絶えず、新しいアイデアを投入し、エスニック、トレンド、カジュアル、ヘルシー、グルメ、アップスケールなどと呼ぶ様々な形態と業態のレストランを生み出してきた。

大人から子供まで幅広い利用ができるファーストフード店やファミリーレストラン、やや重装備の建物で、フルメニューを持ち、アダルトを中心とした客層が利用するディナーレストラン、最も高級に属するファインダイニング・レストラン、はっきりとしたテーマや雰囲気を持つテーマ・レストラン、エンターテイメント性やカジュアルな雰囲気を持ち、ヤング・アダルトたちに好評のカジュアル・レストランなどに区分化されるレストランの業態は、今日ではその境界線が崩れ、経済状況の変化や、めまぐるしく変わるライフスタイルによって、より柔軟化している。

特に、リセッション（景気後退）を境に米国のレストラン業界は大きく変化した。高級レストランが次々と閉店し、多大な投資を一時的に避け、それに変わって価値（バリュー）や品質（クオリティ）、健康や娯楽（エンターテイメント）が求められるようになった。本書に紹介するレストランのように、オーナーの考えや姿勢が強く反映し、より個性化を追求する料理や店舗のデザインが前面に出てきている。

多国籍の人々が集まり、住むアメリカでは、当然のことながらイタリア、フランス、メキシコ、タイ、中国、ベトナムといったエスニック料理が人気を呼び、汎アジア、カリブ、地中海までも取り入れ、今や、世界中の料理が食べられる。加えて、トレンディな料理の登場もみられる。店内には、オープンキッチン、メスキート・グリル、ウッドバーニング・オーブン、ディスプレイ・カウンターなどが設置され、視覚に訴えるイメージ作りと共に巾の広い調理法が導入されてきた。

店舗デザインの面では、ハイテクデザインのコンテンポラリーな店、自然の素材を強調し、活かした店、アーティストたちの作品を飾る店、異国文化や地域の特色を取り入れた店、車やモーターサイクル、潜水艦、自家製ビールなどをテーマとした店など、多岐にわたる。

ニューヨークと共に、トレンドにうるさいと云われるロサンゼルスやサンフランシスコのレストランを中心に、ラスベガスに於ける最新のホテルなどのレストランを含めて紹介した。尚、本書の最後に各レストランの特徴ある料理写真を、店舗のインフォーメーションとして紹介しているので参考にして戴きたい。

1997年9月

American Restaurant Design

Author/Photographer: Gen T. Saito

Publisher: Mitsuo Tada

Executive and Editorial Office:
PROTGALAXY Inc.

[address partially obscured by sticker] 5640-1755

[partially obscured] om/

Editorial Management and Design:
Miwako Ito

Adviser: Hiroshi Tsujita

Translator: Shintaro Okazaki
        (Okazaki Benavent Asociados S.L.)

[partially obscured by sticker] by

All rights reserved.
ISBN 4-89460-042-0 C3052 Y9800E

C.H.I.P.S.
1307 Golden Bear Lane
Kingwood TX 77339 U.S.A.
Tel: 281 359 2270
Fax: 281 359 2277
www.chipsbooks.com

NEW YORK NEW YORK HOTEL & CASINO ＜ Las Vegas ＞
ニューヨーク・ニューヨーク・ホテル&カジノ＜ラスベガス＞

Address: 3790 Las Vegas Boulevard, Las Vegas, Nevada 89109
Phone/702-740-6969 FAX/702-740-6510
Owner: MGM Grand, Inc., Primadonna Resorts, Inc.
Design: Architecture/Gaskin & Bezanski, Interior/Yates Silverman

New York New York Hotel & Casino in Las Vegas, Nevada, was inspired by Manhattan's skyline as seen from the Brooklyn Bridge and designed as a theme-park-hotel featuring a roller coaster around the building. It took approximately two years to complete this 460 million-dollar project.

The hotel includes 2,034 guest rooms and a 7,800m² (84,000 sq.ft.) casino space with 2,400 slot machines and 71 game tables. Such typical Manhattan views as Park Avenue, Broadway, Times Square, Wall Street, Greenwich Village and Central Park were recreated in the casino, which is surrounded by bars, restaurants, and shops. The second floor consists of a 2,600m² (28,000 sq.ft.) entertainment area with game machines as well as a fast-food restaurant. In addition to the gambling facilities, the hotel includes a variety of facilities, such as an outdoor pool, a wedding chapel, party/meeting rooms and a spa, in order to emphasize its concept of creating a family-oriented hotel atmosphere enjoyable not only for adults but also for children. All food service facilities are provided by extremely popular and prestigious restaurants in New York and Los Angeles, including the following:

ニューヨークのブルックリン橋から見るマンハッタンのスカイラインの外観をイメージ・テーマとするテーマパーク型のカジノ・ホテルである。総工費4億6,000万ドルを投じ、約2年をかけて建築された。8haの敷地に2,034室の客室と2,400台のスロットマシーンや71台のゲームテーブルなどを置く、7,800㎡の［セントラルパーク・カジノ］がある。このカジノエリアはマンハッタンのパークアベニューやブロードウエイ、タイムズ・スクエア、ウォール街、グリニッチ・ビレッジ、セントラル・パークなどの街並みの雰囲気が見事に再現されている。その周辺にはバーやレストラン、ショップなどがある。

2階には［コニーアイランド・エンポリアム］と名付けた2,600㎡のゲームコーナーを設け、ハイテク機器を用いたゲーム機や乗物などの娯楽施設、ファストフード・レストランなどで構成している。

その他、アウトドア・プール、ウエディング・チャペル、宴会/会議室、スパなどの施設を備えており、ギャンブルだけでなく、子供も大人も楽しめるファミリー向きのホテルのコンセプトを強調している。また、このホテルの飲食施設はすべて、代表的な繁盛店のテナント導入を計っているのが特徴である。それらの中から大型店の7店を紹介する。

Hotel exterior, looking over 12 landmark buildings, a 46-meter high Statute of Liberty and the Brooklyn Bridge.
ラスベガス大通りとトロピカナ通りの交差するコーナーにマンハッタンが移ってきたかのようなホテルの外観。12のランドマークタワーや46mの自由の女神、ブルックリン橋などが見える。

Night view of famous skyscrapers in New York, including the Empire State Building, Chrysler Building, AT&T and CBS. A roller coaster named "Manhattan Express" runs around the building.
47階建てのエンパイア・ステートビルをはじめクライスラービル、ＡＴ＆Ｔ，ＣＢＳ．などＮＹの有名なタワービル群の夜景。それらの周りを走るローラーコースター［マンハッタン・エキスプレス］の施設。

■ : Restaurant Area. レストラン・エリア

Opposite: "Empire Lounge" produces 1930-1940's American nightclub shows. The two-football-stadium-sized "Central Park Casino" is behind.
右ページ：フットボール場を２つ合わせた広さの［セントラルパーク・カジノ］。1930～40年代の米国のナイトクラブを演出する手前の［エンパイア・ラウンジ］中央にはＮＹを象徴するビッグ・アップルがある。スロットマシーンが並ぶ奥にセントラルパークの森が見える。

NEW YORK NEW YORK HOTEL & CASINO ＜Las Vegas＞
"Il Fornaio Cucina Italiana"
「イル・フォーナイオ・クチナ・イタリアーナ」

Opposite: Overview of the (150-seat) interior space from the entrance area. This Italian restaurant is one of 12 in California. The main branch is located in San Francisco.

右ページ：ダイニングエリアの入口あたりから見る、高い空間を持つ店内（150席）。サンフランシスコに本社を置き、カリフォルニア州を中心に現在12店舗をチェーン展開するイタリアン・レストラン。

Restaurant facade.
セントラルパーク内の小川や橋、木々などを取り入れたカジノエリアに面したレストランのファサード。

Open kitchen.
桝状にレイアウトされた客席の仕切りには透明のガラスが用いてある。その奥にオープンキッチンを設けている。入口あたりに置かれた数種類の自家製パンのディスプレイが店内の色に溶け込んでいる。

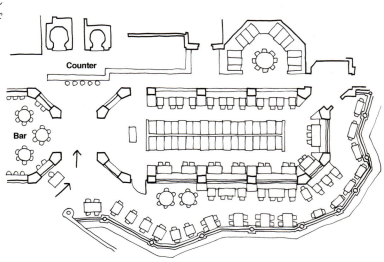

Above: Bar area. Inside the iron door, there's a wine cellar located in the central part of the counter.
Above right: Dining area in the rear.
Right: Open kitchen with counter seats.

上：大理石の円形テーブルとハイ・スツールを配したバーエリア。カウンター中央部にある鉄製扉の奥はワインセラーとなっている。
上右：イタリアの風景や人々を撮ったモノクロ写真を飾る後方に設けたダイニングエリア。
下右：カウンター席を設けるオープンキッチン。このように単独の客にも配慮し、カウンター席やコーナーを設ける店が多くなっている。

NEW YORK NEW YORK HOTEL & CASINO ＜ Las Vegas ＞
"Il Fornaio Panetteria"
「イル・フォーナイオ・パネッテリア」

Guest seats with marbled tabletops and merchandise shelves on the wall.
大理石のテーブルトップを配した客席と大きな鏡を組み込む壁面の商品棚。

Facade of the coffee shop managed by "Il Fornaio Panetteria" restaurant.
[イル・フォーナイオ・レストラン]の経営によるコーヒーショップのファサード。自家製パン、サンドイッチ、エスプレッソ・コーヒーなどを売る。

Interior space of a (32-seat) take-out corner.
左右対象にレイアウトされたテイクアウト方式の店内(32席)。一日平均700〜800人の利用がある。

NEW YORK NEW YORK HOTEL & CASINO ＜ Las Vegas ＞
"Chin Chin"
「チン・チン」

Below: Facade of Chin Chin. This Chinese restaurant has expanded with five branches around Los Angeles.
Opposite: Casual cafe-style (150-seat) interior space.
下：現在ロサンゼルスを中心に５店舗を展開している中華レストランの［チン・チン］は、ホテル内への最初の出店となる。上部にセントラルパークの風景画の壁面を見る。箸をネオンサインに組み込んでいる開放的なファサード。
右ページ：店頭部にのみ円形のテーブル席を設けている。テーブルをスポットライトに沿って配列したカジュアルなカフェスタイルの店内（150席）。

Stainless steel open kitchen. White, green and plum are the uniform colors for all restaurants in the chain.
クリーンでコンテンポラリーのスタイリッシュな店内。奥にステンレススティールを配したオープンキッチンを設けている。ホワイトやグリーン、プラムなどの色を全店の共通したテーマカラーとしている。

Ceiling designed with copper sheets. Terrazzo floors powdered with gold dust.
Mirrors on columns and walls give an illusion of unifying two separate dining rooms.
コパー(銅)の板を貼った天井のデザイン。金粉をあしらったテラゾーのフロア。柱や壁面の鏡は、
2つに分かれているダイニングルームを1つの空間として感じさせる。

NEW YORK NEW YORK HOTEL & CASINO < Las Vegas >

"Restaurant America"
「レストラン・アメリカ」

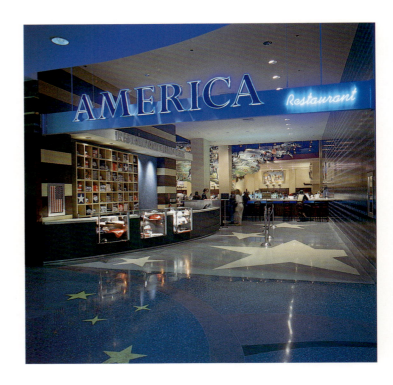

Right: 24-hour open family restaurant. Gift corner and facade. The design of the sign was based on the blue stripes of the American flag.
Below: Bar area (20-seat) near the entrance. Various local specialties are offered at the family restaurant, whose images were inspired by traditional Americana.
Opposite: Famous speeches delivered by American presidents cover the blue walls in the bar area.
右: 24時間営業のファミリー・レストラン。国旗の中のブルーをサインに取り入れているファサード。星条旗のイメージを持つキャラクター商品を売るギフトコーナーを店頭に設ける。
下: レセプションの近くに設けるバーエリア (20席)。「アメリカ」をテーマとする店舗のイメージと各地の郷土料理をメニューに加えるなどが特徴のファミリー・レストラン。
右ページ: バーエリアのブルーの壁面は、米国大統領の有名な演説文で構成する。柱の上部のショーケースを照らす数多くのスポットライトが見える。

Large showcase (27 x 6 meter) in the shape of the United States. This restaurant has its main branch in New York with 4 branches in Washington, D.C. and Nevada.
アメリカの地図を型取った大きなショーケース(27m×6m)を店内中央部に置く。ニューヨークに本店を持ち、ワシントンD.C.とネバダ州に4店舗を経営する。

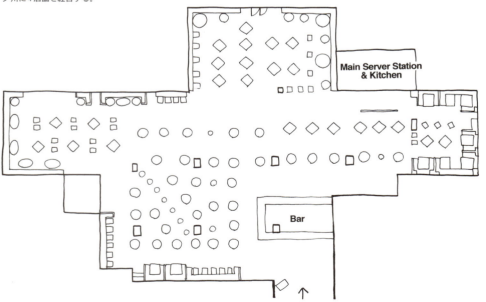

Opposite: Dining area and the showcase indicating local products and places throughout the United Sates.
右ページ：米国各地の特色を示す名産や地名を表示したショーケースと壁面で構成するダイニングエリア。

NEW YORK NEW YORK HOTEL & CASINO ＜ Las Vegas ＞
"Gallagher's Steakhouse"
「ガラガーズ・ステーキハウス」

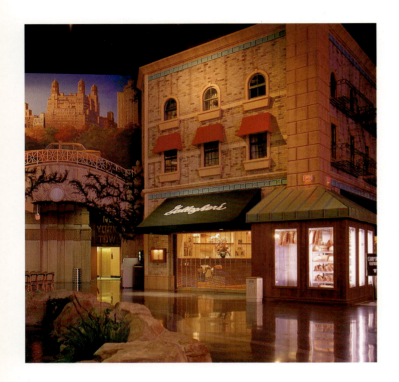

Left: Premises in Greenwich Village, with background of Central Park. The first floor is a steak house, with a showcase for aged beef in the front.
Below: Bar (40-seat) facing the street.
左：イエローキャブが走るセントラルパークの中から見える風景を背景にして建つ、グリニッチ・ビレッジの建物。その一階にあるステーキレストランの店頭にステーキ肉のショーケースを設けている。
下：外の通りに面して設けたバーコーナー（40席）。食事のサービスもしている。

Long-established (185-seat) steak house opened in 1927 in New York.
1927年にニューヨークにオープンした老舗のステーキハウスの出店。有名人の写真を飾った壁面で構成する店内（185席）は、ＮＹ店と同じ雰囲気のダイニングエリア。

NEW YORK NEW YORK HOTEL & CASINO ＜ Las Vegas ＞

"Hamilton's"
「ハミルトンズ」

Interior room with 1930-1940's club setting.
1930〜40年代のクラブの雰囲気を持つ奥の別室。カーテンのある窓は透視ガラスを備え、カジノエリアを見渡せる。

Opposite: Cigar bar and lounge owned by the actor George Hamilton.
左：俳優のジョージ・ハミルトンが経営するシガーバー。中央の夜空を想わせる天井とＮＹの夜景を見下ろす窓の造りを設けたラウンジ。

NEW YORK NEW YORK HOTEL & CASINO ＜ Las Vegas ＞
"Coney Island Food Pavilion"
「コニー・アイランド・フード・パビリオン」

Entrance to the food court attached to the game corner on the second floor.
2階のゲームコーナーに併設しているフードコートの入口。朝食時から午前2時までの営業。

Restaurants include "Nathan's" which has chains in New York area and fast-food shops, which are managed by "Haagen-Dazs". Interior decorations of the restaurant (100-seat) inspired by Grand Central Station and metro station yards in New York.
ＮＹを中心にチェーン展開しているファミリー・レストランの［ネイザンズ］や［ハーゲンダッツ］が経営するファストフード店の集まり。ＮＹのグランド・セントラル駅や地下鉄駅の構内をモチーフにした店内（100席）。

THE ORLEANS ＜Las Vegas＞
ジ・オーリンズ＜ラスベガス＞

Address:　4500 West Tropicana Avenue, Las Vegas, Nevada 89103
　　　　　　Phone/702-365-7111　FAX/702-365-7499
Developer: Coast Hotels & Casinos, Inc.
Designer:　Architecture/Leo A. Daly　Interior/Yates-Silverman, Inc.

The design theme of this casino hotel, The Orleans, was taken from one of the most popular cities for American tourists, New Orleans, Louisiana. Its facade and interior facilities remind visitors of the streets of the French Quarter as well as French and Spanish colonial plantations.

　The 38 ha (88 acre) site includes a 8,600m² (92,000 sq. ft.) public space and various buildings, including casinos, restaurants and party rooms, a 22-story hotel with 840 rooms as well as a parking space for 4,000 cars. On the first floor, the casino area has 2,100 slot machines, 60 game tables, poker tables, a keno lounge, four bars, gift shops, and seven restaurants. On the second floor, the 3,700m² (40,000-sq. ft.) area consists of a banquet room, a convention room, a wedding chapel, a bowling center and a beauty salon. A pool with full-service bar facilities will be completed soon while additional plans for a movie theater, several restaurants and retail shops are under consideration.

米国のツーリストたちに人気のある都市の1つ、ニューオーリンズをデザイン・テーマにしたカジノ・ホテルである。フレンチ・クォーターの街並みをはじめ、フレンチ、スパニッシュ、プランテーション・コロニアル（農園スタイル）などの雰囲気をファサードや内部に取り入れている。38haの敷地内に4,000台のパーキングスペースと22階建て840室の宿泊棟、カジノやレストラン、宴会場などが集まる8,560㎡のパブリック施設の棟とで構成している。1階のカジノエリアには、2,100台のスロットマシーンや60台のゲームテーブル、ポーカールーム、キノ・ラウンジ、4つのバー、ギフトショップなどがあり、その周辺に77つのレストラン施設を設けている。2階には合計3,720㎡の宴会場と会議室、ウエディング・チャペル、ボーリングセンター、ビューティサロンなどがある。フルサービスのバーを併設したプールも近く完成の予定であり、更に、ムービーシアターや幾つかのレストラン、リテイルショップなどの増設も計画されている。

　ここではファーストフード・レストランを除く5つのレストランを紹介する。

Hotel exterior. 宿泊棟とパブリックエリアの集まるニューオーリンズ・スタイルの建物で構成するホテルの外観。

Atrium with 12-meter high ceiling in the central area of the casino, which represents typical streets in New Orleans. "The Alligator Bar" is one of four bars on either side of the game tables.
天井高12mのカジノエリア中央部のアトリウムは、ニューオーリンズの典型的な街並みを表現する。ゲームテーブルを挟んで両側に、［アリゲーター・バー］をはじめ4つのバーが設けてある。

THE ORLEANS ＜ Las Vegas ＞
"Canal Street Grill"
「カナル・ストリート・グリル」

Right: Vaulted entrance, consisting of copper chandeliers, marbled cylinders, round design-floor and a door with circular glass.
Bottom: Booths around wall paintings of canals and forests with sunset-colored ceiling above. The (194-seat) interior atmosphere changes in accordance with the lighting conditions.

右：雲と青空を配した円形ドームのエントランス。銅製のシャンデリア、大理石の円柱、円形のデザインフロアー、円形ガラスを用いたドア周りなどで構成し、重厚さを感じさせている。
下：運河と森を描いた壁画の周りにブース席を配し、その上部の天井は夕焼けを表現するような色を取り入れて、調光の変化と共に店内（194席）の雰囲気が変えられるようになっている。

The most upscale restaurant in the hotel.
レストランの後方にはファイアープレイスと豪華なシャンデリアがあるエレガントな客席を設けている。このホテル内の最も格調高いレストランである。

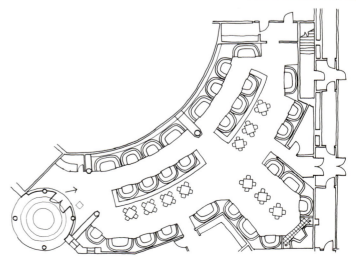

THE ORLEANS ＜Las Vegas＞
"Courtyard Cafe"
「コートヤード・カフェ」

Opposite: 302-seat interior space with keno game board on the wall.
左：グリーンを強調した302席の店内。壁面にはキノ・ゲームの表示ボードが設置されている。

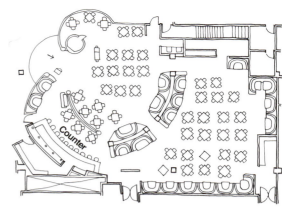

Entrance of the 24-hour open coffee shop.　ニューオーリンズにはコートヤードがたくさん見られる。そのような雰囲気を取り入れた24時間営業のコーヒーショップの入口あたり。

Counter seat area.　四角いパターンのタイルの壁面やフロアーを配したカウンター席のあたり。天井は石膏のデザインを施してある。

THE ORLEANS ＜Las Vegas＞
"Vito's Itarian Restaurant"
「ヴィトス・イタリアン・レストラン」

Opposite: Dining room (120-seat).
右：レストランをテーマとした絵が壁面を飾るダイニングルーム（120席）。

Reception area of the Italian restaurant on the second floor. Corinthian columns separate the dining area.
2階にあるイタリアン・レストランのレセプションあたり。コリント式の支柱を設けてダイニングエリアを仕切る。

Table seats and booth seats in the interior space. 店内はテーブル席とブース席の他にピアノバーを加え、バーエリアからはアトリウムのあるカジノが見える。

THE ORLEANS < Las Vegas >
"Don Miguel's"
「ドン・ミゲルス」

Right: Entrance area of the restaurant. Glass-cased tortilla displays in the front and reception area.
Below: Margarita bar lounge (30-seat).
右：レストランの入口あたり。店頭に設けるガラスで囲んだトルティーヤのクッキングディスプレイとレセプションを見る。
下：円形の天井部に鏡を配した［マルガリータ・バー］のラウンジ（30席）。

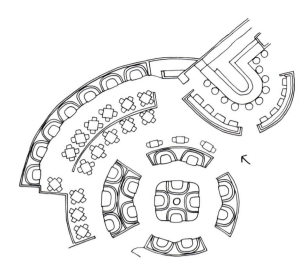

Dining area (158-seat) of the Mexican restaurant and booth seats surrounded with illusory walls.
メキシカンレストランのダイニングエリア（158席）は、だまし絵のある壁面構成でブース席も設けている。

THE ORLEANS ＜ Las Vegas ＞
"French Market Buffet"
「フレンチ・マーケット・ビュッフェ」

Below: Entrance area. This (344-seat) buffet restaurant was designed with bricks and iron works in the popular style of New Orleans.
Opposite: Self-service buffet counter.
下：ニューオーリンズに見られる、レンガやアイアンワークのデザインを取り入れた建物を想わせる造りのビュッフェ・レストラン（344席）。
右ページ：セルフサービスの料理カウンター。ブラスのフレームを用いた素ガラスの覆いを配し、明るい照明で照らす。

MONTE CARLO RESORT & CASINO ＜Las Vegas＞
モンテ・カルロ・リゾート&カジノ＜ラスベガス＞

Address: 3770 Las Vegas Boulevard, South Las Vegas, Nevada 89109
Phone/702-730-7777
Owner: Circus Circus Enterprises, Inc., Mirage Resort, Inc.
Designer: Architecture/Dougall Design, Los Angeles., Gaskin & Bezanski, Las Vegas

This 344 million-dollar resort hotel development, Monte Carlo Resort & Casino, was modeled after Place du Casino, Monte Carlo, Monaco.

The interior space consists of an arched hall with a high ceiling, a dome with chandeliers, beautifully marbled floors, carved fountains, a promenade lined with gas lights and gothic windows, all of which display graceful stateliness.

The site includes a casino space with 3,200 rooms, 2,200 slot machines, and 95 game tables as well as a 550-seat bingo room, 1,800m² (20,000-sq. ft.) retail shopping area, 1,400m² (15,000-sq. ft.) meeting space, river-like pools, a wedding chapel, a health center and seven restaurant facilities. Except for the steak restaurant, the facility includes the following six restaurants.

モンテカルロ（モナコ）の［カジノ・パレス］をモデルにして、総工費3億4,400万ドルを投じて建造された、豪華さを誇るリゾートホテルである。

内部にはアーチを用いた高い空間、シャンデリアを配したドーム、マーブルが美しいフロア、彫刻を凝らした噴水、ガスライトの並ぶプロムナード、ゴシック調のガラス窓などで重厚さと優雅さを表現している。

このホテルは、3,200室の客室と2,200台のスロットマシーン、95台のゲームテーブルをはじめ550席のビンゴルームなどを含むカジノスペース、1,860㎡のリテイル・ショッピングエリア、1,400㎡の会議・宴会場、川や波の演出をしたプールエリア、ウエディングチャペル、ヘルスセンター等と7つのレストラン施設で構成している。ここではその中のステーキ・レストランを除く6つのレストランを紹介する

Hotel entrance with European design and atmosphere.
ヨーロッパ・スタイルのデザインと雰囲気を取り入れたホテルのエントランス。飾りを凝らした噴水やアーチ、巨大な芸術作品の像などで格調を高めている。

Opposite: Stained-glass dome and bar area in the casino space.
右ページ：カジノ・スペースの中に設けたステンドグラスのドームとバー。

MONTE CARLO RESORT & CASINO ＜Las Vegas＞
"Buffet"
「ビュッフェ」

Buffet restaurant with images of a Moroccan palace. Buffet counter offers various dishes.
モロッコの宮殿をイメージした造りのビュッフェ・スタイルのレストラン。後方奥に料理を並べたカウンターが設けてある。

Central part of (700-seat) dining area, consisting of columns with arches against a blue-sky background.
ブルースカイとアーチを配した柱で構成するダイニングエリア（700席）の中央部。

MONTE CARLO RESORT & CASINO ＜Las Vegas＞
"Cafe"
「カフェ」

Below: Entrance to the 24-hour coffee shop, "Cafe".
Opposite: Open-air (350-seat) garden terrace dining in European style, where customers enjoy themselves under the open sky.
下：24時間営業のコーヒーショップ［カフェ］のエントランス。開放的な造りで、カジノから店内が見える。
右ページ：青空の下で食事を楽しむ、ヨーロッパのガーデン・テラスを設定したダイニングルーム（350席）。天井部に設けた空の感じは星空にも変化する。

MONTE CARLO RESORT & CASINO ＜ Las Vegas ＞

"Dragon Noodle Company"
「ドラゴン・ヌードル・カンパニー」

Counter area with open kitchen, as seen from the front. Inner (200-seat) dining area was designed with various Chinese images in mind.
強烈な朱色を使用した店頭部からオープンキッチンを備えたカウンター方向を見る。奥にあるダイニングエリア（200席）は中国をイメージした造りとなっている。

MONTE CARLO RESORT & CASINO ＜ Las Vegas ＞
"Monaco Gardens Food Court"
「モナコ・ガーデンズ・フードコート」

Next to the casino area, there is common dining space shared by five restaurants, including the neighboring "McDonald's", which has adopted a palace courtyard setting.
カジノエリアに隣接し、"夢の通り"と名付けた場所にある。宮殿のコートヤードの中の雰囲気を取り入れ、210席のテーブル席を設ける。併設する［マクドナルド］などを含む5店のファストフード店の共用ダイニングのスペースとなっている。

MONTE CARLO RESORT & CASINO ＜ Las Vegas ＞
"Market City Caffe"
「マーケット・シティ・カフェ」

Casual Italian restaurant with terraced seats. White-tiled pizza oven and wooden counter seats.
テラス席を設けたカジュアルなイタリアンレストラン。店頭部には白いタイルのピザ・オーブンと木製のバーカウンターを備えている。

At central right, antipasto bar with images taken from a local Italian brassiere. Dining area (250-seat) with trattoria setting.
イタリアで見かける食料品店を演出したアンティパスト・バーを右側中央に見る。奥にはトラットリアの雰囲気を取り入れたダイニングルーム（250席）がある。

MONTE CARLO RESORT & CASINO ＜ Las Vegas ＞
"Monte Carlo Pub & Brewery"
「モンテカルロ・パブ＆ブリュワリー」

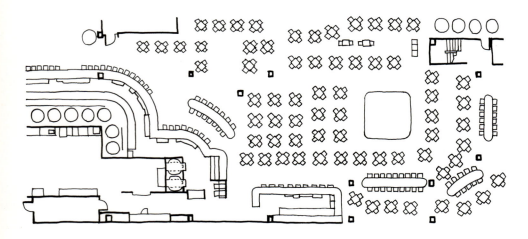

Below: Bar corner, looking from the high ceiling of the second floor.
Opposite: This pub restaurant, under the hotel's direct management, recalls a brewery restaurant. Bar area, as seen from the table seats with custom-made iron chairs.
下：2階から見る店内。トランプゲーム機を組み込むカウンターバーを含む2つのバーコーナーを設けている。
右ページ：ホテルの直営パブ・レストラン（420席）はビール工場の中のレストランの雰囲気。鉄製のカスタムメイドのチェアーを備えるテーブル席からバー方向を見る。カウンターの中にレンガ造りのウッドファイアード・オープン/グリルを設けている。

Interior space of one of the largest brew pubs in the United States.
米国で最も規模の大きなブルー・パブの1つとされる店内には、ライブ演奏のステージが設けてある。広い店内の数多くのTVモニターでは、ライブの様子やスポーツ番組の中継などを流している。

Opposite: The brewery, behind the bar corner, produces six kinds of homemade beer. Big copper barrels and pipes create a brew pub atmosphere.
右ページ：バーコーナーの後方に設置したビール工場では6種類の自家製ビールを製造する。ビッグサイズのコパーのバーレルや管を配してブルー・パブの雰囲気を演出している。

THIRSTY BEAR ＜San Francisco＞
サースティ・ベアー＜サンフランシスコ＞

Address: 661 Howard Street, San Francisco, CA 94105
　　　　　Phone/415-974-0945　FAX/415-974-0955
Designer: Architecture/Roddy Creedon,
　　　　　Allied Architectire And Design

Left: Facade with huge logotype which is also used on the coasters.
Below: Bar area in the central part of the first floor.
左：コースターにも使用している巨大なロゴを配したファサード。
下：1階中央部に設けたバーエリア。暖かな照明の店内は高い天井を支える木製のコラムやビーム、古いレンガの壁、コンクリートのフロアーなどでビアレストランの雰囲気を醸し出している。

Behind the bar corner, six stainless barrels are displayed and visible from every seat on the premises.
バーコーナーの後方には6基のステンレス製バーレルが、ショーケースのように店内のどの席からも見えるように置かれている。

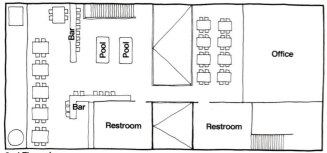

2nd Floor plan

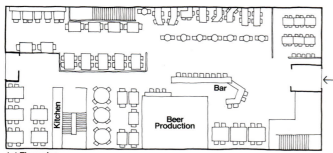

1st Floor plan

The raised dining area, which has wheelchair access, and the open kitchen.
車椅子用のスロープを設け、一段高くなった奥のダイニングエリアとオープンキッチン。

This brewery and restaurant is located in a renovated brick warehouse in downtown San Francisco, California.

The interior space extends far back, and it has two floors with 4.6 meters (15-foot) ceilings. The first floor includes a bar area (80 seats), a dining area (120 seats), a brewery and an open kitchen, while the second floor, which is mainly used for parties, consists of bars, a banquet room, pool tables and an amusement area with darts boards. The Thirsty Bear offers eight different kinds of beer as well as Spanish foods from the Catalan and Basque regions. Small dishes called "tapas" are the most popular entrees.

サンフランシスコのダウンタウンのブリュワリー/レストラン。コンベンションセンターから半ブロック東に位置し、近くにはモダンアート美術館もある。

レンガ造りの倉庫を改装した奥行きのある店内は2層構造で、天井高4.6mの空間を持つ1階はバーエリア（80席）とダイニングエリア（120席）、自家製ビール製造工場、オープンキッチンなどで構成している。2階はバーとバンケットルーム、プールテーブルやダーツのプレイエリアが設けられ、主にパーティ席として使用している。

8種類の自家製ビールとスペインのカタロニアやバスク地方の料理を提供し、特に小皿のタパス料理が好評である。

Opposite: Bar and entrance areas, looking from the center of the skylit staircase.
前ページ：自然光の入る階段中央部から見るバーと店頭方向。

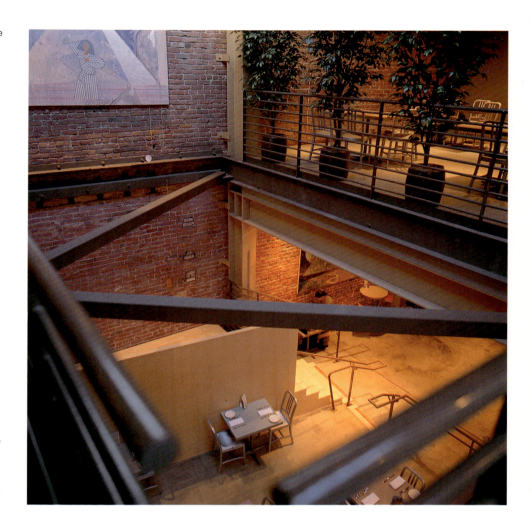

Right: Space on the second floor, separating the play area and the banquet room.
Below: Pool bar, with 40-seat banquet area behind.
右：プレイエリアとバンケットルームを分ける2階の空間部。
下：手前のプール・バーとその向こう側に40席のバンケットエリアがある。

HAWTHORNE LANE ＜San Francisco＞

ホーソーン・レーン＜サンフランシスコ＞

Address: 22 Hawthorn Street (at Howard), San Francisco, CA 94105
Phone/415-777-9779 FAX/415-777-9782
Designer: Architecture/Valerio, Dewalt, Train Associates, Chicago
Searl and Associates, Chicago
Graphic/Hunt-Weber Clark Associates, San Francisco

The establishment is located on the first floor of a brick building, the historic Crown Point Press, which was built in 1922. Its exterior is covered with ivy and has a stately wrought iron gate entrance.

The interior space has been divided into two different spaces: a 120-seat casual cafe with a central cherry-wood bar area and a 140-seat slightly formal dining room with natural lighting. In the latter space, the spacious area has two centered elliptic service stations, and the tables are covered with white tablecloths.

The open kitchen has wood-burning brick ovens and grills. Sufficient daylight is provided from the northern side. The owners and chefs, Ann and David Gingrass, who are particular about the quality and freshness of their locally produced food, offer a creative Californian menu influenced by Asian and European cuisine.

店名の"ホーソーン・レーン"はこのレストランの入口にある通りの名前を指す。1922年に建造されたレンガ造りのクラウン・ポイントプレスビルの1階に位置する。外壁はアイビーに覆われ、重厚な鉄製のゲイトがあるエントランス廻りなど、歴史を感じさせる建物である。

店内は1つの建物のスペースの中に2つのレストランシーンを展開している。それらは、中央部にチェリーウッドのバーを設けたカジュアルなカフェ（120席）とコリドーの奥にある自然光を取り入れた、ややフォーマルなダイニングルーム（140席）で構成する。ナプキンとパン皿を置くウッドトップのテーブルを配したカフェでは簡単な食事ができる。一方のホワイト・テーブルクロスを配したダイニングエリアは、中央に2つの楕円形のサービス・ステーションを設けて広いスペースをうまく仕切っている。北側に設ける自然光を十分に取り入れたオープンキッチンには、ウッドバーニングのレンガのオーブンとグリルを備えている。

オーナーシェフのアン＆デイビッド・ジングラス夫妻は、名シェフ・ウルフガング・パック氏の下で名を上げた人たちであり、ローカルの新鮮な食材と質にこだわり、アジアとヨーロッパの料理に影響された独自のクリエイティブなカリフォルニア料理を提供している。

Cafe with cherry-wood bar in the central space, where booth seats are lined alongside white walls.
広々とした空間の中央部に楕円形の天井デザインとチェリーウッドのバーを設けるカフェ。白い壁面に沿ってブース席が並ぶ。

Cafe, looking from the entrance area. 入口あたりから見るカフェ。手前の木の仕切りに窓を設け、木の枝をデザインした鉄製のオブジェを配している。

Premises in a historic building.
1922年に建てられた歴史のあるレンガ造りのビルの1階に出店したレストランは、重厚な鉄製のゲートのエントランスを設けている。

A central, short corridor leads to a dining room.
ウッドトップのテーブルを配したカフェ。中央のダークウッドの床から短かいコリドーを通ってダイニングルームへ導く。

Service area under a loft-like ceiling. ロフト状の天井の下に設けたサービスエリア。

Open kitchen. 自然光を取り入れた広いスペースを持つオープンキッチン。

Dining room, looking at the open kitchen. 手前に円形の大型テーブル、向こう側に四角のテーブルを配したダイニングルーム。正面奥にオープンキッチンが見える。

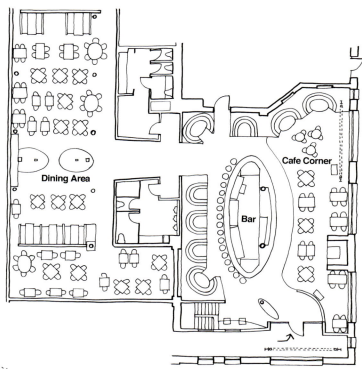

Fine Art Prints by Crown Point Press, Inc. decorate white walls with columns.
円柱を配した白い壁面に飾る絵は、クラウン・ポイントプレス社のファイン・アートプリントのコレクション。

ROSE PISTOLA ＜San Francisco＞
ローズ・ピストーラ＜サンフランシスコ＞

Address: 532 Colunbus Avenue, San Francisco, CA 94133
Phone/415-399-0499 FAX/415-399-8758
Designer:Architecture/Cass Calder Smith

Rose Pistola is a sophisticated cafe bar located in the Italian immigration area of North Beach in San Francisco, California. Its interior space recalls Trattoria in Milano or the well known Harry's Bar in Venezia.

The (130-seat) premises have a deep interior space and a ceiling made of Douglas fir beams. In the central area, a 9-meter (30-ft.) mahogany counter bar faces an open kitchen with counter seats. In the dining areas on both sides, wood tables provide a warm and casual atmosphere.

James Goodman coordinated the color scheme, choosing brown, tan and cream as theme colors which were frequently used in 1940's and 50's.

The owner chef, Reed Hearon, specializes in Italian home cooking of the Genova and Ligurian Coast region.

サンフランシスコのノースビーチ地区の、イタリア人移民街に立地する都会的なカフェ・バーである。ミラノのトラットリアやベニスの有名な［ハリーズ・バー］を想わせる。

奥行きのある店内(130席)は、白く明るい天井に米松の梁を配している。中央部に7.5mのマホガニー製のカウンター/バーを置き、そのバーに向かい合う様にカウンター席を設けたオープンキッチンを備える。店内の前後にあるダイニングエリアはウッドトップのテーブルを配し、カジュアルな暖か味のある雰囲気をつくっている。

カラーコーディネートはジェイムズ・グッドマン氏が担当し、1940〜50年代に多く使用されたというブラウン、タン、クリームなどの色彩をテーマカラーに取り入れている。

オーナーシェフのリード・ヒーロン氏が提供する、イタリアのジェノバやリグリア海岸地方の家庭料理が親しまれている。

Front with large glassy windows. 約100年の歴史を持つサンフランシスコのイタリア人街に出店。大きなガラス窓を設けた店頭。

Opposite: Deep interior space, with all floors mosaic-tiled.
右ページ：奥行きのある店内全体に広がりをみせるグレイ、イエロー、ホワイトなどのモザイクタイルを用いたフロア。

Mahogany bar counter. Curved beams of the ceiling are made of Douglas fir and painted in honey gold.
マホガニー製のバーカウンターにはタンやクリーム色を配したスツールが並ぶ。天井部にハチミツ色に塗った米松をアーチ状にした梁が見える。

Looking at the pizza ovens in the open kitchen.
バーエリア近くのテーブル席とレセプション、ピザオーブンを備えるオープンキッチン方向を見る。

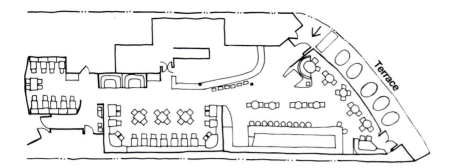

Antipasto tables and counter seats in front of the open kitchen, with dining area in the back.
オープンキッチンの前に備えたアンティパストのテーブルとカウンター席。奥にダイニングエリアがある。

Dining area.
ベンチシートの上方に鏡を配し、モノクロの写真を飾る壁面の構成。

BABALOO ＜San Francisco＞
ババルー＜サンフランシスコ＞

Address: 2030 Lombard, San Francisco, CA 94123
Phone/415-346-5474
Designer: Architecture/Doug Cain Libbi Ziegler-Ekwall
Laura Lyons and Michael Breen

Babaloo is a Latin American restaurant located in Marina, the northern side of Van Ness Avenue, San Francisco. The passionate mustard color of its facade eloquently expresses its Caribbean nature. Close to the entrance, the two-floor premises have a bar area with an oval counter and ocean blue floor. Beside the bar area, a slightly sloped entry leads to a (100-seat) sunken dining area. While the interior walls have been painted in the same color as the exterior, several paintings by local artists are displayed, creating a gallery-restaurant atmosphere.

One of its unusual presentations is cutlery wrapped with napkins and found with the menu in various cigar boxes on the cherry-red tables. Also, reggae, Latin and Spanish music are played in order to emphasize the regional character of the Caribbean Ocean. Babaloo offers "new Latin-American foods" influenced by Cuban cooking. The menu features approximately 15 items or tapas-like small dish entrees.

サンフランシスコのヴァンネス通りの北側、マリーナ地区に出店したラテン・アメリカ料理店。強烈なマスタード・イエローのファサードが、いかにもカリブを連想させる。店内は2段構造で、入口近くに、青い海の色を配したフロアーのバーエリアがあり、楕円形のカウンターを置く。バーエリアとダイニングエリアの間に緩やかなカーブを持たせたスロープを設け、一段下がったダイニングルーム（100席）へ続く。店内の壁面は外装と同じ色で統一し、ローカルのアーティストたちによる絵画を飾るギャラリー・レストランの雰囲気。チェリー・レッドのテーブル上に置かれた様々なシガーボックスの中には、メニューとナプキンに包まれたナイフ、フォークが入っていて、ユニークな演出をしている。また、レゲエやラテン、スパニッシュなどのBGMを流しカリブ海地方の雰囲気を出している。キューバ料理に影響された"新ラテン・アメリカ料理"を提供し、特に、常時15種類前後のタパス風小皿料理を中心としたメニューの構成をしている。

Facade. マスタード・イエローが特に目立つファサード。

Slightly curved and sloped aisle, also easily accessible for the handicapped, leads to the dining room. Paintings on the walls lit by halogen lights are changed every two months and available for sale.
手前の緩やかなカーブを持たせたスロープは車椅子などにも配慮したダイニングルームへの通路。ハロゲンライトに照らされる壁面の絵画はローカルのアーティストたちの作品を飾り、2カ月毎に入れ替え、販売もしている。

Sangria bar, looking from the entrance area.
入口近くから見る、カリブの海を想わせるブルーを配したフロアのサングリア・バー。

Bar corner with (7-seat) counter, 40 cm wide, set alongside a slope toward the dining room.
ダイニングルームに向かって、スロープに沿うように設けた巾約40cmのカウンターを置くバーコーナー（7席）。

Looking at the entrance area from the rear. Gregory Gordon did the color coordination and finishing for walls, floors and tables.
店内奥より入口方向を見る。ブース席と丸テーブルをタイルのフロアーに配している。壁、床、テーブルなどの配色と仕上げはグレゴリー・ゴードン氏が担当。

Mirrors on one side of the walls expand the space, creating picture-window images.
片側の壁面に大きな鏡を配し、空間の広がりとウィンドー・ピクチュアのイメージを造っている。

Unique tabletop presentations with cigar box collections.
シガーボックスのコレクションを置く、ユニークなテーブルトップのプレゼンテーション。

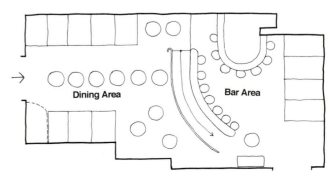

VERTIGO RESTAURANT & BAR <San Francisco>
バータゴウ・レストラン&バー<サンフランシスコ>

Address: 600 Montgomery Street, San Francisco, CA 94111
Phone/415-433-7250
Designer: Architecture/Jennifer Johannson
Engstrom Design Group

Landmark tower, looking from a residential area.
サンフランシスコの住宅地から見たランドマークタワー。

Interior structure built on three levels. 3レベルの店内構成。

Dining area on the second floor, facing the atrium. アトリウムに面した2階のダイニングエリア。

The name of the restaurant comes from Alfred Hitchcock's 1972 "Vertigo". It is located in the basement of the 48-floor pyramid Transamerica Building, a San Francisco landmark tower.

The 725m² (7,800-sq. ft.) site includes a (30-seat) bar space, a two-floor (150-seat) dining areas as well as a (45-seat) banquet room, with an open kitchen and a desert station. The glazed ceiling designed like a pyramid provides the illusion that it reaches the galaxy. In contrast to the exposed concrete studs and the base of the building, the interior has been designed with polished wood and curved details, softening the atmosphere with a color scheme of pram, saffron and pumpkin.

Vertigo Restaurant & Bar offers its own style of cuisine, blending Italian, French and Asian cooking methods.

店名は、ヒッチコック監督の1972年作品"めまい"と同名。サンフランシスコのランドマークタワー［トランスアメリカ・ビルディング］(ピラミッド形48階建て)の地階にある。

725㎡のスペースに、バー(30席)、2層のダイニングエリア(150席)と、半地下のバンケットルーム(45席)で構成し、オープンキッチンとデザート・ステーションを設けている。ピラミッド状にデザインされたガラス天井を透して見上げると、天まで延びているような錯覚にとらわれる。露見するビルのコンクリート製支柱や土台とは対照的に、店内には、磨きをかけた木や曲線のディテールを多用し、プラム、サフラン、パンプキンといったソフトな配色と共に店内のイメージを和らげている。

料理はイタリア、フランス、アジアを加えた、新しいスタイルの料理を提供する。

Dining area and open kitchen, looking from the upper part. 上部より見たダイニングエリアとオープンキッチン方向。

Desert station in the inner center. 中央奥に設けるデザート・ステーション。

Bar area. バーエリア。

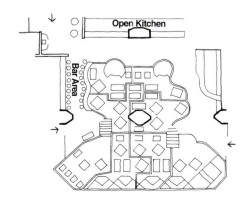

Looking at bar and entrance areas in the rear.
奥にバーとエントランスエリアを見る。

GRAND CAFE ＜San Francisco＞
グランド・カフェ＜サンフランシスコ＞

Address: 501 Geary Street, San Francisco, CA 94102
Phone/415-292-0101 FAX/415-292-0150
Designer: Ron Lieberman, David Lieberman

Entrance area of petit cafe, creating an early 20th century atmosphere.
［プティ・カフェ］の入口あたり。20世紀初期のヨーロッパの雰囲気を取り入れている。

Main dining room, looking from the reception area. メイン・ダイニングルームをレセプションあたりから見る。

Restaurant on the corner of the first floor of the Hotel Monaco, with Terra-cotta exterior.
［ホテル・モナコ］と1階角のレストラン。テラコッタの外装。

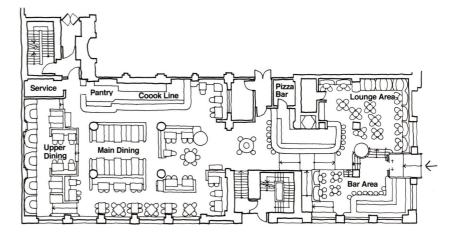

Grand Cafe is a restaurant situated inside the Hotel Monaco, a boutique hotel in downtown San Francisco, California. On the corner of the first floor, a large banquet hall with a 9-meter (30-ft.) high ceiling was remodeled for a European brassiere style restaurant.

Near the entrance, there is a (88-seat) bar & petit cafe with a small kitchen under a coved ceiling, while the (178-seat) main dining room can be found further inside. Local artists completed the decorations, including Art Deco lighting and mirrors for the 3-meter (9-foot) columns, bronze statutes, pen drawings, Terrazzo floor designs and brown-velvet booths separated by walnut partitions.

サンフランシスコのダウンタウンにあるブティック・ホテル［ホテル・モナコ］内のレストラン。1階の角にあった、天井高9mの大宴会場を、ヨーロッパのブラッセリー風レストランに改装した。

入口近くにバー＆プティ・カフェ（88席）とコーブ（折り上げ）の天井の下に設けた小キッチンを備え、その奥にメイン・ダイニングルーム（178席）がある。3mの円柱、アール・デコの照明や鏡、ブロンズ像、ペン画、テラゾーのフロアデザイン、ウォールナットの仕切りを用いたブラウン・ベルベットのブースなど、すべてがローカルのアーティストたちの手で制作されている。

Dining area. ダイニングエリア。

Looking at the open kitchen at the lower right. 右下にオープンキッチンを見る。

Bar area. バーエリア。

Small kitchen and entrance area. 小キッチンと入口方向。

MONSOON CAFE ＜Santa Monica＞
モンスーン・カフェ＜サンタモニカ＞

Address: 1212 Third Street, Santa Monica, CA 90401
　　　　Phone/310-576-9996 FAX/310-576-9988
Designer: O'Brien and Associates Designers

This Asian food restaurant is located on the 3rd Street Promenade, a shopping area in Santa Monica, California.
　According to the designer, Peg O'Brien, the design for the premises was inspired by the Orient, including Southeastern Asia, and includes a space where visitors can feel the tropical breeze.
　Its 1,070m² (11,500-sq. ft.) interior space has a two-floor structure built in the wellhole style. The first floor consists of a bar area, a (129-seat) dining area with an open kitchen, and the first floor of a (170-seat) dining area with a balcony and a lounge on the second floor.

サンタモニカのショッピング街、サードストリート・プロムナードに出店するアジア料理レストラン。
　オリエントや東南アジアをイメージ・コンセプトにし、「トロピカルとそよ風を感じる空間を創造した」と設計者のペグ・オブライエンはいう。
　1,070㎡のスペースに中央吹き抜け部を設けた2層構造の店内。入口近くのバーにオープンキッチンを設ける1階のダイニングエリア（129席）、バルコニーを周囲に設ける2階の客席（170席）とラウンジなどで構成する。

Facade facing the promenade. プロムナードに面したファサード。

Reception and bar area. レセプションとバー。

Open kitchen and interior structure built on two levels. オープンキッチン（手前）と2層の店内。

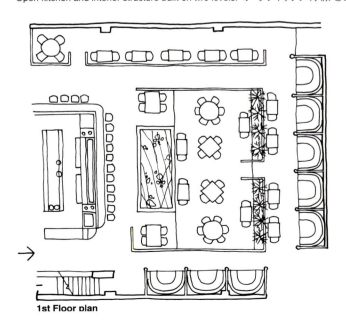

1st Floor plan

2nd Floor plan

First floor dining area, looking from the second floor balcony. 2階のバルコニーから見る1階ダイニングエリア。

Above: Balcony area. Oposite: Central part built in wellhole style. 上：バルコニー周り。右：中央吹き抜け部。

2424 PICO ＜Santa Monica＞
2424・ピコ＜サンタモニカ＞

Address: 2424 Pico Boulevard, Santa Monica, CA 90405
Phone/310-581-1124 FAX/310-581-1338
Designer:Michael Whitehouse/Space Design

Open kitchen and reception area. オープンキッチンとレセプションあたり。

Facade. ファサード。

The name of this restaurant is directly adopted from that of its location. The same color scheme was used for both exterior and interior spaces, which was inspired by villas in Toscana, Italy. A simple linear design without any decorative elements dominates the premises.

Simon Maltby has designed benches and partitions in front of the open kitchen as well as a service station that also serves as a wine station. 2424 Pico consists of a 64-seat dining area and a 10-seat mahogany bar area.

所在地をそのまま店名にした、無国籍料理店。イタリアのトスカーナ地方の邸宅によく見られる色を外観及び店内に使用。直線的で飾りのないシンプルなデザインでまとめている。オープンキッチンの前のベンチや仕切り、ワインラックを兼ねるサービス・ステーションはサイモン・マルビィが手掛ける。64席のダイニングエリアと奥のマホガニーのバーエリア（10席）で構成。

Looking at the entrance area. 入口方向を見る。

Above and left: Service station which also serves as a wine station.
上・左：ワインラックを兼ねたサービス・ステーション。

French bar in 1960's style. 1960年代の雰囲気を残すフレンチバー。

WOLFGANG PUCK CAFE ＜Santa Monica＞
ウルフガング・パック・カフェ＜サンタモニカ＞

Address: 1323 Montana Avenue, Santa Monica, CA 90403
Phone/310-393-0290 FAX/310-393-6892
Designer:Barbara Lazaroff

Wolfgang Puck is an owner and chef of the famous "Spago" restaurant and is now classified as one of the best cooks in the United States. This cafe is a branch of the 11-restaurant chain which he created in order to offer more affordable prices in an informal setting.

This (90-seat) cafe was the fourth to be built and is located on Montana Avenue, where many other unique and professional restaurants can be found. Especially the mosaic tiled facade stands out in the area. Mr. Puck's wife and business partner, Barbara Lazaroff, designed the interior in a colorful and casual manner, which brings back childhood memories to the customers. The premises are filled with art objects and images, like building blocks, collages of broken tiles, various shaped mirrors reminiscent of Antonio Gaudii's architectural works and bright loud colors found in painters' palettes.

ウルフガング・パック氏は［スパゴ］レストランのオーナー/シェフであり、今や、米国の料理界でトップクラスの存在でもある人。このカフェは彼の料理をもっと気軽にそして安価に食べられるようにという発想から生まれたコンセプトであり、目下、南カリフォルニアを中心に店舗展開している。

サンタモニカ店はその第4番目に開店した店舗（90席）である。ユニークなレストランや専門店の集まるモンタナ通りにあって、モザイクのタイルでデザインしたファサードはひときわ目立つ。店舗デザインは彼の奥さんでありパートナーのバーバラ・ラザロフさんが担当。積木のようなオブジェがあったり、ガウディの作品に見られるような壊れたタイルの寄せ集めや丸や四角、三角の鏡、パレットの中の絵の具を想像するような強烈な色彩が店内を埋め尽くす。

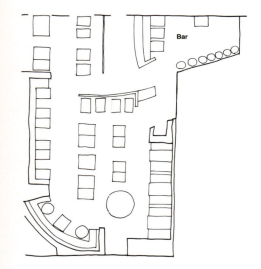

Freestanding facade.
フリースタンディングの店舗ファサード。

Entrance area, looking from the inner part. 店内奥より店頭方向を見る。

Entrance and reception area. 入口レセプションあたり。

Opposite: Colorful dining room. Above: Looking at the inner bar. 左：カラフルなダイニングルーム。上：奥のバーを見る。

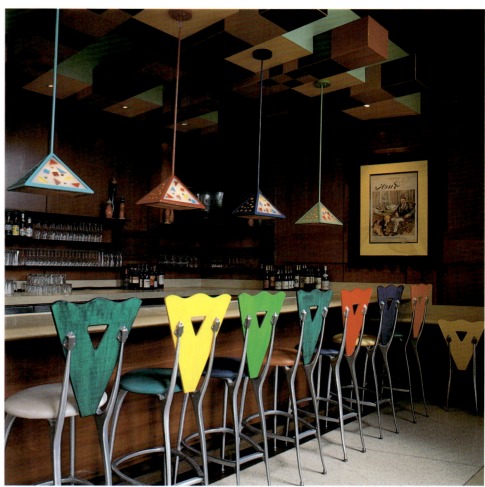

Bar corner. バーコーナー。

OBACHINE ＜Beverly Hills＞
オバシン＜ビバリーヒルズ＞

Address: 242 N. Beverly Drive, Beverly Hills, CA 90210
　　　　　Phone/310-274-4440　FAX/310-274-2611
Designer:Barbara Lazaroff

Facade with terraced seats. テラス席を設けるファサード。

Bar area, looking from the entrance. 入口から見るバーエリア。

The name "Obachine" was coined from a Japanese word meaning a beefsteak plant and a French word meaning China. This Asian-theme restaurant, located close to Rodeo Drive in Beverly Hills, offers innovative foods, combining various recipes and ingredients from China, Thailand, Vietnam, India, Japan and so forth.

Visitors encounter a large beefsteak-plant-shaped signboard on the facade, while the backs of the chairs are designed after the same plant. The first floor has a bar area, featuring a huge copper counter and ranges, and the second floor consists of a (180-seat) main dining area and an open kitchen with a marble-tiled counter under a vaulted wooden ceiling, which is surrounded by tables and booths. In spite of the partially skylit ceiling, the entire dining is kept dim by a lighting system that is controlled by beam lights. Painted in a terra-cotta color, enormous ducts run over visitors' heads. The kitchen walls are uniquely decorated with laser-printed tiles, displaying vegetable drawings as well as children's picture books of 1930-1940's.

店名は大葉（しそ）と中国を意味するフランス語を結びつけた造語。アジアをテーマとし、中国、タイ、ベトナム、インド、日本‥‥といった国々の料理と食材を取り入れ、新しいトレンドの料理を生み出している。ビバリーヒルズのロデオドライブにも近い立地。

ファサードの大きな大葉のサインボードが目に付く。店内の椅子の背もたれにも、大葉のデザインを取り入れている。店舗は2層で構成し、1階は巨大なコパーのカウンターやレンジを配したバー。メインダイニングエリア（180席）は2階にあり、木製の円形ドーム状天井の下に、大理石のタイルのカウンターを設けたオープンキッチンを置き、その回りにテーブルとブース席を配置している。天井部の一部にスカイライトを取り入れているが、全体に暗い感じの部屋でありビームライトによる調光がなされている。テラコッタ色にペイントされた大きなダクトが頭上に流れるように配置してある。1930～40年代の子供の絵本や野菜の絵をレーザープリントにしたタイルを貼ったキッチンの壁面構成がユニークである。

Bar area, looking from the upper part of the staircase which leads to the dining area. ダイニングエリアへ上がる階段の上部から見るバー。

Opposite: Open kitchen and central part of dining area. Above: Interior space, looking from the open kitchen side.
左：ダイニングエリア中央部とオープンキッチン。上：オープンキッチン側から見る店内。

Walls with laser-printed tiles. レーザープリント処理のタイル壁。

LE COLONIAL ＜West Hollywood＞
ル・コロニアル＜ウエストハリウッド＞

Address: 8783 Beverly Boulevard, West Hollywood, CA 90048
Phone/310-289-0660

The main branch of this Vietnamese restaurant is in New York. The interior space was inspired by hotels popular in Saigon in the 1920-1930's and is decorated with tropical trees such as palms, green Asian tiles, cream-colored wall paintings, shuttered windows and ceiling fans.

　The first floor includes a (80-seat) dining room and a (40-seat) patio in a French-colonial atmosphere which are decorated with old photographs of scenery and people in Indochina, and the second floor consists of a(60-seat) bar and lounge.

ニューヨークに本店を持つベトナム料理店。ヤシの木や熱帯樹、緑のエイシャンタイル、クリーム色の壁面、シャッタード・ウインドー、シーリングファンなどを配した、1920～30年代に見られたサイゴンのホテルを想わせる造り。

　壁面にインドシナの風景や人々の古い写真を飾る、フレンチ・コロニーの雰囲気を持つダイニングルーム（80席）とパティオ（40席）、2階のバー／ラウンジ（60席）で構成。

Above: Patio. Opposite: Entrance.　上：パティオ。　右ページ：エントランス。

Dining room. ダイニングルーム。

Staircase area, leading to the bar and lounge on the second floor.
2階のバー/ラウンジへ上がる階段あたり。

Looking at the reception area. レセプション方向を見る。

99

MONDORIAN HOTEL ＜Los Angeles＞
モンドリアン・ホテル＜ロサンゼルス＞

Address: 8440 Sunset Boulevard, Los Angeles, CA 90069
    Phone/213-650-8999
General Designer: Philippe Starck

Facing Sunset Boulevard, the 16-story building includes 245 guest rooms situated in a lively setting. The objective of this urban resort hotel is to offer both entertainment and excitement for clients by adopting natural and simple elements that alternate between reality and illusion.

Among its 6 different restaurant facilities, the multipurpose (36-seat) The Lobby Diner has a floating bar without any bartenders. In the outdoor dining area alongside the pool, there are terra-cotta pots as tall as a person. The Pool Bar, a (40-seat) spacious area with a ceiling made of logs and plywood, and Coco Pazzo, a (120-seat) main dining room decorated in white, are based on the aesthetic sense of Philippe Starck.

Hotel entrance with 9-meter mahogany doors.
9mのマホガニー製ドアを置く、ホテルのエントランス。

サンセット大通りに面した16階建て、245室のアーバン・リゾート・ホテル。現実と幻想の間に、自然さやシンプルさを取り入れ、エキサイトメントとエンターテイメントが存在する"ホテルづくり"を追求している。

6つの飲食施設があり、多目的利用の［ザ・ロビー・ダイナー］（36席）には、バーテンダーのいない"フローティング・バー"を備えている。プールサイドにあるアウトドア・ダイニングエリアには、等身大のテラコッタのポットを置く。オープンエアの中に、ログとトタン板で構成する［ザ・プールバー］（40席）の天井部、白い木と布の調和をはかるメインダイニングルームの［ココ・パッツォ］（120席）。これらはすべてスタルク氏の理論と美意識に基づいている。

Lobby area, attempting to eliminate the barriers between the interior and the exterior. ロビー。

MONDORIAN HOTEL ＜Los Angeles＞
"The Lobby Dinner"
「ザ・ロビー・ダイナー」

"The Lobby Diner"［ザ・ロビー・ダイナー］

"Floating Bar" where customers can move about freely. 移動が自由にできる "フローティング・バー"。

MONDORIAN HOTEL ＜Los Angeles＞
"Coco Pazzo"
「ココ・パッツォ」

New York-based Italian restaurant, which has expanded throughout the United States.
ニューヨークを中心に全米展開している、イタリアンレストラン。

White wine racks in accord with interior decoration. 白で店内と統一したワインラック。

Booth seats. ブース席。

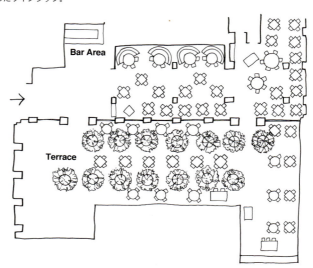

"COCO PAZZO". Outdoor dining area. ココ・パッツォのアウトドア・ダイニングエリア。

MONDORIAN HOTEL ＜Los Angeles＞
"The Pool Bar"
「ザ・プール・バー」

Open-air structure facing poolside.
プールサイドに面したオープンエアのつくり。

Inside of the bar area. バーの内部。

JIRAFFE ＜Santa Monica＞
ジラフ＜サンタモニカ＞

Address: 502 Santa Monica Boulevard, Santa Monica, CA 90401
Phone/310-917-6671 FAX/310-917-6677

Giraffe is a rustic American-French restaurant that faces Santa Monica Blvd., 5 blocks east from Santa Monica beach. Situated in a corner of a building with a glass window facade, the two-floor urban cafe has a bright atmosphere.

The interior has large full-height windows with the upper parts rounded, dark-wood chairs and furniture, and white tablecloths in harmony with the white walls. The restaurant space includes a (46-seat) dining area built in wellhole style, a loft-like (34-seat) upper dining space as well as a beverage station and a small waiting area beside the entrance. There is no bar area. Many stuffed giraffes, the restaurant's mascot, are displayed throughout the establishment.

サンタモニカ海岸から東に5ブロックのサンタモニカ通りに面し、大きなガラス窓を配した白いビルのファサードが並ぶ。そのコーナーに位置する素朴なアメリカン・フレンチ料理のレストラン。2階建ての明るい都会のカフェの雰囲気で、天井から床までの上部に丸みを持たせた大きなガラス窓を設けている。

白壁の店内は、ホワイトテーブルクロスとダークウッドの家具や椅子を備え、シンプルな感じ。2階吹き抜けのダイニングエリア(46席)と、ロフト状になった上部の客席(34席)、入口近くのドリンクのサービスステーションと小スペースのウエイティングエリア等で構成し、バーコーナーはない。店名にもなっているキリンがマスコットとして店内の所々に飾ってある。

Facade. ファサード。

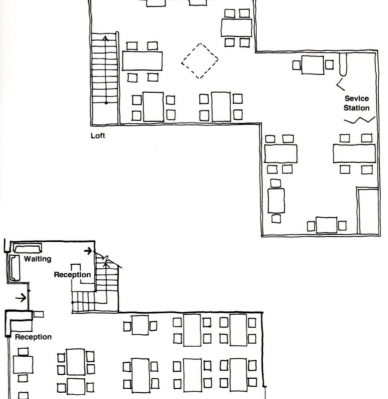

Entrance with a small waiting area. 小スペースのウエイティングエリアを設ける入口あたり。

Reception area.
レセプションあたり。

Opposite: Interior space in the loft style. Above: Interior space, looking from the second floor.
左ページ：ロフト状の店内。上：2階から見る店内。

Looking at staircase to the second floor. 2階への階段部分を見る。

FENIX ＜West Hollywood＞
フェニックス＜ウエストハリウッド＞

Address: 8358 Sunset Boulevard, West Hollywood, CA 90069
Phone/213-848-6677

Facing Sunset Boulevard in West Hollywood,"The Sunset Tower" (constructed in 1929) was formerly an apartment building, which is now designated as a historic monument. In 1985, it was first remodeled, in a 40 million dollar development, into a hotel called "The St. James's Club", which was then converted to a (64-room) small luxury hotel called "The Argyle" in 1994.

Art Deco was adopted for its architectural style while an interior designer, David Becker, has selected the furniture, most of which was reproduced by Italian artisans based on furniture exhibited in the Beaux Arts Museum in Paris and the Metropolitan Museum in New York. The restaurant, alongside the hotel pool, has a panoramic view of Los Angeles. The premises consist of a (30-seat) bar lounge,"Grand Salon", and a (75-seat) dining area with a patio,"Terrace Room", both of which are well lit by a skylight and decorated with contemporary as well as art deco art works.

ウエストハリウッドのサンセット大通りに面した歴史的建造物に指定されている、［ザ・サンセット・タワー］（1929年建造）は、ハリウッドのスターも住む高級アパートメントであった。1985年に4000万ドルを投じて［ザ・セント・ジェイムズ・クラブ］というホテルに変わり、更に、1994年に［ザ・アージャイル］と名付ける、スモール・ラグジュアリィホテル（64室）になった。

　アール・デコの建築様式を取り入れ、インテリア・デザイナーのデビッド・ベッカー氏によって家具や調度品が集められ、そのほとんどがパリのボザール美術館やニューヨークのメトロポリタン美術館にあるものから選び、イタリアの名工たちの手によって復元されたものが使用されている。レストランはホテルのプールサイドにあって、ロサンゼルスの景色がパノラマのように見える位置にある。［グランド・サロン］（30席）と名付けたバー・ラウンジと、パティオの付いた［テラス・ルーム］（75席）で構成する。スカイライトをふんだんに取り入れ、コンテンポラリィとアールデコの要素を導入している。

Exterior of "The Argyle". ホテルの外観。

Bar lounge in Art Deco style. アール・デコのバーラウンジ。

Bar lounge. バーラウンジ。

Bar lounge, looking from the entrance area. 入口あたりから見るバーラウンジ。

Dining area facing poolside, looking from the bar lounge.
バーラウンジから見るプールサイドに面したダイニングエリア。

Interior space. 店内をみる。

Terraced seats at poolside. プールサイドのテラス席。

NICOLA ＜Los Angeles＞
ニコラ＜ロサンゼルス＞

Address: 601 S. Figueroa Street, Los Angeles, CA 90017
Phone/213-485-0927 FAX/213-485-0931
Designer: Michael Rotondi

Opposite: Terraced seats in the atrium.
右ページ：アトリウム内のテラス席。

Nicola is located in an atrium of the Sanwa Bank Plaza, a new high-rise building in the commercial area in downtown Los Angeles.

The premises consist of a (58-seat) casual dining area, constructed of wood, iron, brass, marble, cloth and stones, and a (42-seat) upscale indoor dining room. Utilizing wooden pieces, rib-like frame structure and other flexible light fixtures, the interior space recalls the internal body of a whale. It offers contemporary American cuisine with an ethnic presentation.

ロサンゼルスのダウンタウン商業地域の新しい高層ビル、［サンワ・バンク・プラザ］のアトリウム部分にオープンしたレストラン。

木、鉄、ブラス、大理石、布、石などでクリエイトされたカジュアル・アウトドア・ダイニングエリア（58席）とアップスケールなインドア・ダイニングルーム（42席）で構成。木材のピースを組み合わせ、あばら骨のような骨格状のデザインを取り入れたり、自由な形態の照明器具を用いて、クジラの体内を見るような店内構成をしている。

エスニック調のコンテンポラリーなアメリカン・キュイジーヌを提供。

Atrium. アトリウム。

Terraced seats and interior seats alongside the windows. 店内の窓側客席とテラス席方向。

Looking at private dining area at right, with open kitchen in the rear.
右側にプライベート・ダイニングエリアと奥にオープンキッチンを見る。

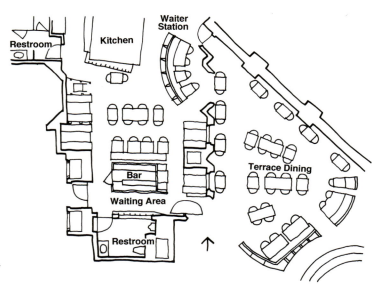

Dining room. ダイニングルーム。

Bar area close to the entrance.
入口近くのバー。

CAFE PINOT ＜Los Angeles＞
カフェ・ピノ＜ロサンゼルス＞

Address: 700 West 5th Street , Los Angeles, CA 90071
　　　　 Phone/213-239-6500 FAX/213-239-6514

This French cafe restaurant is located next to Macguire Gardens, a central library in downtown Los Angeles.
　The freestanding structure has a (110-seat) dining room surrounded with large windows, a bar counter, and a (70-seat) outdoor dining area. Interior walls are decorated with fresco paintings displaying scenery, vines (ivy plants) and birds in Toscana, all of which emphasizes a natural atmosphere. The premises have received two architectural and design awards.

　ロサンゼルスのダウンタウンにある［セントラル・ライブラリー］、［マクヴァイアー・ガーデンズ］などに隣接するフランス料理のカフェ。
　フリースタンディングのレストランは、四面に大きな窓を設けたダイニングルーム（110席）とバーカウンター、アウトドア・ダイニングのエリア（70席）で構成。店内壁面には、トスカーナ地方の風景やバイン（つるの植物）、鳥などを描くフレスコ画を配し、自然の中に溶け込む雰囲気を強調。2つの建築・デザイン賞を受けている。

Restaurant, looking from Macguire Gardens.
［マクヴァイアー・ガーデンズ］から見るレストラン。

Entrance. エントランス。

Patio seats, facing central library (behind).
［セントラル・ライブラリー］（後方）に面したパティオ席。

Looking at open kitchen near the reception. レセプション近くのオープンキッチン方向を見る。

Dining area close to reception. レセプションあたりのダイニングエリア。

Central area of restaurant with fresco paintings. フレスコ画のあるレストランの中央部。

Bar area facing the patio. パティオに面したバーエリア。

ECLIPSE ＜West Hollywood＞
イクリプス＜ウエストハリウッド＞

Address: 8800 Melrose Avenue, West Hollywood, CA 90069
Phone/310-724-5959
Designer: Lambert Monet and Henk Rijkers

This mansion-style restaurant is surrounded by West Hollywood and has a stately door inspired by the sun shining at its entrance. A 700-sq.m. ft. bar lounge also functions as a waiting room, while the lounge and dining area have large glass windows through which one can look into the kitchen area. Entering from an aisle between the wine cellar and the bar, visitors encounter the (120-seat) elegant dining room, which was designed by Lambert Monet, a grandchild of a famous painter, Claud Monet, and his partner, Hank Rijkers.

The interior space has been decorated with many original art works painted by a modern neo-classical artist, Alexander Mihaylovich, creating an art-museum setting. A wooden vaulted ceiling provides sufficient lighting so that customers can enjoy the interior decoration and paintings in various ways, depending upon the angle of view and quantity of daylight.

The outside terrace seats 40 and has large umbrellas. At Eclipse, the menu, called "Cuisine of the Sun," combines Provence-style seafood diet from southern France with traditional Californian cooking.

ウエストハリウッドの木々に囲まれた邸宅風のレストラン。入口には太陽の光をイメージした重厚な扉がある。60㎡のバーラウンジ（28席）はウエイティングルームも兼ねる。ラウンジやダイニングルームから、キッチンの中が見えるように大きなガラス窓を設けてある。画家クロード・モネの孫にあたるランバート・モネと、彼のパートナーであるハンク・レイカーズがデザインした120席のエレガントなダイニングルーム。

店内には、現代的なネオクラシカルアート画家のアレキサンダー・ミハイロビッチ氏が描いたオリジナル作品が数多く飾られ、美術館の雰囲気がある。

丸みを持たせた木製の天井から自然光を取り入れ、店内や展示された作品の感じが、光の変化にともなって異なって見える効果を計算しデザインされている。

店名の"イクリプス"とは太陽の陰を表現する意味。外のテラスには40席のテーブル席が大きなアンブレラと共に配置されている。

"太陽の料理"とうたった南仏プロバンス地方の魚介料理とカリフォルニアの食材や料理法を合わせたメニューを提供する。

Opposite: Terraced dining area. 右ページ：テラス・ダイニングのエリア。

Facade. ファサード。

Above: Looking at the bar lounge and kitchen. Opposite: Dining room.
上：バーラウンジとキッチンを見る。右ページ：ダイニングルーム。

Aisle between the bar and dining areas. バーエリアとダイニングエリアの間の通路。

THE ORIGINAL SONORA CAFE ＜Los Angeles＞
ジ・オリジナル・ソノラ・カフェ＜ロサンゼルス＞

Address: 180 South La Brea, Los Angeles CA 90036
Phone/213-857-1800
Designer: Roslyn Smith

Above and below: Facade. 上・下：ファサード。

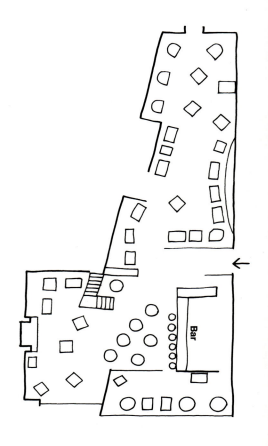

This Southwestern and Mexican restaurant, which opened in downtown Los Angeles in 1986, has been recently moved to the present location near Hollywood and Beverly Hills.

The Original Sonora Cafe had a southwestern atmosphere. An attractive (130-seat) dining room is decorated with fabrics of an American Indian motif and Western taste such as paintings of aloes and cacti, ceramic lizards, and pots, while the wood floor is covered with antique carpets. Because of chandeliers and dried vines twisted around the wooden ceiling beams, the ceilings look lower than they actually are. Parasols of flying-bird-shaped canvas are used to decorate the (30-seat) bar area.

サウスウエスタン/メキシカン料理のレストランで、1986年にロスのダウンタウンに開店し、最近、ハリウッドやビバリーヒルズに近い現在の場所へ移ってきた。

サウスウエスタンの雰囲気を持ち、アメリカン・インディアンのモチーフのファブリックやウエスタンカラーを活かしたダイニングルーム（130席）が中心。ウッドフロアーには古いアンティークのジュータンが敷かれ、アロエやカクタスの絵、セラミックでできたトカゲ、壺などが飾ってある。太い木の梁をめぐらし、枯れ枝が絡まるデザインのシャンデリアが天井の高さを意識させない。バーエリア（30席）には鳥が飛んでいる形のカンバスの傘を配している。

Dining room, looking from the entrance area. 入口あたりから見るダイニングルーム。

Looking at the dining room from the bar area. バーからダイニングルーム方向を見る。

Looking at the bar area from the inner dining room.
ダイニングルームの奥よりバー方向を見る。

Bar area.
バーエリア。

Interior space, looking from the staircase to the banquet room.
バンケットルームへの階段から見下ろす店内。

Looking at the entrance area and bar tables.
バーエリアのテーブル席と入口方向を見る。

BERNEY GREENGRASS ＜Beverly Hills＞
バーニィ・グリーングラス＜ビバリーヒルズ＞

Address: 9570 Wilshire Boulevard, Beverly Hills, CA 90212
Phone/310-777-5877 FAX/310-777-5760

Located at the top (5th) floor of "Barney's", a high-class department store in Beverly Hills, Barney Greengrass is a New York-based restaurant/ delicatessen with a long and distinguished history.

Upon arrival, customers immediately encounter a (13-seat) vodka bar with marbled counters. Next to the bar, long glass showcases feature approximately 180 food items, such as caviar and potato salad, for sale. In the center of the shelves on the walls of the deli corner, water runs down the black walls behind the vegetables and fruits.

The inner (52-seat) dining room has white ceilings and walls, with sufficient lighting and wonderful views from the large windows. Tables have Italian armchairs and white paper tablecloths. In the patio, there is another (60-seat) dining area, while New York jazz tunes are played for background music throughout the premises.

ビバリーヒルズにある高級デパートの［バーニーズ］の最上階（5階）に出店したニューヨークの伝統あるデリ/レストラン。

エレベーターを降りると目の前に大理石のカウンターを配したウオッカ・バー（13席）がある。その隣には長いガラスのショーケースが置かれ、キャビアからポテトサラダなど約180種類のアイテムが売られている。物販コーナーにある壁面を利用した棚の中央部に、野菜や果物が置かれ、その後方の黒い壁の上方から水が流れ落ちている。

奥に設けたダイニングルーム（52席）は、白い天井と壁、大きなガラス窓の見晴らしの良い明るい部屋。イタリア製のアームチェアーと白いペーパークロスを掛けたテーブルを配している。他に、パティオのダイニングエリア（60席）があり、店内にはニューヨーク・ジャズのＢＧＭが流れている。

Bar area. バーエリア。

Opposite: Walls beside the take-out corner. 右ページ：テイクアウト・コーナー横の壁面。

Opposite: Dining room. Above: Looking at take-out corner from the dining room.
左ページ：ダイニングルーム。上：ダイニングルームからテイクアウト・コーナー方向を見る。

Take-out corner. テイクアウト・コーナー。

CAVA ＜Los Angeles＞
カバ＜ロサンゼルス＞

Address: 8384 W. Third Street, Los Angeles, CA
Phone/213-658-8898 FAX/213-658-8998

Cava, which means "champagne" in Spanish, is located on the first floor of the Beverly Plaza Hotel. Offering Spanish specialties, the premises have two levels: the first floor consists of a (110-seat) cafe and a (60-seat) "tapas" bar in the Barcelona style and the second a (250-seat) nightclub restaurant.

The "tapas" bar has a circular layout built in a two-level wellhole style, while the walls are painted a mustard color with the lower parts of the bar counters and walls hand carved and painted. Other unique decorations include chandeliers made of cutlery and a lighting system projecting bull images on the walls. There are impressive paintings of red roses on the walls of the dining room. Only the first floor is explained here.

［ビバリー・プラザホテル］の1階に出店するスペイン料理店。店名はスペイン語で"シャンパン"の意。1階のバルセロナ・スタイルのカフェ（110席）＆タパス・バー（60席）と、2階のナイトクラブ・レストラン（250席）で構成。

2層吹き抜けの円形にレイアウトされたタパス・バーは、マスタード・カラーの壁面を配し、バーカウンターや壁の下方に手描きの浮彫と彩色がしてある。ナイフ、フォーク、スプーンなどで造るシャイデリアや壁面の牛を表現した照明がユニーク。ダイニングルームの真紅のバラを描いた壁面が印象的。ここでは1階部分のみを紹介する。

Entrance and signboard. エントランスとサイン。

Left: Bar corner.
Opposite: Customer seats at the "tapas" bar.
左：バーコーナー。右ページ：タパス・バーの客席。

Looking at the tapas bar from the cafe. カフェよりタパス・バー方向を見る。

Above: Interior space of the cafe. Opposite: Cafe at left side beyond the entrance.
上：カフェの店内。右ページ：エントランスを挟んで左側にあるカフェ。

DAILY GRILL ＜Los Angeles＞
デイリー・グリル＜ロサンゼルス＞

Address: Tom Bradley International Terminal at LAX Airport, CA
　　　　　Phone/310-215-5180
Designer: Project Design/Michael Czysz

From the check-in counter below at right, escalators lead to the restaurant entrance. 右奥下のチェックイン・カウンターからエスカレーターで結ぶレストランの入口。

This is the only full-service restaurant in Tom Bradley International Terminal at Los Angeles Airport, which has been recently remodeled.

Its 750㎡ (8,000-sq. ft.) premises have two bars, an upscale buffet corner, and a dining area inspired by passenger trains. Although located in the airport, the restaurant purposely uses images of trains and ships. Daily Grill offers traditional American home cooking as well as international dishes.

新築なったロサンゼルス国際空港の、インターナショナル・ターミナルに出店した唯一のフルサービス・レストラン。

750㎡の店内（250席）に、2つのバー、アップスケールのビュッフェ・コーナー、客車をイメージしたダイニングエリアなどで構成。空港内のレストランであるが、あえて、汽車と船のテーマを持ち込んでいる。伝統的な米国の家庭料理とインターナショナルなメニューを提供。

New International Terminal at LAX Airport.
新しい国際線専用ターミナル。

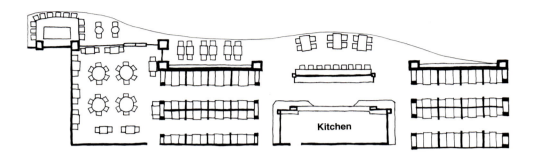

Layout which extends far back. 奥行きのあるレイアウト。

Bar area, inspired by a ship, with stainless steel canopy. ステンレス・スティールのキャノピーを配し、船をイメージするバー。

Inner bar area.
店内奥のバー。

Open kitchen and counter seats in the central area.
中央部に設けるオープン・キッチンとカウンター席。

Dining inspired by train, with luggage racks made of wood and bronze.
木やブロンズで造る荷物用ラックを配した、客車をイメージするダイニングエリア。

Dining area.
ダイニングエリア。

TWIN PALMS ＜Pasadena＞
ツイン・パームス＜パサデナ＞

Address: 101 West Green Street, Pasadena, CA 91105
Phone/818-577-2567 FAX/818-577-1306

Reception area. レセプションエリア。

Facade. ファサード。

Central patio. パティオの中央部。

The site has two old palm trees, each approximately one hundred years old. Twin Palms consists of a (210~300-seat) dining area in the patio, which has a flexible canopy made of yacht canvas, and a (110-seat) main dining room, which was remodeled from an old car repair shop. The bar area and rotisserie grill is located between them. This restaurant offers Provence home cooking.

樹齢約百年のパームツリーが2本ある敷地に建てられたレストラン。セイルボートの帆を開閉可能なキャノピー状にしたパティオのダイニングエリア（210～300席）と、元自動車修理工場であったスペースを改装したメイン・ダイニングルーム（110席）で構成。両エリアの中間にバーとロティセリー・グリルを設けている。プロヴァンス風家庭料理を提供。

Heaters with shades, placed beside table seats. テーブル席の脇に傘の付いたヒーターを並べる。

Kitchen and bar area in the center. 中央部に設けたキッチンとバー。

Main dining room. メイン・ダイニングルーム。

Bar area. バーエリア。

IL FORNAIO CUCINA ITALIANA ＜Pasadena＞
イル・フォーナイオ・クチナ・イタリアーナ＜パサデナ＞

Address: 24 West Union Street, Pasadena, CA 91103
Phone/818-683-9797 FAX/818-683-0789

Entrance area of take-out corner. テイクアウト・コーナーの入口あたり。

Victorian and Art Deco buildings were restored and renovated to create "One Colorado", a specialty shop street, located in Old Town, Pasadena, California. Il Fornaio, Cucina Italiana is a sophisticated Italian restaurant in Milano style in this redevelopment project. In the center of the premises, there is a (200-seat) dining area with an open kitchen, a (14-seat) bar area and a take-out counter with a bakery shop.

パサデナのオールドタウンに完成した専門店街［ワン・コロラド］－ビクトリア様式とアール・デコの建物を保存・修復し、再開発された－の中に出店の、洗練されたミラノ・スタイルのイタリアン・レストラン。店内中央部にオープンキッチンを備えるダイニングエリア（200席）とバーエリア（14席）、ベーカリー・ショップを備えるテイクアウトエリアとで構成。

Aisle between restaurant and take-out corner. レストランとテイクアウト・コーナーを結ぶ通路。

Take-out corner with eat-in seats. イートイン席を備えるテイクアウト・コーナー。

Above: Reception area in inner center. Opposite: Central dining area and open kitchen.
上:中央奥に設けるレセプション。右ページ:ダイニングエリア中央部とオープンキッチン。

Bar. バー。

CHART HOUSE ＜Malibu＞
チャート・ハウス＜マリブ＞

Address: 18412 Pacific Coast Highway, Malibu, CA 90265
Phone/310-454-9321

Chart House, which means "house which makes navigational charts", is an upscale dinner restaurant, whose branches are located in resorts with breathtaking views such as California, Hawaii and Colorado. Both the exterior and the interior are emphasized with wooden materials in line with surrounding natural setting. The premises have a (150-seat) dining area and (50-seat) bar and lounge. Magnificent views from large windows are highly integrated into the interior design, which in turn the interior provides customers simple impressions. Charts are placed on each tabletop. Fresh seafood dishes are highly recommended.

店名は"海図を作る家"の意。カリフォルニア、ハワイ、コロラド州などの眺望の良い、リゾート地に出店するアップスケール・ディナーレストラン。

　エクステリアとインテリアは木で強調し、周辺の自然との融和を計っている。オープンキッチンを備えたダイニングエリア（150席）とバー/ラウンジ（50席）で構成。大窓を透して見る景色を、インテリア・デザインの大きな部分に取り込み（借景）、店内をシンプル化し、各テーブルトップに海図を加工する。料理は特に新鮮な魚介類のメニューを提供。

Exterior view facing the Pacific coastline. 太平洋に面した外観。

Wooden facade. 木造のファサード。

Reception area. レセプションあたり。

Dining area and surroundings.
景色に融け込むダイニングエリア。

Looking at inner dining area with open kitchen from the bar lounge. バー/ラウンジより奥のオープンキッチンを備えたダイニングエリアを見る。

Table seats in the shape of an amphitheater. 階段状に設けるテーブル席。

Service area with point-of-sale and bar lounge. ＰＯＳを備えたサービスエリアとバー/ラウンジ。

RIVIERA ＜Redondo Beach＞
リビエラ＜レドンド・ビーチ＞

Address: 1615 Pacific Coast Hwy, Redondo Beach, CA 90277
Phone/310-540-2501 FAX/310-316-6412
Designer:Ben Burkhalter L. A. Design

Facade with parking space. パーキングスペースを店頭に持つファサード。

Patio with electric heaters above. 上部に電気の暖房機を備えるパティオ。

Looking at the patio and reception area from inside. 店内よりレセプションとパティオ方向を見る。

This Mexican restaurant is located in Redondo Beach, approximately 16 km (10 miles) south of Los Angeles International Airport. The premises consist of a (28-seat) patio, a (10-seat) bar and a (90-seat) dining room. The colorful interior space is decorated with surfboards and ocean fish.

ロサンゼルス国際空港の南、約16kmにあるレドンド・ビーチのメキシカンレストラン。店内はパティオ (28席)、バー (10席)、ダイニングルーム (90席) で構成。サーフィンと海の魚を飾るカラフルなインテリア。

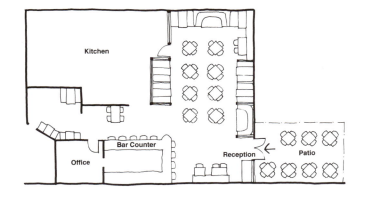

Kitchen, looking from the latticed windows of the inner dining area. ダイニングエリアの奥のガラス格子からキッチンが見える。

Looking at bar corner at right. 右にバーコーナーを見る。

Looking at bar area with skylights from the inner dining area. 奥のダイニングエリアから天窓を配したバーエリアを見る。

CHIMAYO GRILL ＜Newport Beach＞
チマヨ・グリル＜ニューポート・ビーチ＞

Address: 327 Newport Center Dr., Newport Beach, CA 92660
Phone/714-640-2700

Facade. ファサード。

Dining area from the reception area. レセプションあたりから見るダイニングエリア。

Dining area with wood frame ceilings. 木組みの天井を配したダイニングエリア。

Chimayo Grill, which specializes in southwestern foods, is located in Fashion Island Shopping Center, Newport Beach, California. The interior space was inspired by the streets of Santa Fe, New Mexico, which consists of a (140-seat) dining room decorated with contemporary art works and a (20-seat) tequila bar vividly lit by a burning fire place.

ニューポート・ビーチの［ファッション・アイランド・ショッピング・センター］内に出店したサウス・ウエスタン料理の店。ニューメキシコ州のサンタ・フェの街を想い起こす店内の造り。温かな夕日の色彩を配した壁に、コンテンポラリーなフォークアートを飾るダイニングルーム（140席）とファイアープレイスが燃えるような雰囲気の照明を施す"テキーラバー"（20席）で構成。

Upper part of bar, with views of the New Mexican landscape. ニューメキシコの風景を描くバーの上方部。

Bar area decorated with folk art.
フォークアートを飾るバーエリア。

Contemporary folk art and booth seats. コンテンポラリー・フォークアートとブース席。

ROUTE 66 ＜Pasadena＞
ルート・66 ＜パサデナ＞

Address: 425 S. Fair Oaks Avenue, Pasadena, CA 91105
Phone/818-793-8462

Entrance at parking side. 駐車場側に設けるエントランス。

Reception area. レセプションあたり。

Bar area. バーエリア。

The gallery-style Route 66 has an "automobile" theme. The old brick garage was renovated to create a (125-seat) restaurant/bar, displayed with original prints, paintings, photographs and sculptures, all inspired by automobiles such as antique sports cars. Those are all priced for sale. It offers creative Californian cuisine.

"車"をテーマとした店舗デザインのレストラン/バー。レンガ造りのガレージをギャラリー風に改装した店内 (125席) に、アンティークのスポーツカーをはじめ、車を題材としたオリジナルの版画や絵画、写真、彫刻品などを飾る。すべて価格が表示され、販売もしている。料理はクリエイティブなカリフォルニア・キュイジーヌ。

Dining area. ダイニングエリア。

THUNDER ROADHOUSE CAFE ＜West Hollywood＞
サンダー・ロードハウス・カフェ＜ウエスト・ハリウッド＞

Address: 8363 Sunset Boulevard, West Hollywood, CA 90069
Phone/213-650-6011 FAX/213-650-3705

Signboard. サインボード。

Facade. ファサード。

Counter seats. カウンター席。

Dining room. ダイニングルーム。

Facing Sunset Boulevard in West Hollywood, Thunder Roadhouse Cafe is a (225-seat) cafe bar with a "motorcycle" theme. Attracting motorbike fans, the premises display antique motorbikes and their posters. It consists of a counter area with Harley-Davidson motorcycle seats, polished pine tabletops, chandeliers made of gasoline tanks and lamps made of race trophies. There is also a sales corner selling a wide-range of products such as T-shirts and motorcycles.

ウエスト・ハリウッドのサンセット・ストリップに面し、"モーターサイクル"をテーマとしたカフェ/バー（225席）。バイクファンにとっては魅力の、アンティークのバイクやポスターが飾ってある。ハーレイ・ダビッドソンのシートが並ぶカウンター席、磨きのかかったパインツリーのテーブルトップ、ガソリンタンクで造るシャンデリア、レースのトロフィで造ったランプなどがある。Tシャツからモーターサイクルまで売る、物販コーナーを併設する。

Opposite: Dining room. Above: Bar area. 左ページ：ダイニングルーム。上：バーエリア。

Sales corner. 物販コーナー。

169

DIVE ＜Los Angeles＞
ダイブ＜ロサンゼルス＞

Address: Century City Shopping Center, 10250 Santa Monica Boulevard, Los Angeles, CA 90067
　　　　 Phone/310-788-3483　FAX/310-557-0705
Designer: Architecture/Meisel Associates, Ltd., Chicago
　　　　　Dale Mason and Phil Hettema

Submarine-shaped facade in the Century City Shopping Center.
ショッピングセンター内に出店したサブマリン（潜水艦）のファサード。

Entrance with a hatch. ハッチを設けたエントランス。

Reception area. Computerized circular floors project logotypes of light-emitting diodes. レセプションあたり。円形の床はコンピューター制御で、発光ダイオードのロゴが映し出される。

Totally produced by the movie director, Steven Spielberg, Dive is an entertainment/theme restaurant in a food complex in Century City Shopping Center, Los Angeles, whose main theme is a "submarine".

The 1,000-m² (11,000-sq. ft.) floor space consists of a 300-seat dining area (on the first and the second floors) with state-of-the-art audiovisual equipment. The first floor includes a lounge area, a semicircle bar and an open kitchen, while the second floor includes a dining room decorated with inside images of an underwater submarine. The theme colors are red, blue and yellow. The most popular menu item is a submarine-shaped gourmet sandwich.

ロサンゼルスの［センチュリーシティ・ショッピングセンター］内のフード・コンプレックスに出店。映画監督のスチーブン・スピールバーグの総合プロデュースによる、潜水艦をテーマとしたエンターテイメント/テーマレストラン。

1,000 ㎡の床面積に、最先端のオーディオ・ビジュアル装置を駆使した300席のダイニングスペース（1, 2階）を設ける。1階にラウンジエリアとセミサークルのバー、オープンキッチンを置く。2階は海中の潜水艦の内部を演出したダイニングルーム。テーマカラーはレッド、ブルー、イエロー。サブマリンの特製グルメ・サンドイッチが売り物。

Bar stools, the design for which was inspired by torpedoes, with booth seats behind.
魚雷をデザインしたバースツールと奥にブース席を見る。

Lounge area.
潜水艦の先端部にあたるラウンジエリア。

Open kitchen area designed with images of a galley (a long low single-decked ship propelled by oars and sails, used by old American navy).
ガリィ（galley＝昔の米国海軍の喫水の浅い帆船）をイメージしたオープンキッチンあたり。

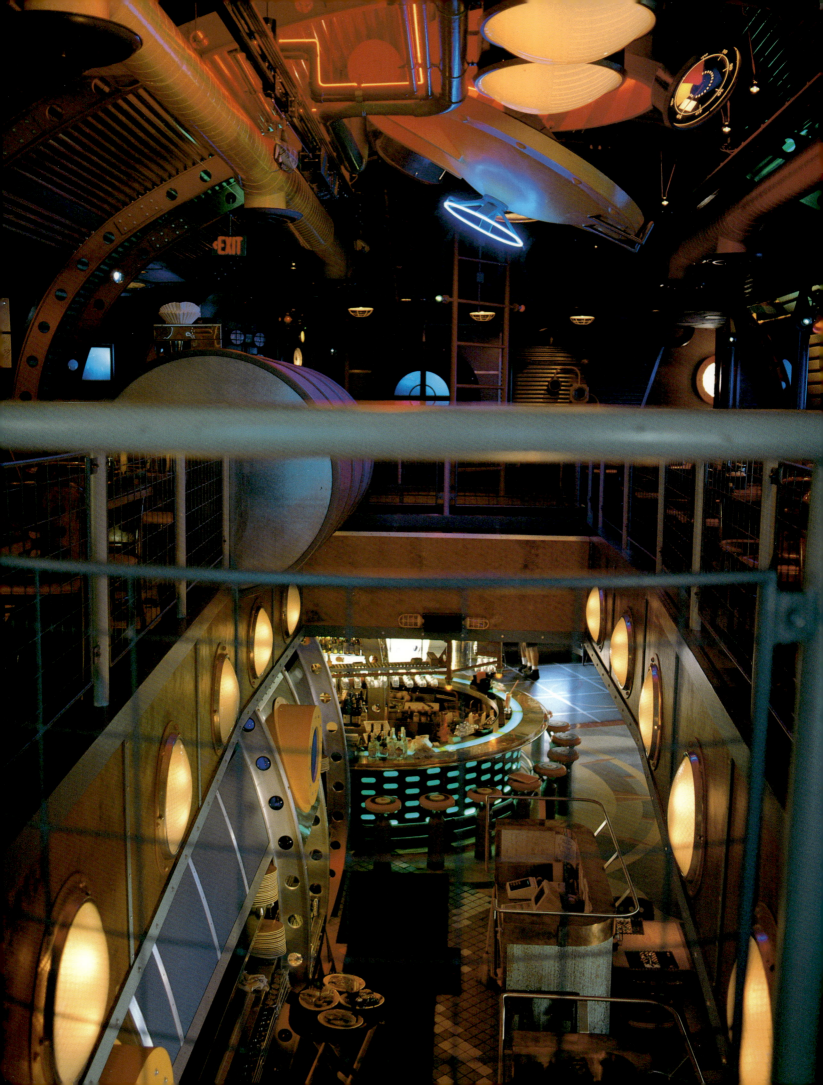

Opposite: Looking at the bar area from the stairwell of the central area on the second floor.
左ページ：2階中央部の吹き抜けからバー方向を見る。

Interior space with computerized programs for lighting and sound control.
コンピューター制御により照明や音響が変わる2階店内。

THE STINKING ROSE ＜Los Angeles＞
ザ・スティンキング・ローズ＜ロサンゼルス＞

Address: 55 N. La Cienega Boulevard, Beverly Hills, CA 90211
Phone/310-652-7673

Exterior. 外観。

Entrance. エントランス。

Entrance with images of garlic farms. ガーリック畑の風景を演出するエントランス。

Sales corner and restaurant entrance. 物販コーナーとレストランの入口。

A theme restaurant, The Stinking Rose, specializes in Italian garlic cooking and faces North La Cienega Boulevard, which is called "Restaurant Law" in Beverly Hills. The name of the restaurant refers to garlic.

The interior space consists of various parts: the European courtyard setting (60~190-seat) "The Piazza" with canopy tents, trees and an Italian-cafe-style facade; the semicircular Renaissance (62-seat) "Michelangelo Room" with scarlet canopies lined with miniature bulbs; the wine-cellar-shaped (36-seat) "Dracula's Grotto" designed to look like Dracula's residence; the small Italian (36-seat) cafe/restaurant "Chianti Room" decorated with decanter bottles and corks; the (60-seat) "Garlywood" parody of Hollywood with wall paintings of garlic characters and rodeo drives, Venice beach scenes and Sunset Strip atmosphere; and the (50~100-seat) bar lounge "The Garbar" recalling an Italian style turban. Other facilities include sales corners and cigar bars.

ビバリーヒルズのレストラン・ローと呼ばれるノース・ラ・シエネガ通りに面した、イタリア風ガーリック料理のテーマレストラン。店名は"異臭を発する薔薇"つまり、ガーリックの意。

店内は、スペースによりそれぞれ異なったテーマでデザインされている。キャノピー・テント、木々やイタリアン・カフェのファサードを配する、ヨーロッパのコートヤードを設定した［ザ・ピアッツァ］（60～190席）。20cm×160cmのコンピューター・グラフィックスによる壁画と、豆電球を配した真紅のキャノピーのあるルネッサンス調の半円形の部屋は、［ミケランジェロ・ルーム］（62席）。ワインセラーにドラキュラが住むという設定の［ドラキュラズ・グロット］（36席）。キャンドルだけの照明で、キャンティボトルとコークを飾る、小さなイタリアのカフェ/レストランの造りは［キャンティ・カフェ］（36席）。ロデオ・ドライブやベニス・ビーチ、サンセット・ストリップなどと、ガーリックのキャラクターを配した壁画で構成しハリウッドを捩って名付けた、ブース席の［ガリィウッド］（60席）。イタリアン・スタイルのタバーンを想わせるバー/ラウンジ［ザ・ガーバー］（50～100席）。他に、物販コーナー、シガーバーなどで構成。

"THE PIAZZA". [ザ・ピアッツァ]

"THE GARBAR". [ザ・ガーバー]

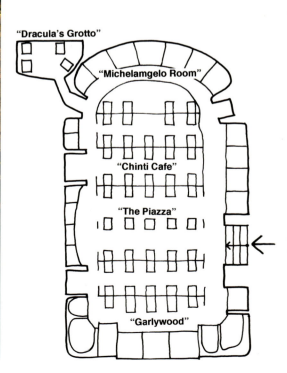

"GARLYWOOD". [ガリィウッド]

"MICHELANGELO ROOM". [ミケランジェロ・ルーム]

"DRACULA'S GROTTO". [ドラキュラズ・グロット]

Opposite: "CHIANTI CAFFE". 右ページ：[キャンティ・カフェ]

INDEX インデックス （地名別・店名＝アルファベット順で、掲載ページを表示しました。）

●Beverly Hills／ビバリーヒルズ

BARNEY GREENGRASS　バーニーズ・グリーングラス／130
Add: 9570 Wilshire Boulevard, Beverly Hills, CA 90212
Phone/310-777-5877　Fax/310-777-5760

OBACHINE　オバシン／92
Add: 242 N. Beverly Drive, Beverly Hills, CA 90210
Phone/310-274-4440　Fax/310-274-2611

●Las Vegas／ラスベガス

MONTE CARLO RESORT & CASINO
モンテカルロ・リゾート&カジノ／42
Add: 3770 Las Vegas Boulevard, South Las Vegas, Nevada 89109
Phone/702-730-7777
BUFFET　ビュッフェ／44
CAFE　カフェ／46
DRAGON NOODLE COMPANY
ドラゴン・ヌードル・カンパニー／48
MARKET CITY CAFFE　マーケット・シティ・カフェ／50
MONACO GARDENS FOOD COURT
モナコ・ガーデンズ・フードコート／49
MONTE CARLO PUB & BREWERY
モンテカルロ・パブ&ブリュワリー／52

NEW YORK NEW YORK HOTEL & CASINO
ニューヨーク・ニューヨーク・ホテル&カジノ／7
Add: 3790 Las Vegas Boulevard, Las Vegas, Nevada 89109
Phone/702-740-6969　FAX/702-740-6510
CHIN CHIN　チン・チン／16
CONEY ISLAND FOOD PAVILION
コニー・アイランド・フード・パビリオン／28
GALLAGHER'S STEAKHOUSE
ガラガーズ・ステーキハウス／24
HAMILTON'S　ハミルトンズ／26
IL FORNAIO CUCINA ITALIANA
イル・フォーナイオ・クチナ・イタリアーナ／10
IL FORNAIO PANETTERIA
イル・フォーナイオ・パネッテリア／14
RESTAURANT AMERICA　レストラン・アメリカ／20

THE ORLEANS　ジ・オーリンズ／30
Add: 4500 West Tropicana Avenue, Las Vegas, Nevada 89103
Phone/702-365-7111　Fax/702-365-7499
CANAL STREET GRILL　カナル・ストリート・グリル／32
COURTYARD CAFE　コートヤード・カフェ／34
DON MIGUEL'S　ドン・ミゲルズ／38
FRENCH MARKET BUFFET
フレンチ・マーケット・ビュッフェ／40
VITO'S ITARIAN RESTAURANT
ヴィトス・イタリアン・レストラン／36

●Los Angeles／ロサンゼルス

CAFE PINOT　カフェ・ピノ／118
Add: 700 West 5th Street, Los Angeles, CA 90071
Phone/213-239-6500　Fax/213-239-6514
CAVA　カバ／134
Add: 8384 W. Third Street, Los Angeles, CA
Phone/213-658-8898　Fax/213-658-8998
DAILY GRILL　デイリー・グリル／138
Add: Tom Bradley International Terminal at LAX Airport, CA
Phone/310-215-5180

BARNEY GREENGRASS

OBACHINE

MONTE CARLO RESORT&CASINO

BUFFET　CAFE

DRAGON NOODLE COMPANY　MARKET CITY CAFFE

MONACO GARDENS FOOD COURT　MONTE CARLO PUB& BREWERY

NEW YORK NEW YORK HOTEL & CASINO　CHIN CHIN

CONEY ISLAND PAVILION　GALLAGHER'S STEAKHOUSE

HAMILTON'S　IL FORNAIO CUCINA ITALIANA

IL FORNAIO PANETTERIA　RESTAURANT AMERICA

THE ORLEANS　CANAL STREET GRILL

COURTYARD CAFE　DON MIGUEL'S

FRENCH MARKET BUFFET　VITO'S ITARIAN RESTAUTANT

CAFE PINOT

CAVA

DAILY GRILL

DIVE　ダイブ／170
Add: Century City Shopping Center 10250, Santa Monica Boulevard, Los Angeles, CA 90067
Phone/310-788-3483　Fax/310-557-0705
NICOLA　ニコラ／114
Add: 601 S. Figueroa Street, Los Angeles, CA 90017
Phone/213-485-0927　Fax/213-485-0931
MONDRIAN HOTEL　モンドリアン・ホテル／100
Add: 8440 Sunset Boulevard, Los Angeles, CA 90069
Phone/213-650-8999
COCO PAZZO　ココ・パッツォ／102
THE ORIGINAL SONORA CAFE
ジ・オリジナル・ソノラ・カフェ／126
Add: 180 South La Brea, Los Angeles, CA 90036
Phone/213-857-1800
THE STINKING ROSE　ザ・スティンキング・ローズ／176
Add: F55 N. La Cienega Boulevard, Beverly Hills, CA 90211
Phone/310-652-7673

● Malibu／マリブ

CHART HOUSE　チャート・ハウス／150
Add: F18412 Pacific Coast Highway, Malibu, CA 90265
Phone/310-454-9321

● Newport Beach／ニューポート・ビーチ

CHIMAYO GRILL／チマヨ・グリル／158
Add: F327 Newport Center Dr., Newport Beach, CA 92660
Phone/714-640-2700

● Pasadena／パサデナ

IL FORNAIO CUCINA ITALIANA
イル・フォーナイオ・クチナ・イタリアーナ／146
Add: 24 West Union Street, Pasadena, CA 91103
Phone/818-683-9797　Fax/818-683-0789
ROUTE 66　ルート・66／162
Add: 425 S. Fair Oaks Avenue, Pasadena, CA 91105
Phone/818-793-8462
TWIN PALMS　ツイン・パームス／142
Add: 101 West Green Street, Pasadena, CA 91105
Phone/818-577-2567　Fax/818-577-1306

● Redondo Beach／レドンド・ビーチ

RIVIERA　リビエラ／154
Add: 1615 Pacific Coast Hwy, Redondo Beach, CA 90277
Phone/310-540-2501　Fax/310-316-6412

● San Francisco／サンフランシスコ

BABALOO　ババルー／68
Add: 2030 Lombard, San Francisco, CA 94123
Phone/415-346-5474
GRAND CAFE　グランド・カフェ／76
Add: 501 Geary Street, San Francisco, CA 94102
Phone/415-292-0101　Fax/415-292-0150
HAWTHORNE LANE　ホーソーン・レーン／60
Add: 22 Hawthorn Street(at Howard), San Francisco, CA 94105
Phone/415-777-9779　Fax/415-777-9782
ROSE PISTOLA　ローズ・ピストーラ／64
Add: F532 Colunbus Avenue, San Francisco, CA 94133
Phone/415-399-0499　Fax/415-399-8758
THIRSTY BEAR　サースティ・ベアー／56
Add: 661 Howard Street, San Francisco, CA 94105
Phone/415-974-0945　Fax/415-974-0955

DIVE

NICOLA

MONDRIAN HOTEL　　COCO PAZZO

THE ORIGINAL SONORA CAFE

THE STINKING ROSE

CHART HOUSE

CHIMAYO GRILL

IL FORNAIO CUCINA ITALIANA

ROUTE 66

TWIN PALMS

RIVIERA

BABALOO

GRAND CAFE

HAWTHORNE LANE

ROSE PISTOLA

THIRSTY BEAR

VERTIGO RESTAURANT & BAR
バータゴウ・レストラン&バー／72
Add: 600 Montgomery Street, San Francisco, CA 94111
Phone/415-433-7250

● Santa Monica／サンタモニカ

JIRAFFE　ジラフ／106
Add: 502 Santa Monica Boulevard, Santa Monica, CA 90401
Phone/310-917-6671　Fax/310-917-6677
MONSOON CAFE　モンスーン・カフェ／80
Add: 1212 Third Street, Santa Monica, CA 90401
Phone/310-576-9996　Fax/310-576-9988
2424 PICO　2424・ピコ／84
Add: 2424 Pico Boulevard, Santa Monica, CA 90405
Phone/310-581-1124　Fax/310-581-1338
WOLFGANG PUCK CAFE
ウォルフガング・パック・カフェ／88
Add: 1323 Montana Avenue, Santa Monica, CA 90403
Phone/310-393-0290　Fax/310-393-6892

● West Hollywood／ウエストハリウッド

ECLIPSE　イクリプス／122
Add: 8800 Melrose Avenue, West Hollywood, CA 90069
Phone/310-724-5959
FENIX　フェニックス／110
Add: 8358 Sunset Boulevard, West Hollywood, CA 90069
Phone/213-848-6677
LE COLONIAL　ル・コロニアル／96
Add: 8783 Beverly Boulevard, West Hollywood, CA 90048
Phone/310-289-0660
THUNDER ROADHOUSE CAFE
サンダー・ロードハウス・カフェ／166
Add: 8363 Sunset Boulevard, West Hollywood, CA 90069
Phone/213-650-6011　Fax/213-650-3705

VERTIGO RESTAURANT & BAR

JIRAFFE

MONSOON CAFE

2424 PICO

WOLFGANG PUCK CAFE

ECLIPSE

FENIX

LE COLONIAL

THUNDER ROADHOUSE CAFE

アメリカのレストランデザイン

著者・写真：斎藤　武

発行日：1997年11月25日

定価：4,700円

発行所：
株式会社　プロトギャラクシー
〒103 東京都中央区日本橋蛎殻町1-38-12
電話 03-5640-1751　FAX 03-5640-1755

発行人：多田光雄

編集・デザイン：伊藤美和子

編集協力：辻田　博

翻訳：岡崎伸太郎

印刷：今井書店印刷工場

本書の収録内容の無断掲載、複写、引用を禁じます。

Night of Death and Flowers

Rebecca L. Garcia

Night of Death and Flowers

Copyright © 2024 by Rebecca L. Garcia

The characters in this book are fictitious. Any similarity to real persons, living or dead, is coincidental and not intended by the author.

All rights reserved.

No part of this publication may be reproduced, stored in a retrieval system, or transmitted, in any form or by any means, electronic, mechanical, photocopying, recording or otherwise, nor translated into a machine language, without the written permission of the publisher.

The moral right of the author had been asserted.

This was a work of fiction. Any resemblance to actual persons, living or dead, events, and organizations was purely coincidental.

Line edits and proofreading by Lunar Rose Editing & V.M.

Developmental edits by Renee Polkinghorne

Cover Design by Jamila Jariwala (@acourtofjamila)

AUTHOR'S NOTE

Thank you for picking up your copy of Night of Death and Flowers! Access the in-depth glossary of terms on my website by clicking the link below. It can also be found at the back of the book for those who like a quick reference of terms, however, it is not necessary to read to understand the story.

www.rebeccagarciabooks.com/worldbuildingguide

This book is intended for readers 18 and older and contains sensitive subject matter that may be triggering for some readers.

Content Warnings:

Animal death, blood and gore, child death by choking (with resurrection, flashback, on page), execution by hanging, graphic violence, emotional parental abuse, human sacrifice, multiple character deaths, profanity, religious oppression and trauma, physical parental abuse (open hand slap, one scene, on page), sexual content, snakes, spiders, and strangulation.

May you find magic and courage in all things,
Amanda E. Hughes, Bradley Bolt,
Amanda Eschmeyer, Hannah and Megan Long.

To V, for your keen eye and fierce soul!

For those of you who dream of villains, magic, and love,

may you find your home within these pages.

PLAYLIST

Black Sea by Natasha Blume

Wicked Games by RAIGN

Warfare by Katie Garfield

Glass Heart by Tommee Profitt and Sam Tinnesz

Darkness by X V I

Where Your Secrets Hide by Klergy and Katie Garfield

Dark in my Imagination by of Verona

Darkside by Neoni

Not Afraid Anymore by Halsey

Blood//Water by grandson

War of Hearts by Ruelle

Breathe by Tommee Profitt and Fleurie

Legends Never Die by League of Legends and Against the Current

Man or a Monster by Sam Tinnesz and Zayde WØlf

Game of Survival by Ruelle

12 Rounds by Bohnes

Yellow Flicker Beat by Lorde

Fates by Kaia Jette

You've Created a Monster by Bohnes
Enemy by Tommee Profitt, Beacon Light, and Sam Tinnesz
Living in the Shadows by Matthew Perryman Jones
The Foundations of Decay by My Chemical Romance
All the Things She Said by Ponette
Cravin' by Stileto and Kendyle Paige
Couldn't Stop Caring by The Spiritual Machines
Haunted by ADONA
Up in Flames by Ruelle
Don't Let Me Go by Raign
Bad Dream by Ruelle
Burn by 2WEI and Edda Hayes
I'm Yours by Isabel LaRosa

ENNISMORE

CAL

THE CHURCH

ABANDONED HOUSE

THE INCARCURI

...OUSE

TOWN SQUARE

THE BLACK SEA

THE STONES

NIGHT MARKET

SACRIFICE'S WALK

ABANDONED HOUSE

DOCKS

CEMETARY

TENENOCTI

DARK RIVER

DEATH'S TEMPLE

PRONUNCIATION GUIDE

Arabella (Ari-belle-ah)

Astraea (As-tray-ah)

Azkiel (Az-keel)

Calista (Cal-ee-stah)

Cyna (Sin-ah)

Dahryst (Daw-wrist)

Dephina (Deaf-ee-nah)

Essentria (Ess-en-tree-ah)

Everist (Ever-ist)

Guildre (Gill-druh)

Gurger (Gurj-ur)

Incarcuri (In-carss-ure-eye)

Knog (Nog)

Libren (Lee-brun)

Morcidea (More-sid-ee-ah)

ONE

Calista

The Harvest is coming, and soon, eleven of us will be sacrificed.

The cold air seeps into my bones, settling beside the slither of unease in my stomach. I gaze out my window into the rich night that promises such wonder, yet I can't settle my nerves.

No. We will not be chosen. We are the daughters of an elder.

Yet, as I tilt my head, gazing into the still silhouette of the forest behind our house, I cannot shake the dread threading through my every thought.

I kneel, hiking up the skirt of my navy blue dress, and glide my onyx dagger into its sheath, the blade never fully warming to my thigh.

"I hope you're not planning on using that tonight." My sister's voice resonates, and I jolt, whipping my head around to watch as she crosses the threshold into my room, swaddled in a purple, velvet cloak.

I tug the fabric of my dress down until it lands around my ankles—the blade hidden behind layers of linen and woven wool. "I will act according to people's behavior," I say, and lower my gaze to her heavy, black dress. At least she took the advice to wear darker colors tonight. "You should bring a blade, too."

Her gentle touch lands on the sides of my forearms, her lips stretched into a painted-peach smile. "I never thought I'd be the one calming you down." Her tone softens, but the sharp edge of impatience is enunciated in each word. "Tonight is supposed to be a night of merriment. It's unlikely anyone will hurt us."

I nod, my lips forming a tight line. "There are a lot of visitors right now, many of whom don't know who our father is."

"I know," she says, then turns to us, blocking the view of the wardrobe behind her. "Anyway, I have taken *some* precautions." She plucks one of the purple flowers speckling her long, golden braid, and hands it to me. "Night Blossom," she announces, as if

NIGHT OF DEATH AND FLOWERS

I don't know what the poisonous plant that flowers outside of our home looks like.

I take the bud between my pinched fingers, my expression souring as I examine it. The tear where it was recklessly pulled from its black vines will make the poison inside far less potent, but at least the silver veins threading through the five dark-purple petals are still vibrant enough to cause some damage. "I see," I say. "It seems you're wearing your weapon tonight."

She grins, her cheeks balling, wrinkling her delicate features. "I learned from the best. I'm surprised you're not bringing several vials of poison with you, too."

I tap the fabric over my thigh, feeling the bulge of the dagger under my fingers. "The blade is laced with enough to kill ten men."

"I'm joking," she says with a roll of her eyes. "Let's go before we miss all the festivities."

"If only," I mumble under my breath, but fortunately, my sister doesn't hear me. I shouldn't be so pessimistic. She's been looking forward to this for weeks and experiencing some change will come as a relief. Every day here is the same: propagated speeches every three days at the church, the daily market of fresh bread, fish, and meat, and now that we have graduated from the academy, monthly dinners with potential suitors and their families.

I'd rather stab myself in the eye than sit through another one of those. But it is my future, my fate, and I can do nothing about it except make myself as unworthy a match as possible.

Ari's eyes drop to the corset cinching around my waist. "When did you get that?"

"I wanted to try something different."

Her blonde hair sweeps to one side when she tilts her head. "Is that blush on your cheeks?"

"What of it?"

Her lips curve into an amused grin. "I'm assuming Drake is going to be at the market."

"Stop talking," I warn, and she laughs.

"Okay, okay," she says, waving her hand in the air.

I hug my cloak around me, covering my dress and corset. "Let us go before Mother hears us."

"I'm so excited," Ari whispers as we walk out the door, our steps quiet as we pull the hoods of our cloaks over our heads and take the servant's entrance to the gardens.

The fresh, cold air brushes my face as we walk, keeping to the shadows of the tall plants and trees. We slide between two Night Blossom vines, the thorns snagging against the fabric of my cloak as I shuffle my way down the narrow path on the side of our house.

My stomach dips when we hit the bustling cobblestone streets, illuminated by the soft, blue glow of lanterns. While it is widely accepted that the six covens—each boasting thousands of families across the entire continent of Dahryst—live in harmony in large communities of witches, I know too well how easily fights can break out between the coven factions. I will not be caught off guard, especially when countless visitors have fallen into Ennismore, our usually sleepy town on the east edge of the country. But I promised Ari we would go. I am curious to see it myself. The Harvest, and the Night Market erected to celebrate it, only happens every ten years, and I was too young to experience the last one at thirteen years old.

As we reach the town square, a drizzle of rain descends like a curtain, obscuring everything in a mystical, silver mist. Through the glittering fog, laughter interspersed with conversation fills the air. Gradually, the mist dissipates, revealing a cavern of booths sparkling under the canopy of twinkling stars.

"It's really here," Ari whispers, her jaw slacking. "The Night Market."

I white-knuckle my coin purse, then whisper, "Stay close to me."

She nods, but anticipation threading her eyes is enhanced by the current of excitement charging into the air as the first night of festivities unfolds.

"You hear that?" I ask as we push our way through the bustling crowds.

At first, the music is faint, but as we near the center of the market, the melody grows louder. Blue light spills through the aisles as a quartet of musicians perform like songbirds, their harmonies echoing through the air. A man's hand glides across a silver, enchanted harp, and two women in flowing black robes complement the harp's melodic sound with their flutes.

My gaze snaps to a gangly man as he walks in front of us. He snips the ties of another man's leather coin pouch into his nimble fingers, before disappearing seamlessly into the crowd.

"Don't let your coin out of your sight," I warn Ari.

The darkness whispers secrets wherever we walk, offering glimpses into the depravity hidden underneath the performances. Because no matter how they dress it up, this is a celebration of the upcoming slaughter of eleven people—one of whom may be my best friend. He, along with my sister and I, must volunteer for The Harvest. Our mother has assured us we will not be chosen, because our father is an elder. But, unlike us, Drake does not have anyone other than me to protect him.

NIGHT OF DEATH AND FLOWERS

Arabella catches hold of my hand as I push my way through crowds of witches, many of whom have traveled from the various provinces of Dahryst to our town.

Ari pulls on my arm, her fingers gripping around my elbow. "I've never seen so many people."

I grimace as I cast my eyes around the newcomers clad in crimson robes, to signify the upcoming Harvest. Dressing up like sacrifices is one thing, but some even have red paint slathered over their shoulders and faces, representing the blood that will be spilled.

"A travesty," I state.

"It's also quite beautiful," Ari counters.

The people are as eccentric as the items on their tables, many wearing masks fashioned from clay or plaster, decorated with silver leaves, crow feathers, and the flowers of the Night Evedelain plant. I wonder if they realize the rose heads they have torn from their stems induce insanity when properly crushed. They are beautifully arranged around the mask's edges, the layers of blood-red petals slowly turning black the closer they get to the midpoint.

Located in the center of the square, where we normally barter with local farmers and bakers, stand tall, pointed tents decorated with paints depicting the scales of the shadow viper, and the sigil of the God of Death.

He is everywhere—his symbol embroidered into people's tunics, and painted on their bare arms, his likeness forged in stone effigies, and depicted on canvases. He is ethereal, with flowing silver hair, and predatorial eyes glistening like stars. Even those who are not in his coven worship him this week.

Not me. I grimace as his essence surrounds me, surfacing a painful reminder of the magic I harbor. Arabella's hand tightens around mine, her grip conveying a silent comfort as I am transported back to the night that changed my life forever.

Even now, seven years after the incident, I can still feel the icy tendrils of death as I remember that night—the pointless fighting and panic as I was dragged into the forest by the deadliest creature of them all: a Phovus. I shudder, recalling the shapeshifting shadow creature and how it first appeared in human form, its wide, yellow eyes resembling those of a cat. Then it morphed into a serpentine shape, made of darkness and mist, as if it were crafted from the essence of the night itself.

The sound of my bones snapping under the Phovus' tight hold will forever be imprinted into my mind along with the relentless agony that followed and made me wish it would hurry and kill me. But I wasn't so lucky.

NIGHT OF DEATH AND FLOWERS

As the creature's final squeeze brought me to the brink of death, it was my best friend, Drake, who saved me. An illusion, born from his powers from the Goddess of Dreams, bathed the forest in a bright light, distracting the creature.

I'd waited sixteen years to find out which of the Goddess of Creation's powers I would possess. When my magic presented itself for the first time, and the Phovus crumbled, falling like ash between my fingers, I realized I instead harbored one of the most dangerous powers possessed by the God of Death himself. Magic, that if discovered, will see me at the end of a rope.

The gods gifted witches many powers, but never their ethereal magic, and for Azkiel, his decay magic gives him the ability to kill anything with one touch.

My fingers pulse, as if my magic can sense my dark thoughts, and I quickly pull my hand from my sister's.

"Get your hands on the Choosing's list of volunteers," a man's voice rings out into the crowd, with a cart filled with rolled-up papers.

I grimace, shooting the man daggers through the crowd. My glare penetrates his aura enough that his eyes lift to meet mine.

"Don't," Ari warns as I step forward, gritting my teeth. Her hand lands on my arm, and she swings me toward a small booth.

"I wasn't going to do anything," I whisper as we stop in front of Eren's table.

She shoots me an incredulous glare, and I smile.

Eren watches me as I lean over the stall. Her hands slam on the table between us, her over-shaped face etched with wrinkles, each a reminder of the irritation and stress from having witnessed seven Harvests.

"I'm not selling to ya," she says, and sweeps her long, silver braid hanging below her stomach, over her shoulder.

I sigh, and I climb my eyes to meet hers. "Coward."

Eren's thin lips curve as she leans back, shaking her head when we both let out a clipped laugh. "Your father will have my head."

I roll my eyes, then tug Arabella closer. "Hear that, Ari?"

I direct my words to my sister, whose eyes brim with anxiety as the night darkens and the blanket of stars glitters.

"He would never," she snaps, then pulls her hand from mine, crossing her arms. "Excuse us, Eren. You have a uh… lovely display of… medicines?"

"Poisons," Eren corrects, then smirks at me. "Suppose I should be grateful your father won't allow his daughter to become a potioneer." She points a long finger at me as my sister ushers us along. "Might put me out of business. Ya got talent, child."

"See, Ari?" I tease. "Someone thinks it is a talent."

"Goodnight, Eren," my sister says, then pushes me toward the Weaver's tents erected outside of the Grumpy Gurger Tavern. Once we're out of earshot, her scent of vanilla and jasmine wafts towards me as she leans in and whispers, "Are you trying to get us in trouble?"

I shrug. "Eren's harmless. I wasn't actually going to buy any."

"No," Ari says, her full lips slanted. "But you would buy ingredients for your own collection."

I swing the coin purse, then tuck it away inside the bosom of my dress, guildre and libren coins jingling inside. "It isn't against our laws," I point out.

"It isn't," she concedes, huddling closer, and pulling the hood of her dusky-purple cloak over her head, her golden curls tumbling down either side of her heart-shaped face. "However, it is frowned upon. Let us hurry, please. I want to see everything before Mother discovers we have snuck out."

"She won't check on me," I say, casting a glance at Ari and gauging her reaction. She rolls her eyes. It is uncanny how she shares the strongest resemblance to our mother, with her golden hair and violet eyes, yet is nothing like her.

However, I look most like our father, with blue eyes and chestnut-brown hair, and according to Ari, I'm just as stubborn as he is. Our two youngest sisters are somewhere in the middle. Cecilia, the youngest, took on mother's violet eyes, but father's dark hair and sharp features while Emilia inherited Mother's blonde waves, paired with her soft, dainty features.

I wiggle my fingers as the deadly magic threatens to surface again, and I shake my head, dispelling the thoughts of our mother, itching at the crevices of my mind.

"Look," Ari squeaks from beside me, and I trail my gaze to the opening of the main area of the market, with erected wood pillars reaching twenty feet in the air, tapestried with a canopy of silver and blue, woven from the fabrics of those skilled in embroidery and animation magic. The dream magic pulsing through every thread dances in purples and blues.

My breath catches in my throat as we enter. I may hate everything about The Harvest, but the elders truly have put on quite a show.

"Father didn't tell us it would be this spectacular," Ari announces as we walk past hordes of witches, all coming from different covens, wearing the colors and sigils of their gods with pride.

"No," I state, drawing Ari close. "He's good at keeping secrets."

NIGHT OF DEATH AND FLOWERS

I scan the witches, noting the colorful fashions. We are not required to dress in the colors of our coven, just as Ari and I are not wearing the colors of Essentria, the Goddess of Creation. But tonight, it seems everyone is dressed in the colors of their covens—various shades of green shimmer over the fabrics and skin paint of those in Cyna's coven, their discerning eyes evaluating the stalls lining the sides of the cobblestone street, transformed by this large tent. Members of our coven are distinguished by their gold adornments, a stark contrast to the black and silver worn by those in Azkiel's coven, the God of Death.

The dream witches, practicing Astraea's magic, the Goddess of Dreams, are beautiful in various shades of blue. Concurrently, those in Volan's coven, the God of Will, are bold and frightening in deep shades of red and orange, their warrior glares softened by the gentle glow of flickering lanterns.

Nyxara's coven stands out above the rest. The witches walk, adorned with the color attributed to destiny—purple. Their orb-like eyes wander, as if they're lost in thoughts and futures we cannot see.

A symphony of laughter and melodies erupts into the night from strong musicians accompanying us as we hurry through the labyrinth of teeming crowds. I inhale sharply, slowing my pace as we pass a crowded booth, peering over the shoulders of a group of witches. Cauldrons simmer with potions, bubbling in a kaleidoscope of colors, creating a mesmerizing dance of smoky swirls that interweave with the enchanting aroma of herbs and incense.

"So beautiful" Ari states as we stop by a stall filled with enchanted talismans. The gold chains and glistening gems lay on top of the vibrant tapestry covering the vendor's table. He waves us over, his weathered hands covered in silver rings, welcoming us with golden eyes, twinkling with a hint of mischief.

"This'll look pretty around your neck at your witch ball," he tells Arabella, and I shake my head.

"She's already had her ball, *four* years ago," I state, and before he can shove another amulet under our noses, I swiftly pull my sister to the booth next to his, where the most mouth-watering aromas permeate the air.

Her eyes flick up to meet mine. "Do I really look sixteen?"

"No," I say with a laugh.

I turn my attention to a young woman handing out pastries to two witches dressed in dark, floor-length robes. They walk away after handing over their coin, leaving the booth empty save for the two women standing behind it. They share the same raven-black hair and blue eyes, so I assume they are mother and daughter. I notice they're both adorned in the golds of Essentria's coven.

"Ooo," Ari coos, leaning over the stall, a mosaic of culinary enchantments.

Delicate, golden-crusted pastries dusted with a flurry of powdered sugar entice from a display that rivals an artist's canvas. Crystal jars filled with sugared petals and glistening chocolates beckon me, and my tongue instinctively slides between my lips.

The sweet aroma of buttery pastries and candied fruits mingles with the heady fragrance of smoke and magic, tantalizing my senses, unlike anything I've ever experienced at the local bakery.

"Want to try one?" The older of the two witches asks.

"Are they spelled?"

"These are not, but if you want our enchanted cakes, we have a selection here."

I put my hand up before she can disappear behind her stall and into a crate. "No, I'm good with the normal baked goods."

I glance at Ari, who tilts her head, the curiosity lacing her expression making me nervous. I lean closer, then whisper, "The last thing we need is to have our inhibitions lowered while surrounded by strangers in the middle of the night."

She nods, then lets out a small, relenting sigh.

The woman leans over, offering me a sample of a delicate strawberry tart. I bring the crumbly crust to my lips, breathing in its mouthwatering blend of buttery richness and blooming garden of berries.

My teeth sink into the soft, layered pastry, and my eyes flutter shut as all the flavors dance unrestrained upon my tongue.

"That," I say, after the last crumb has tumbled between my lips, "Is pure magic."

Ari lets out a soft moan beside me, finishing the last of a slice of cake, a waft of cinnamon drifting from her breath. "Pure magic," she agrees and pulls eight small bronze coins from her leather pouch. "What can I get for eight knogs?"

"Two more slices of that cake," the woman says, then folds them into brown paper.

I hold a single heavy silver coin between my fingers. "I'll take as many tarts as a guildre can afford me."

I turn as she hands me my confectionaries, and my gaze lands on a muscular figure standing three stalls up, wearing a tattered, brown cloak I'd recognize anywhere. Drake said he'd be here, but I thought perhaps he'd changed his mind.

His tousled black hair falls effortlessly across his forehead as he runs his fingers through it. A subtle tan adorns his skin, a tribute to his days of training in the sun. Most believe he wants to become an Enforcer, despite how few outside of Cyna's coven are being invited to be a protector, but I know the truth. Drake's family isn't influential, and when the Choosing happens, it's likely that his name will be drawn.

I swallow thickly as a lump forms in my throat, and Ari links her arm with mine, then waves at Drake. "Let's go say hi," she says. "Take your hood down and show off how pretty your hair looks tonight."

I bat her hand away when she attempts to touch my cloak. "He doesn't care how I look," I hiss, but straighten my posture.

"So? He can always change how he sees you."

"Stop meddling," I whisper.

I watch as he engages in conversation with a stall vendor, his eyes trailing over tomes of leather-bound books. The moment he leans over to take a closer look, his cloak parts and reveals his toned thighs, snugly hugged by a pair of fitted pants.

I know I shouldn't stare, but I can't resist stealing a glance now and then. A flush of heat creeps into my face, and I scowl at the obvious display of my emotion. Gods, I hate wearing my feelings so glaringly.

He waves to the vendor, his smile reaching his eyes and crinkling the corners. He turns, his baggy leather boots, worn and scuffed, then runs a hand over the stubble framing his rugged features.

He turns his attention in our direction, and then waves as he spots us. He hurries toward us with that charming wide smile. "Hey, Wildflower." He pauses, raking his eyes over my body with open appreciation. "You look different."

"*Good* different," Ari says, crossing her arms over her chest, and Drake arches his brow at me in a way that makes me want to shrink into the crowd.

"Yes," he drawls, his gaze focused on mine. "You're always beautiful to me."

Ari looks up at me, her eyes widening. She thinks she's being so subtle, as if we can't both see that told-you-so smile. Gods fucking kill me right now.

He drops his gaze to Ari, changing the subject. "I'm surprised *you're* out. Is your mother finally loosening those reins?"

Ari beams up at him, pride sharpening her expression. "She doesn't know. We snuck out."

"Such a rebel," he says, and his lips curve into a smirk as he turns from Ari to me, drinking me in with his emerald eyes. "Just like your sister."

"Anyway," I say, "we must get you home."

Ari's shoulders slump. "So soon?"

"Mother will murder me if she knows I brought you here."

She rolls her eyes. "I am twenty years of age and old enough to meet suitors. I can leave the house."

I lick my dry lips. "I agree but save your reasonings for her."

Drake's eyes lock onto mine. We both know I didn't sneak out tonight to just attend the Night Market. Tonight, the entirety of Ennismore is distracted, and it is our only chance to destroy it all.

His stare drops to Ari. "We'll walk you home. Cali's going to stay out a little late with me."

Ari shoots me a knowing look, then presses her lips in what I assume is an attempt to suppress a smile. "*Oh,* I see. In that case, I'll cover for you, Cali," she says, though I'm certain Mother won't notice my absence until we're due to make a public appearance, like at The Choosing ceremony.

My gaze flickers from Drake to my sister. Tonight changes everything. If we succeed in our plan, then we will have committed one of the greatest treasons in Dahryst. I look up at the star-speckled sky, grateful that Death has long since abandoned us.

TWO

Azkiel

The dead are so needy.

I lift my stare to a group of mortals as they're dragged deeper into the caverns of The Darklands by my reapers, begging for salvation as if they deserve it. They know nothing of repentance. Especially with the God of Judgment missing. Although, that last part is my doing.

A concave of gray stone surrounds us as I watch from the towering window of my castle. Wisps of dim light dance against the dark backdrop, each mortal's soul a fleeting echo of who they were when they were alive.

The small group falls into hysterics as they gaze upon the bleak, rocky landscape stretched out before them. A sea of shadows creeps over the ground below, hiding layers of jagged cliffs.

I shift position and place one arm against the stone, leaning forward. Every day is the same, watching from this window as more are brought here, an afterlife where hope is snuffed out in place of sorrow and regret. Here, they will suffer, just like the rest of them.

One soul falls to his knees, and a woman sobs into her translucent hands next to him as if they've been told a lie. As if life was supposed to have a happy ending.

The group scatters, and the cloaked, skeletal beings of my reapers walk back into the caves, sealing it behind them with their scythes.

A smile curves my mouth as a howl sounds in the distance. My Phovi are preparing to hunt the newly harvested souls. They have no idea what awaits them.

The seven souls stand upon a scarred rock looking into the abyss, unaware of how deep the cliffs go. As they glance around them, a haunting symphony of whispers fills the air, carried from the gnarled trees that make up the forest of remorse behind them. From here, I can discern the skeletal branches interwoven with skulls and bones in the distance.

One mortal points at my castle, and two press their hands together in prayer as if they may have found a haven.

A chuckle leaves my lips as the overlapping, distorted voices of my Phovi sound from the depths of the caverns. My shapeshifting, shadow creatures will drag the souls into the darkness before they can make it here.

It is a beautiful irony to witness souls gradually transform into the very beings they once feared, shedding their humanity until they barely resemble the witches or warlocks they once were.

I glimpse a flutter of iridescent dark blue in the corner of my eye, then step back as a flurry of ebony feathers crowds the view. The crow lands on the narrow ledge of the window, balancing on the stone before hopping inside.

"Well done," I praise as she tilts her head, her intelligent, beady eyes meeting mine. I retrieve the rolled-up parchment, which she fetched from a threader in the mortal world, from her pointed beak. She flies onto the top of my bone-white dresser and watches as I carefully unravel it.

My heart stammers as the inked words sink in. *The witch is alive. The prophecy will come to fruition.*

NIGHT OF DEATH AND FLOWERS

Shadows whip from my hands like ribbons as the prophecy lingers in my mind, words written by my sister, the Goddess of Destiny. The crow takes flight, likely fearing becoming collateral to the anger that quakes through my muted chambers.

Words that have appeared in countless dreams circle my mind: *Death shall betray his family and seek to prevent his fate. For one hundred and fifty years, Death shall hide, and all monsters and gods will be left in a slumber. Until the lost ones are reborn and on the fifteenth harvest, a daughter of creation, doomed with death, shall free those trapped and destroy Death's domain.*

A throbbing pain spears through my skull. If only I had a single memory before finding myself back at The Darklands. All I have are elusive dreams and a cryptic note I left myself one hundred and fifty years ago: *Never let them awaken.*

Since then, I've only learned dregs of information through my crows in the mortal world: I trapped the gods within my domain on Tenenocti island, a place we once called home.

No matter how much I've tried, my memories linger out of reach, like hazy smoke that can never be grasped. Yet, the emotions remain intact. Whatever caused me to leave and imprison my family was rooted in heartbreak and betrayal.

I have picked apart the prophecy countless times, carefully deciphering each phrase. My sister loved nothing more than giving double meaning to her words.

Daughter of creation.

As we cannot have children, it must mean the witch was born into Essentria's coven.

I mull over Nyxara's next words.

On the fifteenth harvest.

The sacrificial tournament—The Harvest—closes the last days of my one hundred and fifty years. From what I discovered while in the Darklands, I had used sacrificial magic to bind the magic spelling them to sleep. Therefore, if the prophesied witch is killed on that island, then it will undo the spell.

A daughter of creation, doomed with death, shall free those trapped and destroy Death's domain.

The witch will be amongst them, this Harvest. She will free them.

Draperies of silk woven from shadows cascade from the pillars that surround the chamber, their threads glistening with silver as if they were cut from the night sky.

I glide my fingers down one of the eight columns, each one an artistry of death, carved from bones and skulls of the sacrifices sent here. They are my only companions in this somber existence, where I remain as a sentinel of some modem of balance.

I flex my fingers, sensing the powers of my sibling's rage inside me. Each of them is a distinct and tumultuous entity that pushes and pulls against one another, yet all of them vie for release. Nyxara's tricky magic blazes through my veins, aching to weave destinies and timelines again.

Intertwined with hers, Astraea's muddied hue of dream powers haze my mind while Volan's fiery power of will singes my body. Essentria's surge of tempestuous magic crackles beneath my skin with electrical force to join the rest before Cyna's judgment and truth powers stir within me with a blast of primal fury. As always, I restrain and tighten them to my core, despite their futile attempt to rebel against my darkening thoughts.

I will not allow the prophecy to unfold, even if it means destroying everything and anyone on my path to prevent it.

I command my shadows to form a bridge and carefully step through it, leaving the ether behind, a place that exists between the Darklands and the mortal world.

In a swirl of mist and shadow, I fall through time and space until the familiar burn of the veil slices through me. Twinkling stars appear among the blur of darkness, like pinpricks of silver against the black canvas. Below, houses and trees grow larger as my body descends in a rapid spiral towards the mortal world. My lungs burst when I draw the first breath of the night, only for it to be knocked out of me the second I hit the ground with a swift, sharp thud.

The sky slowly comes into focus as I open my eyes. Coughing, I sit upright, my gaze traveling over the familiar, night-pinched meadow on the edge of the forest in the small coastal town of Ennismore.

"Damn mortal bones," I splutter, and press my palm against my shoulder, then massage out a twinge of pain throbbing at the curve of my muscle.

Slowly, I stand. Gusts of wind whip through the tall grass and purple wildflowers, lashing my nude body with icy abandon. A shiver snakes down my spine, and I rub my arms.

Ribbons of power slither between my fingers to knit darkness, shadows and stars into an embroidered, silver and black tunic, midnight pants, and leather boots. The clothes clad around my muscles, shielding my skin from the gusts of Olen, the cold months.

I let out a long exhale as the last of the magic simmers, then recoils in a dark smoke, back into my core. My gaze lifts to the inky sky while my veins singe with an indescribable grief that is only eased by the lingering fog of amnesia in my mind.

NIGHT OF DEATH AND FLOWERS

I leave the meadow, keeping to the shadows as I enter Morcidea Forest, an endless sea of gray, barricading the entire town in a barrier of time-chiseled trees and magic.

Peering through contorted gray branches, knotted like bones, I inhale a deep lungful of the town's air, scented with lavender and smoky incense.

The darkness becomes my cloak as I keep out of sight, peering from the refuge of the shadows.

Booths stand amidst the market cloaked in glittering black, embellished with shimmering silver thread depicting the ancient sigils of the gods.

My lips curl upward when I spot one that stands out among the others—the fine embroidery of skeletal fingers of my reapers curved around three crow's heads.

The God of Death.

"Over ere'," a voice calls as the market dwindles to an end. I tilt my head, my eyes drawn to a woman at the helm of the closest booth, her long gray hair tied in a thick braid.

With a twist of her wrists, shadows rise in an illusory swirl, capturing the merchandise from her stall. She wiggles her fingers, dancing the shadows into submission, and they link through the locks of the chests. One by one, potion bottles are placed inside shadow fingers, the contents inside shimmering with purple and poison.

The sign reading 'Night Market' catches my eye from the front.

They're celebrating the upcoming Harvest. My Harvest.

My eyes close briefly as I press my palm against the trunk of a graywar tree, its gray branches bare as the season of Olen captures the world in a frosty grasp. The cold flurries circle Ennismore like vultures, picking at every drop of life left in nature. Olen, the season named after the mother of all, snatches the harvests and crops cruelly, holding life in her grip for four long months.

Excitement pinches the air of the town as I disappear into the darkness of Morcidea Forest. The shadows become my cloak under the moonlit branches, hiding me from mortal eyes as I navigate the rough terrain.

I pass the stone circle in the heart of the forest, a place now abandoned, where each stone and symbol etched in weathered by the flow of time.

Out of the corner of my eye, I notice a mess of blood-tinged feathers on a patch of (snowy) grass nearby. A small bird, its heart thumping erratically, lays nestled in what remains of its scattered nest. Shell from hatched eggs lay scattered, frost coating them like tiny icy crypts. Spiderwebs glisten, blanketed between the branches high above, the moonlight catching against raindrops. I sigh as I watch a Nighbor Spider climb up a strand of thick web, then settle in the center, awaiting a brave creature to venture too close to their hideout. Within the dead branches, I sense their magic. Much like the Shadow Vipers slithering into my presence, drawn by the familiar tinge of death magic from which they were born. I stride around them, their long, red and black bodies forming a knotted pile on the barren ground.

Their hungry eyes latch onto the dying bird, and I kneel, my leather boots pressing against the frost-bitten mud and moss. "You do not wish to live," I whisper, and lean over, my fingertips darkening, decay magic pulsing under my nails. For her babies are devoured already. Her torn wings tell her story, but she could not save them from my spiders or vipers.

Such hungry little things.

I can at least offer it mercy from the fangs of the Shadow Vipers. My fingertip glides over its feathers, and as my touch presses over its racing heart, the thumps still. Its small eyes find me, and the creature turns to ash.

Quickly carried away by a breeze, my eyes are dragged with the swirling ash to the tree line.

Tenenocti.

I emerge through the dangling vines of the tree line and onto the familiar pebbly shore overlooking the Black Sea. I run my fingers through my silver strands and lift my gaze to the starry midnight black sky. The full moon hangs low behind the silhouette of the small island, casting white light on the turbulent, inky waters surrounding it.

My lips curve in a seldom smile as the wind whips around my ears, knotting through my hair, and the spray of the ocean caresses my face.

As I cast my eyes to Tenenocti Island, cloaked in perpetual clouds, with fog enveloping the trees like a halo, the familiar symphony of death surrounds me. Whispers carry from each wave, and anguished screams cry into the night from the souls trapped within the waters.

From the dense vegetation, a short boat ride from this pebbly shore, I can sense their rage—my family. I have faced countless horrors as the God of Death, and there is little I fear, but as I gaze over Tenenocti, a tendril of dread slides down my spine.

My heart pounds as I stare through the shimmering veil of my domain, cloaking the island and the Black Sea.

My stomach churns as I grow closer to the water's edge. My Skhola holds them captive. The silver band, carved into a skull, glows as I use it to siphon the powers of my siblings. It pulses as

NIGHT OF DEATH AND FLOWERS

I get closer to the water's edge, the magic thrumming through my fingertips.

An unmistakable reminder that if I reach too deeply into my domain, encompassing the island and waters, all the magic I took will return to my siblings. My domain is unlike anything else in this mortal world, a slice of the ether with a sense of home created for me so I could exist to carry out my duties here of guiding the dead.

Without my siblings—the gods and goddesses of dreams, destiny, judgment, will, and creation—Dahryst has descended into darkness. The kind where dreams become nightmares, and destiny refuses to be bound. Even in death, there is no peace.

I pull the hood of my black cloak over my silver hair, blocking out the whipping winds. As I gaze around behind, I bring my fingers to the sky. Carved on the trunks of the trees facing my domain, is my sigil, splintered into gray bark by the locals.

They worship me now. Adore me. Admire me. It was not always this way.

For centuries, in the mortal's eyes, I was the embodiment of lives cut too short—the diseases that killed their children, the arrow that pierced their loved ones' hearts. I was everything nobody wanted, but I was not the bringer of death. Nyxara wove the tapestries of their lives, carefully creating various paths. Yet, I was admonished.

A flash of anguish steals my next breath when I flick my eyes up and over the waters to the island. I clutch the fabric of my tunic and clamp my eyes shut as the pain surfaces. I count the steady beats of my mortal heart thumping beneath my fist. One, two, three, four, five.... When I reach ten, I open my eyes and inhale sharply.

Being back in my physical form, after all these years of not having to feel anything, is torturous.

An acrid, smoky scent mixed with decaying leaves permeates from the soil, transporting me back to a memory of the Ash War. It was simple then, our goal was to aid the witches against those who persecuted them. While my siblings ruled over Dahryst—each taking glory during the war—their power grew as their subjects worshiped their victories. Meanwhile, I was fated to eternal servitude, forever stuck between life and death, guiding souls from this world into the next until I saved this land and imprisoned them.

Only then was I venerated, and as my powers grew, my siblings weakened. Not that it mattered. However much I was worshiped afterward, it did not fill the emptiness that lingered in my mind, which was likely caused by Nyxara and her memory manipulation.

Waves crash in the distance, groaning with each surge of rising tide. Beneath the turbulent surface, the dead form a barricade against any curious mortals who may try to venture to the island.

My fingers tingle as I sense their exhaustion, how they long to leave this world. To allow them their peace is to destroy the protection, stopping anyone from finding my siblings' sleeping bodies.

Breathing in the crisp night air, I kneel on the shore and graze my fingers over the surface of the Black Sea.

I summon the souls of those sacrificed in the fourteen previous tournaments and the unfortunate sailors whose ships were drawn into these treacherous waters, doomed to sink into the depths.

Three spirits draw closer, beckoned by my call. Essentria's magic leaves my fingers in a hue of gold, hovering over the dead in the waters, then drifts like glitter, seeping through a wave.

Slowly, they emerge from the inky sea, drops sliding down their shadowy bodies as they shift into the same creatures that serve me in the Darklands—the Phovi.

Under my hard stare, the humanoid-appearing shifters bow into submission.

"I, Azkiel, God of Death, bring you back to find the prophesied one. She will be amongst those whose names are volunteered. You must guard the church where the ceremony will take place and keep watch on all who enter and leave." The command leaves my lips in a hiss. "Find her."

THREE

Calista

As we slide through the back entrance, we walk into our mother, holding a cup of steaming lavender tea.

Ari gasps, shuffling back, and I scoot over in time so that she doesn't fall into me. "Mama."

Mother's long fingernails tap against the tea bowl as she drags her assessing stare over Arabella, then hovers over the coin purse attached to my sister's leather belt. "Get to bed," she orders with a shake of her head, then runs one hand down her long, blonde braid. "We will talk about this in the morning."

"I'm sorry. It's my fault. I wanted to see the market," Ari says, her voice lightening into submission.

I clear my throat. "That's not true. It was—"

"Bed," she shouts, and Ari glances over her shoulder at me, apology infused in her gaze before she turns and hurries past Mama, disappearing into the corridor. Once she's out of sight, Mother places her cup down on the half-moon table, then presses her hands against her hips, wrinkling the silk of her nightdress.

"Should I go, too?" I ask as she frowns, the wrinkles on her forehead more pronounced despite the powder she uses to attempt to hide them.

"Are you *trying* to ruin our reputation?" she asks, her voice as frigid as the draft leaking in from the door behind me. "Have you not done enough?"

"Nothing bad happened." I press my lips tight, to prevent the spill of poison from my tongue as I caress my argument in my mind.

"You best *hope* no one of importance saw you," she spits through her teeth. "Your sister will provide a strong union with another family. I am sure you're aware the other elders and their families are in town."

All I know is Ari can't be blamed for tonight. She may be the favorite, but that doesn't mean Mother won't punish her still. Not that forcing Ari to meet with suitors twice her age isn't punishment enough. "It's my fault. I'm sorry I took her out," I say, my tone strained, then hug the cloak tighter around me, my heart pounding as I edge closer to the door.

Please let this end quickly. I don't need another lecture, and Drake is waiting for me.

She lifts her fingers to her temple, the tattoo on her hand, emblazoned with Essentria's sigil, shimmering in gold under the candlelight flicking from the wall. The back entrance falls silent, save for the occasional clanking from the kitchen in the next room. My mother leans forward, the smell of lead and lavender choking the air around us. With a low whisper, she says, "The sooner I can rid your sisters of your influence, the better."

I laugh, having heard this a hundred times in private. She'd never dare say it in front of our sisters or my father. I lift my chin, my teeth grinding in my ears. "I know you don't care about me, but must you always be so obvious about it?"

"Do not be dramatic, Calista." She shakes her head, sighing. "You were always so emotional, even as a child."

I take a deep breath, then briefly close my eyes, feeling her baiting me in like she does with every argument. I can't bite. I won't. Not this time. I clear my throat, then look at her. "Don't worry, I plan on being out of this house soon."

"Yes, and your father's position will ensure it. A good marriage is all there is left. Without his name, what worthy suitor will overlook your deficiencies?" She proceeds to list off the numerous flaws I apparently possess, ones I have already memorized by now from her constant repetition. "You are twenty-four years of age and unmarried through your perseverance. Then there's your lack of manners and social graces, your reckless reputation and, of course, your magic—" she pauses, then closes her lips over her venomous tongue briefly. I know what she was going to say. My lack of power. Like the rest of the town, she believes I don't have any magic. That I was one of the rare few born without magic, deemed unworthy by the gods. If only she knew the truth. She'd hate me even more.

She sighs, dragging my focus back to her. "If you choose to destroy your reputation piece by piece, the least you can do is not to drag your sisters down with you. You took Arabella out tonight, alone! Anything could have happened. She could have been spotted."

I roll my eyes up. "Even if we were spotted, Ari wasn't alone. I was with her, and so was Drake."

She huffs a breath through her nose, then steps back, placing a few feet between us. "The farmer's son with *dream* magic?" Her hand slaps against her forehead, her eyes closing for a moment. "You should pray no one saw her with him. He is a nobody."

"He is not," I reply, my tone raising an octave. "Drake's a good man, and we have been friends for years. I care about him and won't have you say a bad word against him."

Suspicion crowns her eyes. "So this is what your defiance is truly about. I hope you do not plan on marrying *him*. He has no status. Unless he's lucky enough not only to be chosen for the Harvest, but win it and become an elder, there is no world that you two can be together."

Something inside of me snaps. I close the distance between us, my finger pointed, but a faint voice in my mind reminds me she is still my mother. As much as I wish she wasn't. "He would not be *lucky* to be chosen! No one is," I say breathily.

"It is an *honor*," she enunciates.

My brows knit together as I tilt my head. "If it's such an extraordinary honor to be selected, why is Father keeping us from participating in The Choosing, then? What power does an elder have to prevent a fate determined by the God of Death himself?"

"Enough!" She snaps. "You dare talk back to me like this? Show me some respect. I am your mother," she barks, as she always does when she can't answer something. "You will go to bed now, before your father finds out about your shenanigans."

"Gods forbid," I state and walk up the stairs.. She follows me, then turns into her room. As soon as her doors close, I creep back down the stairs, tears dissolving into my eyes.

Despite the years of building a wall around my heart, each brick created from anger, jealousy, hurt, and apathy, occasionally my mother still hurts me with her words.

I shake the pain away, reminding myself that I have Ari, my other sisters, and Drake and tonight, he needs me.

The cold air hits my hot cheeks and tear-pinched eyes as I walk out into the gardens, slide between the vines and wall, then the gate and into the dark street where Drake waves me over from the other side.

"What's wrong?" Drake asks when I reach him.

"Nothing… I—" I touch the back of my neck, grazing my fingertips over the raised hairs. "I was just thinking about the Harvest," I lie, then glance up at my house before turning and walking with him down the cobblestone road.

"You don't have to do this," Drake says for the thousandth time since we formed this plan.

NIGHT OF DEATH AND FLOWERS

"Yes, I do." My mother's words taunt me as I walk. *Lucky.* She called him fucking *lucky.* "If this is the last thing I do," I say breathlessly. "Then my life will have meant something."

The music and festivities of the Night Market fade as Drake and I walk across town, hidden under the anonymity of the hoods of our cloaks. No one can place us at the church tonight. Otherwise, by this time tomorrow, our hoods will be replaced by nooses.

"You can still turn back," Drake whispers before we walk through the wrought-iron gates of the ancient, stone church, illuminated by the full moon. "I know Ari loves you, but we both know she is devout to your father, and the gods. When she hears about this tomorrow, she'll know we were behind it."

"She won't say anything. She'll never put me in danger like that, even if she doesn't like it."

After a quick glance to check we are alone, he pulls down the hood of his cloak, then runs his hands through his rain-soaked hair. Raven-black curls form against his forehead, and his green eyes widen when they finally meet mine. "This is my fight. They're never going to pick you."

I avert my gaze to the entrance as we walk through the gates, the heavy metal screeching in protest.

"It doesn't matter," I murmur as thoughts of being trapped on Tenenocti Island, forced to kill other witches or warlocks, carousel through my mind. I could think of nothing worse, except for Drake or Arabella being sent there. "Ari and I may not be, but what about Cecilia and Emilia? They'll be of age at the next Harvest and father won't be around forever. And even if he is, what about the later generations? This will go on forever unless we stop it. Something has to change."

He lets out a long sigh. I'm not the only one with young siblings. Like me, he has three sisters. "I just don't want you to lose control," he says, softening his tone.

Thick droplets of rain land on my face as I turn my gaze to the cloud-stricken night sky, pin-pricked with silver stars. The icy gusts seep through my black, traveling cloak, and I tighten the fabric around my navy blue dress, camouflaging me against the darkness.

Lowering my voice, I whisper, "I won't."

Drake follows me up the path. "You don't know that."

"I've got it under control," I state, flexing my fingers as the familiar sensation of decay magic taunts me. Drake has always been worried that the darkness inside of me will somehow take over.

"You're upset," he observes.

"I'm not," I reply, but I can feel his eyes on me, so I relent. "My Mother caught us sneaking back inside."

His hand lands on my shoulder, and with a gentle squeeze, he whispers, "You can turn back if you want. This could get us both killed.."

I shrug. "It wouldn't be the first time I almost died."

"Nor the first time I have to save your ass," he jokes..

My thoughts flit to his illusion that distracted the Phovus last time. "You helped."

The corner of my mouth tips upwards slightly, and he brushes his thumb across it, wearing a smirk. "My gods, is that a smile?"

"No." I clear my throat, then touch the side of my neck. His dimples deepen as he flashes me a toothy smile. There's something so carefree in his expression that I secretly envy. I assess the face I've seen so much of since I was five, illuminated by the full moon. I run my gaze over his tanned, rugged features. The scar from when he'd fallen off a tree when we were children is still visible down one side, but faded, and pink now. His heavy-lidded eyes widen as he watches me, the sparkle within the moss-green irises reflecting my stoic face. His full lips, always tilted, with a ghost of a laugh always etched upon them.

"See something you like, Wildflower?" he asks, using the nickname he'd passed onto me since he discovered my affinity for making poisons from foraged flowers and plants.

"Nothing new," I tease, my lips forming back into a hard line. "Let's go. And before you say anything else, we both know I'm not leaving."

His breath hitches, and he grabs my arm before we can go any further. I cast a brief glance at his hand, where the tattoos come to life, swirling against his skin. Like others in Astraea's coven with illusion magic, his emotions and desires take form through art. Appearing on the top of his hand, a painting materializes of us inching closer, as if we might kiss at any moment. I see myself through his eyes.

My wavy, long hair dances in the breeze, threads of silver speckled within the brown, and Drake lifts a finger, brushing back a few stray chestnut-colored strands. My glacier-blue gaze fixates on him, my hand on his chest. I can only imagine how it would really feel as I watch the moment play out, his arms tightening around my waist, then gliding down to my wide hips, fisting the fabric of my dress as he towers over me, at least a foot higher than my five-foot-two stature.

As he catches sight of the inked scene, he promptly pulls his sleeve down.

NIGHT OF DEATH AND FLOWERS

I avert my gaze, then look around at the stretches of cobblestone surrounding the building, shadowed by graywar trees carpeting the entrance with skeletal leaves. Their low branches reach out, casting shadows over pale tombs housing the dead. Among those graves, a well-known presence draws my attention. Deep in slumber, the creature that haunts my dreams rests in its natural feline-looking form, surrounded by dancing wisps of darkness.

"There's a phovus."

His eyes widen. "What?"

"The elders must have sent the creature to guard the church." I tread carefully over the path and our hushed whispers carry into the night. I gaze around as the familiar tingle of death sparks through my body. The memory paints in my mind as I grow closer to the creature, recalling the one that almost killed me—its predatory eyes finding me in the forest.

"It's sleeping," I say with a shudder, balling my fists. Drake hesitates, but I push forward. I won't let fear paralyze me. Facing challenges head on is the only way to survive in this world. "Let's go."

It's rare the elders would use one and ridiculous that the elder coven thinks they can tame one. Phovi are predators, serving only one being, and the God of Death hasn't been seen in forever.

They are supposed to stay in the Darklands, but some walk in our world. I'm not sure if they escaped, or are spies sent here by Death.

Decay magic sizzles under my skin upon thinking of him, like a dull ache that never fully goes away.

Death's coven practices his magic, but while he has many powers for them to harness, no one I know has inherited the type of magic I possess. As far as I am aware, I am the first.

The sharp scrape of a match against the stone wall pulls me from my thoughts, and a warm, reddish glow replaces the darkness as Drake lights the candles.

Before us, the statue of the God of Death—Azkiel—stands close to seven feet tall, its surface decorated with the small, engraved names of the sacrifices chosen from the last Harvest. Every decade, the names fade right before the next twelve are chosen to compete, as if the possibility of becoming an elder is a prize worth dying for.

I always catch my breath every time I see Death's likeness. Hatred swallows my ability to keep my magic at bay, and in the presence of the statue, containing Azkiel's magic, the decay seeps into my fingers.

"Trying to win a staring contest with a statue, Wildflower?" Drake whispers, and I snap my eyes shut, then shake my hands as if I can somehow will the magic away. Quickly, I shove my hands into my pockets, until the burning sensation subsides from my hands, notifying me the power of Death's Touch has dissipated.

"No," I say with a clipped laugh.

Drake gazes at the burning red candles before glancing up at the ancient passages carved into the stone walls, adorned with portraits of gods. Their ethereal eyes watch us from their frames, each one appearing deceptively mortal.

"Are you certain about this?" Drake asks while his hand glides over the short, dark stubble on his sharp jawline. Once again, several of his tattoos move, depicting terrifying inked images of the Phovus flying over his defined muscles. It chases us in every scene, and in one, I am dead.

I point at the art covering his arms and ask, "Can you at least pretend we have a chance?"

"I do. It's you I'm worried about," he teases, but in many of the animated illustrations, I am protecting him.

"You're hilarious," I drawl, my tone thick with sarcasm. "Seriously. I'd love to see your ability to paint pretty pictures up against a Phovus."

He glances over his shoulder at me, his eyes alight with menace. "Oh, yeah? What are you going to do? Wish it to death?"

he asks, although we both know my powers are far worse than that—just one touch and he will be ash on the ground.

Until now, I've only killed the occasional plant with my touch, but I imagine it does the same thing to people. I have no desire to find out. "I'll wish you to death in a minute," I mumble under my breath, and he smirks.

I stare at the altar in front of the statue, decorated with clay symbols. Candlelight flickers as we step closer.

I fix a piercing stare on the carved face of the God of Death and grimace. Even being close to his statue—infused with his magic—has me on edge.

Like him, I am nothing but decay and death. I was supposed to become a healer, like the rest of my family. My stomach turns as I look at his deceptively angelic, marbled features, proving that some monsters wear the most handsome of disguises. "Let's tear the bastard down," I say, my fists balled at my side. I brush my chestnut hair away from my face, draping it over my shoulder. I regret not putting it in a braid tonight. "It's just a shame it's not the actual god."

Drake murmurs, "I love it when you're murderous."

I almost smile, but I stop myself. Admittedly, my hatred for the God of Death far outweighs Drake's anger at the gods. In reality, I don't hate them all, although I don't like any of the six siblings fated to rule over Dahryst. However, there is something about Azkiel. When I think of him, a wound carved in the crevices of my chest rips open.

"I can't believe we're really doing this," he says as he grabs the dagger from the table. "Ready?"

"Do it."

"Then we run," he adds.

I nod. "We run really fucking fast."

Drake's hiss fills the air as he runs the blade across his hand, creating tiny crimson droplets. "Ready to see something exceptional?"

"Always, but no one else is here."

He rolls his eyes as we both nonchalantly commit the worst sacrilege of all in the most sacred of places. My mother would weep if she were here. It's a shame she isn't.

Using the blood from the wound on his hand, he paints something onto the statue with his fingers.

I've never seen another warlock do anything like this before. Although those with illusion magic can create powerful images, the magic is always temporary—except for Drake's. Blessed with two powers from the Goddess of Dreams, one grants him the ability to conjure illusions, while the other allows him to animate them into tangible objects.

Much like those in Azkiel's coven, with shadow magic, they are the only witches who can create tangible objects. While Death's witches can weave tapestries of fabrics from shadows and darkness, Astraea's witches can bring life to art.

Chains made of blood materialize around the God of Death as Drake finishes painting. There's one hanging around the statue's throat, and six around its torso and legs. Gradually, the chains awaken, shimmering in gold as they tighten their grip.

I wrinkle my nose at the smell of smoke and blood mixing with the musty odor of the ancient building. Loud cracks sound as the marble splits in two. Pieces chip away, flying onto the floor with each crack and splinter of stone echoing throughout the church. Despite straining against the stone, the chains never break until the entire statue tumbles to the ground. Stepping back, I smile as the decapitated head of the God of Death rolls toward me.

My heart races as the last echoes fade away.

Drake mercilessly slices his wound deeper, and I groan. Watching him mutilate himself for the second time tonight is enough to make my stomach turn. I can't help but wonder how he learned that his blood could animate art beyond his body. We've experienced enough emotion for one night, so I tuck the question away for another day.

NIGHT OF DEATH AND FLOWERS

Drake's legs nearly give out as more blood spills onto the altar. I clutch his arm, and he tries to nudge me away. "I'm fine."

"I know," I whisper. "Just maybe sit down for a minute."

Drake stumbles back into me as the magic becomes too much. The tattoos on his skin vanish, as if they never existed.

"This is a bad idea," I state. "We should just…"

He shakes his head. "We have to destroy the stone basin," he says, pointing at the bowl used for The Offering.

The candles flicker as they are snuffed out one by one. Ragged breaths reach my ears before I can see the creature, and a shiver snakes down my spine. Goosebumps spread over my arms as I focus on the vestibule to the church, spotting movement within the blackness.

Hunched over by a pew, made of smoke and night, the Phovus' shifting form is all snarling teeth and glowing eyes, and he's focused on us.

FOUR

Calista

"Drake," I whisper as the creature's yellow stare latches onto me, its intelligent eyes tracking my movements. It stalks the shadows, wisps of a dark body visible under the light of the moon, pouring in through the door and stained-glass windows. "We need light. Now."

Drake's hand is on my arm in a heartbeat, his grip tightening as he pulls himself upright. "What's going o—"

The creature shrieks—the shrill sound searing into my mind. I yell, pressing my hands against my ears, muffling the sound. My ankle curves toward the ground as Drake tugs me against the wall, my bare shoulders hitting the rough, ancient stone. I can barely catch my breath when he's standing in front of me, his toned body pressing against mine.

Flickers of touch run between us as time seems to slow down as the creature slowly stands, shifting into a humanoid form—tall, with long arms and legs, reminiscent of the witch it once was.

His hand slides onto my stomach as he pushes me back further, as if there is any possible space left between us. He turns to face me, his penetrating, wild stare pinning me to the wall. "When I say run…"

"I'm not leaving you," I say, my heart hiccupping at both the closeness of us and the surge of adrenaline preparing me to fight. I peer around him as he shields me from the creature, and decay magic seeps through me, sensing the Phovus, but I don't know if it will even work on them.

Before I can react, Drake releases my hands, then spins quickly. I squint as an illusion of light materializes around us, the harshness of it forcing me to clamp my eyes shut.

When I reopen them, I notice Drake's body slumping forward and his gaze darkening as he focuses every ounce of his magic onto the creature, enveloping it in the thing it hates most: light.

"We have to go. Now," I shout as I take off, grabbing his arm. He runs beside me, his shallow breaths growing hollower.

The sharp edges of the marble shards crunch under my boots as we sprint to the narrow entrance, barely falling outside before the fleeting mirage born from Drake's magic vanishes into darkness.

My hand slaps over my chest, my heart racing under my splayed fingers as I catch my breath. "Gods!"

I glance inside the church, watching the Phovus slink around the walls, skillfully evading the piercing rays, seeking refuge in the darkness.

"Drake?" I say as he sways where he stands, as if the breeze could blow him away with one, harsh gust. The soft glow of the moon highlights his paling features, revealing bare skin where his tattoos once were. "You drained yourself," I realize.

I pull him further from the church entrance, my eyes flicking between his stumbling steps to the vestibule of the church. Shadows emerge from the entrance, like tendrils, vining over the front of the church. My gaze trickles up the building as the shadows dissipate.

The terrifying flap of wings echoes through the air before the dark mass of the Phovus emerges on the church roof, blending into its surroundings.

Drake mumbles between breaths, "Is it gone?"

My gaze travels up along the towering buttress to the imposing spire above. There, the intense stare of the predator's yellow eyes meets mine.

"It shifted again," I say, as puddles form around us. My thoughts turn to the dagger always sheathed on my thigh, but the blade is useless against the Phovi. Reaching for the weapon, or running, will only ignite the creature's hunter instincts. Carefully, I watch the beast, but realize it is too late. It has already regarded us as prey.

With a snarl, it launches forward, sliding over the slated spires of the church. "Fuck," I yell and place my arm around Drake, my legs almost buckling under the extra weight. With one last glance at the church spire, we sprint up the narrow path into the graveyard, winding around the white crypts.

The souls of the dead call to me, their voices whispering in my ears like a haunting melody. The lingering pain and anguish of those who died heightens my powers.

Within a few strides, we halt, our attention drawn to the sound of wings flapping. My gaze swiftly darts back towards the church spire, but it's empty.

A thud shatters the silence. My fingers tremble uncontrollably as I gasp for air, my body frozen in place. I can sense its presence just feet from where we stand.

I paused, eyes flicking to the thick, heavy branch overhead.

Another resounding bang echoes behind us, sending a murder of crows scattering into the sky.

"There's more than one," I whisper.

Thunder roars above, as if the gods have awoken and seen what we've done.

Bolts of lightning crackle between ominous black clouds, casting an eerie glow on the headstones. Spotting a dark silhouette in my peripheral vision, I slowly turn my head. A second flash of lightning illuminates the creature tilting its head as its piercing eyes fixate on me.

"Good gods," I whisper, my breath leaving in a fog.

Light flickers from Drake's fingers as he lifts his hands, willing another illusion, but the sparks quickly fade. He has nothing left, and now the creature knows it.

"Run," Drake yells as the Phovus runs through the darkness on all fours, its needle-like teeth glistening with droplets of saliva.

My ankle twists as I turn to run, and the ground grows closer as I fall. My palms absorb the impact as I land on the dirt, the air knocked from my lungs. Drake's hands are around my waist, urging me to move, but as I stand, pain shoots through my leg into my knee, and I hiss.

"Cali, please," Drake pleads, his wild eyes widening as the creature reaches us.

"Look out," I yell as it stands behind him, moving with the grace and fluidity of a cat. Rustling sounds around us. "There's more."

How many more? Two? Three?

Their death magic resonates with mine, but there are too many Phovi for me to pinpoint how much danger we're in—facing one of them is challenging enough.

The Phovus' hungry stare trickles to my throat. These creatures are faster than us and skilled hunters in the dark. We have little advantage, leaving no room for error.

Drake balls his fist, the wound on his hand still dripping blood. I ready my powers, reaching within until I feel the familiar swell of magic, an extension of myself. It moves, pulling tighter at my core. I stretch it out of myself, like an elastic band that's ready to snap at any moment.

Lightning streaks illuminate the darkened sky, accompanied by the creature's strident screech. The only sound that follows is the Phovus' swift, resounding footfalls, and before I can react, I'm forcefully thrown backward by Drake.

I clamp my eyes shut as I grab the top of the headstone to steady myself, and a surge of energy buzzes through me. Drawing a shaky breath in, I lift my gaze just in time to witness Drake running headfirst into the massive creature.

The ground trembles upon impact, and Drake's subsequent scream pierces through my very soul. His body collides with the ground with a sickening thump, and within seconds, the Phovus has him gasping for air when it lands a hit to his throat.

Leaving Drake lying in a puddle several feet from me, the creature wastes no time and lunges in my direction. Terror roots me to the spot, and I cry out when its large, sharp claws sink into my shoulders.

In the corner of my eye, I spot another Phovus slip down the side of a tree. In a heartbeat, the creature descends upon me.

My legs buckle and I hit the ground with a thud.

"Fuck," I yell, and a jolt of pain shoots up my spine, fuzzing my mind along with the throbbing in my ankle. I shake my head, fighting through the dizziness, but every breath is a constriction around my ribs.

My eyes widen as I kick my legs, watching as shadows pool from the creature's body. A spiral of darkness breaks away from it, slithering up my leg like a serpent.

Drake's yell reaches my ears seconds before his fist connects with the side of the Phovus' head. As the world sharpens into focus, he moves swiftly to grasp its wings—its only vulnerability.

A shockwave thrums up my leg as I deliver a powerful blow with my boot to the creature's face, the snap of its teeth cracking under my heel. I slide a hand up my skirt, then unsheathe the onyx dagger. The blade glides through its wing, and it emits a high-pitched screech.

I leap back, putting some distance between myself and the Phovus I kicked just in case it wakes up and resumes its attack.

The Phovus Drake is fighting morphs into a serpentine shape, winding itself around him in a death hold.

Tears run down my cheeks as Drake desperately gasps for air, his fingers clutching at the writhing form of the Phovus. Panic seizes me as the shadowy mass twists and turns, constricting him until bones snap.

I won't die today. Drake will not die.

It starts as a deep rumble in my core. As the death magic seeps out of me, a bone-chilling coldness envelops me—the foul odor of decay and rot surrounding us.

The power slips through my skin like ink, blackening the ends of my fingers. I stare at them, horrified as I use them again, despite vowing that I would never do so.

Drake cries out, and I force away the shock, acting on instinct. The pain from my injuries dissolves as my power takes over.

Running my hands over the skin of the creature's textured wing, I clutch it to my chest, digging my nails into the wing, releasing a primal roar. The creature squeals, its noise grating through me, as its wing disintegrates in my hands until it falls away into ash. Its eyes widen when it looks at me, and for a second, I glimpse the soul it once was as it lets out a horrified scream.

Winds whip through the graveyard from the forest, sweeping away parts of it as the rest of the creature turns to ash, until there is nothing left.

The second Phovus shifts, the mass of its body swirling like smoke, until it takes the form of a human man. High on adrenaline, I run at it, my fingers poised for its neck.

It should have killed me. It had the chance, but it is frozen in place, as if it is staring at a monster more terrifying than itself.

My brows furrow, but I can't falter. Not even for a second.

NIGHT OF DEATH AND FLOWERS

My heart leaps as I throw myself at the Phovus, as if it's trying to escape the deadly attempt I put us in. My blackened fingers grip the sides of its ribs, and I yell, all of my anguish concentrated into one scream. It struggles as its skin turns ashen, crumbling as it is incinerated within my fatal hold.

Tears run down my cheeks as it crumbles, the ash covering my arms and chest. When it stops screaming, I take my first proper breath, my lungs aching with each gasp. I gaze at the puddle of ash, melting under the rain, and I am reminded that it had once been a witch or warlock before its soul was cast into the Darklands and was forced to become this.

I shake my head, snapping myself out of the trance, and turn my focus to the third as it slips away from Drake. It stares at me for a few seconds, tilting its head with unnerving curiosity, before disappearing into the darkness.

The magic dissolves slowly, curling back into me like an unwelcome visitor. As if it knows the danger has passed. I grab the dagger from the ground, quickly sheathing it, then turn to Drake.

He lies on the ground, his body twitching much like mine had all those years ago after the Phovi attack. I run my hands down my rain-soaked face and press my lips tightly together. It is moments like this that I wish I had my sister's powers to heal, although her magic is different to the other healers—it is beautiful. Unlike mine.

Finally, Drake's bloodshot eyes fling open.

I lift him slightly, and he groans, wincing from the pain. As I look around, making sure no one has come upon hearing the commotion, I let out a tense breath. "I have to get you to Arabella. Stay with me, okay?"

I hate forcing him up, especially when I can see every breath and step is a labor. If we don't move now, we'll both be dead.

FIVE

Azkiel

Birds flock from the trees as my shadows descend upon the Phovus, binding his smoky-black wings. The creature squirms, my shadows crumpling the delicate skin under the swirling darkness coating his entire body.

"Tell me again how they destroyed my statue."

Rage takes the reins as I watch the Phovus panic, my eyes narrowing as he screeches, squirming in the contours of my magic, attempting to shift from his humanoid image to serpentine, so he may slither from my bonds. My magic is a shield, and the harder he fights, the tighter it constricts.

The creature's voice is an echo of distorted voices overlapping. Every word is an unbound offense as he speaks into my mind, like listening to a bow glide across broken strings.

I tried to stop them.

Ropes of darkness drag him to my feet, forcing him to his knees on the pebbly shore.

"Lies. You ran," I growl, then lean over him. While he may appear deceivingly intangible, as if I could put my hand right through his air-like form, underneath the tenebrous outer body, is a physical form—one I can bend and break at will.

He speaks into my mind once again.

One of them, a witch, she holds your power. She killed the other Phovi with one touch, turning them to ash. She would have executed me, too.

"It is impossible." With my eyes fixed on the stormy horizon, I crouch and seize a pebble, pulverizing it within my grasp as I envision it being the witch's fragile bones. Only one strain of magic can kill by touch. Mine.

I wince, my lip twitching as the foreign feeling dips into my core. No one is supposed to hold our ethereal power. It is what makes us gods—it is what makes us who we are.

Realization washes over me. In underestimating Nyxara, I must have misinterpreted the double meaning in the prophecy. Doomed with death.

The witch isn't only fated to die in The Harvest, so her death will undo the spell on them. She is doomed with my power—the power of death.

Slowly, I rise as the Phovus's yellow eyes trail my movements. "Where is she?"

When he doesn't immediately answer, my shadows tighten around him, until he's gasping for air.

I don't know. I...I've told you...everything.

My anger releases from me in the form of my magic, slicing through my skin, leaving an ashen, singed tingling in my fingertips. Darkness pierces his wings in shadow thorns, carving through the thin membrane of his wings, coaxing a blood-curdling scream from his throat.

Clouds roll above us, thunder quaking through the Black Sea. My heart thumps erratically, like a monster trying to escape its cage.

"Do you fear the girl more than me?" I question, my eyes fixated on the Phovus, staring at my creation. What was once a mortal warlock, now a creature of little humanity, possessing my powers of fear induction and shadow manipulation, is supposed to be the strongest of monsters.

He shakes his head, but my nostrils flare when sensing his hesitation.

"She may have killed you," I say, disgust curling my lips. "But I will obliterate you."

Please…

His pleas echo in my head.

I can find her. I will bring her to you.

"Enough," I command. "I will find the witch myself."

Slowly, my shadows tear through him, one by one, each a release of the building anxiety in my chest. Emphatically, the daggers of darkness slash his body into ribbons, hacking at his wings until parts of him shred, then disintegrate.

His screams are a symphony in my mind, lingering on the fringes of every dark thought. Inky blood spills over the pebbles as his screams gurgle into silence, his soul fractured under the denseness of my powers.

Black waves lap hungrily at the shore, as if it can smell the blood of the creature. Piece by piece, the sea drags what's left of him into the murky depths.

I stare blankly as shredded body parts are claimed by the waters, a stark reminder that even the most ferocious of monsters can be destroyed.

The witch will be next to die.

A chorus of hissing caresses the inside of my ear, guiding my attention to Morcidea's tree line. From within the underbrush, a large Shadow Viper edges out onto the shoreline, its intelligent, red eyes fixated on me. Under the dove-gray sky, where a distant storm brews, the body of the creature glistens with red markings patched over black and purple.

Another shuffle sounds in the distance, along with footsteps. The elders are here. I can sense their array of powers.

Closing my eyes, I take a deep breath in and fix my composure before traveling the short distance from the shore of the Black Sea to the stone circle in the heart of the forest.

Their heartbeats are unstable, palpitating when they notice me, and their movements come to an abrupt halt. I observe the seven elders, their heads remaining bowed in reverence at the foot of the tall, weathered stones.

Striding to the center, I breathe in the burning incense from within a clay bowl nested in dry grass. My stare climbs from the bowl to the youngest looking elder. He slowly raises his head, and I notice his fingers trembling under the sleeves of his cloak.

My gaze travels over each of the stones. It has been two centuries since the stones were erected, yet still my sigil remains clearly etched on each of them.

"You no longer worship here," I state, noticing the lack of prayer totems and ivy strangled between the cracks, destabilizing the structures.

Two elders flinch as my sharp tone slices through the winds.

"Azkiel, God of Death and protector of our realm," a lone woman says, positioning herself in front of me first. She pulls her hood down, revealing her elegantly braided hair. Her captivating green eyes demand attention, their presence stressed by the wrinkles around them, a testament to the power she exudes.

All magic takes an exhaustive toll on mortals, but holding the power of all six gods is more than most can handle, even if it is a diluted version of our magic.

Yet, I can take it from her now. I can pull every ounce of magic from her bones until she is depleted. My jaw sets as I stare intrusively into her eyes until she speaks at my silent command.

"I am Dephina, my God."

"Why did you come to me?" I ask, my tone gravelly.

"We caught signs of your return, and we hoped it was true," she says, her wide-eyed traveling every line of my face, her gaze drifting to my tunic, then my blackened fingers. Her eyes snap back to mine, her lips parting, pupils dilating. "Our powers," she says, then clears the croak from her voice. "They grew stronger two days ago. We all felt the surge. Then the crows were acting erratically, and we found what looked like stardust glowing in the nearby meadow."

I hold my breath, suppressing the urge to roll my eyes and dash their hopes now, but the look of anticipation shared in their gazes keeps me silent, reminding me I did not always hate mortals.

In fact, I could swear I even liked them once.

I stare at her until she looks away first.

"We had an incident." Dephina exhales shakily, understanding my silent question. She was correct not to wait for me to ask. Because if it is true, then they did not come to immediately. I can only hope they caught the witch.

She continues. "Two assailants entered the church. One was a warlock with illusion magic. We were not aware that he also possessed the ability to animate objects into reality. It's rare to hold two powers, but—"

"What of the accomplice?" I ask, stepping forward.

"We believe it was a witch or warlock from your coven."

My brows furrow as I wait for a name.

"We, um, we do not know who they are."

"Then you have failed your people," I state, and Dephina falls back in line. "You assume the accomplice is from my coven, yet none of you will speak the truth out of fear."

Another man speaks this time. "I am Vaknor, my most humble god of death," he says with a quick bow, lacking the grace of the others. "We found evidence that this accomplice used… decay magic."

He holds his breath, and a gust of air clips midair, as if the very forest is holding its breath.

A low growl reverberates in my chest, and he watches me cautiously, before speaking, his tone low, and quiet. "We are searching for the accomplice. We have our best enforcers searching for them."

My eyes narrow on the man. His heart races, fluttering in my ears, accompanied by uneven breaths. The longer I stare, sweat beads his forehead. Slowly, he touches the side of his neck, his eyes begging to look away.

"I sense your deception," I say, voice shaking.

His eyes widen. "Me? I know nothing."

"You." I point at the eldest of them. "Come."

Vaknor steps back, and the man steps into his place in front of me. His black eyes reveal his deep devotion to Volan, the God of Will, confirming his abilities of sight. "You saw the accomplice?"

He refuses to meet my stare, as if it might be fatal. "I…" He glances at Vaknor, and I step forward. I inch closer, the magic darkening the tips of my fingers as I bring them slowly toward his face. His gulp is music to my ears as he stares at them, wide-eyed.

"You have one chance," I say, "before I send you to the Darklands."

Vaknor pleads from behind him, "Please, Everist, don't."

"Her name is Calista," Everist splutters as Vaknor falls to his knees, his palms covering his eyes. The elder continues. "Calista Bellevue."

I tilt my head, looking over his shoulder to Vaknor. "You hide her out of sentiment?" I ask, my lips curling into a frown. "A traitor."

With a shaky voice, Everist finally breaks the heavy silence. "She is his daughter, but he just discovered she is behind this. He will punish her for her crimes, familial ties or not. We will send her to the Incarcuri."

"You will do *nothing*. You will leave her to me."

Vaknor's brows pull downward, his lips parting from behind Everist. I interject before he can speak. While they may be the most powerful in Dahryst, they answer to me. "Do you object?"

He leans back as my stare darkens. I know better than to kill an elder. I need them on my side, even if they are weak. But they still hold the power of all six, like diluted versions of myself.

"No."

My eyes focus on him. "No, because I am certain you understand the ramifications a witch holding such deadly magic would have on your society. A society *I* built."

He swallows hard, his gaze objecting, but his lips don't move.

"Should you try to warn her, or tell anyone of this," I say, untapped restraint behind each word, "the rest of your loved ones shall pay the same price as her."

"Yes, I understand," he says croakily, then bows his head, stepping back in line with the others.

The witch's name swims in my mind, again and again—so familiar, yet so poisonous. As if the word, something so unimportant, can destabilize me.

Calista.

Her name becomes my obsession, and I caress the vowels on my tongue until I can taste her essence. The fated one, an echo of myself, and she is here.

So very close.

Dephina presses her hands together in prayer, then bends her knee, snapping me back to the present. "If I may," she says, interrupting my thoughts. "Unfortunately, during this disruption, your statue was… destroyed," she hesitates. "We were hoping, now that you have returned, you will choose the names for The Harvest?"

"You wish for me to complete The Choosing?" I ask, my tone measured, but my fingers flex at my side when I glare at them. "When you cannot even find the perpetrator? The boy?" I tilt my head. "They were allowed to pass into the church."

"We were told Phovi were guarding the entrance," Dephina says.

"Yes, because I sent them," I spit. "You did not protect the church with any spells. Not even a simple curse?"

The elder coven is supposed to be my legacy, a coven built of the strongest of mortals to govern the people and keep them safe from the humans in our absence.

As my gaze travels across each generation, I shake my head as I notice the weakness in the younger ones, born from the false sense of safety they have lived in.

My fingers curl with the violent urge to rid myself of this embarrassment of a coven.

"Are you not more powerful than any other mortal in your world, holding the powers of all six covens? The people will not respect you if the boy is not found and punished. So, what am I to do with you now?"

The youngest of the seven steps forward, his hands shaky as he meets my stare. "We beg for your mercy, our most gracious god of death."

A shadow ribbons from my fingers and Dephina's eyes narrow as she glares at my fingers. A glint of something deadly crosses her eyes when she looks at me, but she quickly looks away. At least she may be my only worthy elder here.

The shadow dances over to Everist, slowly coiling around his throat. My lips curve as I watch him shudder under the embrace, his eyes bulging as he splutters for air and my shadow grows tighter, darker, until his bloodshot eyes latch onto me.

I release him, calling the darkness back into my hands. He drops to his knees, grappling at his throat. The gurgling sounds are music to my ears as the others suppress their gasps.

"Capture the traitor boy before the Choosing," I command. "Else others may believe they can get away with such treason." Dephina lets out a sigh of relief at my statement. "Let us hope this year's crop is stronger than all of you."

SIX

Calista

Lightning intermittently flashes in the sky in blue and purple, illuminating the knot of gray trees surrounding the abandoned mansion that is now our hideout. I breathe in a crisp, icy breath, a welcome reprieve from the musty air inside the mansion in search of my frequent visitor and friend, Thorn.

We've been here for less than a few hours, and while I didn't want to call on my sister, there is little I can do to help Drake. He's still inside, writhing on a bed, and my potions have done little to help the internal damage caused by the constriction from the Phovus.

I cast my eyes to the mansion as I venture further from the door. The mansion, a crumbling testament to the beautiful home it once was, stands strong against the battering storm. Ivy wraps around the weathered, gray bricks, nestling deep into the crevices and cracks, revealing the decaying structure beneath. Broken windows silently overlook the forest with a haunting darkness, and a moss-stricken fountain fills with rainwater.

It's not the first time I've visited the decrepit building, sneaking into its dark corridors with handfuls of deadly ingredients so I can work on my potions in peace. But this morning feels different. No matter what I tell myself, or do, I can't remove the dread growing in the pit of my stomach.

"There you are," I say, holding out my arm as my crow flies down from a branch. "I knew you'd find me out here. You always do." He tilts his head, his ebony eyes searching mine. "I'm okay, but Drake's hurt," I explain. "I need you to deliver something for me."

Thorn squawks as I attach the parchment to his leg, his ebony beak opening when he turns his head to look at me. Crows are mostly a nuisance to those in town and seen as pests. But I've learned they're clever, angry little things with a mischievous sense of humor. So, naturally I've always been drawn to them.

Raindrops glide from his body as he prunes his shiny black feathers, then gives me one last look, his beady eyes boring into mine. "To Ari," I instruct, very much aware that she's probably going to kill me for this, if she's able to sneak out after we were caught last night. Although, I doubt mother is awake.

Thorn takes off, and I watch as he soars into the stormy sky to deliver my note.

I step back from the branches of a graywar tree, then turn my gaze to the morning sky thick with rain and fog.

I run my hands down my rain-slicked face, then push my locks behind my ears. Drake's scream carries from a grimy, shattered window on the second floor, and I clutch the fabric of my cloak, wincing. After weeks of planning, deciding we were going to destroy the statue and basin, so the so-called volunteers couldn't be chosen at The Offering, we failed. The basin remains intact, but without Death's statue to reveal the names, surely they can't go ahead with The Offering.

Rain pelts against the trees, the branches creaking and groaning under the heavy winds. I pull my hood up and walk under the sagged front porch, wooden boards groaning with each step, then reach the door. Mildew and a burned herbal smell leak into the back of my throat as I step into the mansion. The stark echo of my footsteps carries around the large foyer. I track the shadowy corners, and a sense of being watched pricks goosebumps over my skin.

Cobwebs drape dusty chandeliers, and tapestries hanging from the walls depicting fables and lore are faded and torn in places. I hurry up the grand staircase, my boots crunching twigs and skeletal leaves swept in here over time.

"Aghh."

Another scream resonates in synchrony with the old grandfather clock, chiming three times. I splutter out a cough when I halt outside the heavy, wooden door of the room Drake is in. I gaze through the crack, at the flickering candlelight, and my stomach dips.

If I possessed powers like the rest of my family, I could alleviate my best friend's pain. Instead, I only harbor the power to end suffering permanently, rather than healing it.

"Hey," I mumble as I cross the threshold. He turns onto his side, the flame from the candelabra illuminating drops of shimmering sweat coating his face. "Ari is coming." His lips part, as if he wants to speak, but only a shriek of agony uncurls from his tongue. "Don't talk. She won't be long. This'll be over soon."

I don't know how long I've been sitting beside him, his hands in mine, when the door finally creaks behind me. I whip my head around as my sister walks inside.

Her violet eyes narrow, scanning the scene. "You said to come quickly. What happened?"

I stand, then turn my back to her, carefully positioning myself out of Drake's line of sight, sliding into the shadows of the room.

"He was attacked by a Phovus," I explain.

Drake groans, shifting onto his stomach.

"Oh, Gods." In a flurry of movement, Arabella dashes across the room, discarding her black cloak that tumbles to the ground in a pool of silk.

She drops to the side of the bed, her fingers tracing the contours of Drake's face, golden swirls of magic seeping into his skin, offering him slight relief from the pain. I can't help but feel a twinge of jealousy, knowing I can never offer that kind of comfort. It is why I keep my magic buried so deeply, because should it ever surface unexpectedly, I fear I may accidentally destroy them.

"Stay still," Ari says softly, "it's going to be okay." She turns her head towards me, her hand outstretched. I know the routine, having watched it a hundred times.

My sister can use her own energy and health to heal him, but she knows I will never allow it.

Considering Drake's actions, giving up a portion of my health to aid in his healing is a small sacrifice. His roar still echoes in my mind from when he charged at the creature to shield me.

Our hands intertwine, her grip firmer than expected. Creation magic is beautifully dark. Despite being opposing entities, the covens devoted to the Goddess of Creation and the God of Death share similar attributes, although neither group will openly admit it.

Through her magic, my inner vitality is used to charge her healing force. While my physical energy dwindles, being drawn out by Arabella, I can't help but wonder how we healed prior to the god's arrival, when they bestowed their powers upon us. During that time, we considered ourselves folk witches and used the residual energy from nature and the blood of our fallen companions to access magic, though its power wasn't nearly as strong.

Every breath is a labor as my sister channels me. Drake's anguished screams are muffled by the pillow he holds to his face. I wince as a loud crack resonates from his body, signaling the bones being mended.

While struggling to stay awake, I eventually hear Arabella softly utter the words, "It's finished."

Her fingers slip out of mine, and I slowly peel back my heavy eyelids. "Did it work?" I ask, each word croakier than the last.

"Yes, but you both need rest."

I nod, allowing her to guide me into the adjacent room. Our footsteps cause the rotting boards to creak.

Finally, I find a bed and climb onto the mattress, not caring how old it is. Arabella tosses me a blanket I'd brought here several weeks ago when I was creating a new poison, and I curl up into a ball.

I embrace the exhaustion and discomfort as atonement for letting Drake get hurt. "Thank you," I say, lifting my gaze to meet hers.

She shakes her head, staring at the shreds of fabric dangling from the dress she made for me. "Pretty things are wasted on you."

Both our lips curve into half-smiles, but it does nothing to the shine of betrayal and hurt in her expression. "Get some sleep," she says. "It's probably best if you don't come home today."

"You know," I state.

She nods.

"How?" I ask, my heart aching.

"Father," she admits. "Well, he didn't exactly tell me. He was shouting about it downstairs, and I overheard. He left with the elders into the forest about an hour ago. They know you're missing, Cali." She pauses, a frown wrinkling her delicate features. Her lips part, and a brief gasp of air swirls between them. "Did you really destroy Azkiel's statue?" she asks, her voice soft, but broken.

"I had no choice," I say. "Drake would have been chosen otherwise, but I used my magic last night to kill a Phovus."

Her expression softens. We both know our parents will never forgive me if they find out we destroyed the ritual, but if they discover I possess decay magic, they'll be forced to hand me over to die. It's bad enough they think I have no magic, but it's better than having a daughter who holds an ancient power only possessed by Azkiel.

"If anyone finds out you were behind it or killing the Phovi…"

"I know."

"I'll cover for you with Mother and bring you some fresh clothes tonight."

"Don't bother," I say and chew the inside of my lip. "She'll know you snuck out again, and you'll be in more trouble. Besides, they know I'm behind it." I pause briefly. "Save the lecture for later," I tease, trying to ease the tension, but Arabella's stoic look doesn't change. "You do understand why we had to do this?"

Her usually soft gaze hardens, and she averts her eyes to the ground. "I believe you think you had to, but they'll kill Drake for this. He may not have even been picked at The Choosing."

"Ari," I say softly, "Don't you ever question it?"

"What?"

"The Harvest."

Silence hangs between us, but I quickly shatter it, even if it's something she doesn't want to hear. "Our names are in there, too, yet Mother said we wouldn't be selected. If the gods are supposed to choose the sacrifices, then surely the elders would have no say in it?" I question, although I'm wrong. They say the gods choose, but it's only ever one god. It's Azkiel's statue that the names show up on. When I think about it, only his name is ever used in relation to the tournament.

She inhales sharply, then rubs her eyes, forcing back a yawn. "Maybe they just favor us because Father is an elder. It's not a terrible thing to be protected like this."

"And Drake?"

She swallows thickly. "I know. I agree, but this will have far worse consequences. I'm scared for you," she admits. Ari walks to the door, then looks back over her shoulder. "If the elders find out you are behind this, we will all be ruined. Father may not be able to protect you this time. Even if they can, Drake won't be spared. Everist is a Sight Seeker, Cali. He'll be investigating this, and no one can hide the truth from him."

With that, she leaves, closing the door behind her. I just hope she isn't right.

"How are you?" I ask Drake as he enters the bedroom.

The last rays of the sunset stream through the moth-bitten drapes, but I've barely slept—only minutes between each panicked awakening. The silence hangs heavy in the room when he doesn't answer right away. "Drake?"

He clears his throat and responds, "I went home. You were asleep, and I didn't want to wake you."

I notice his fresh clothes—a clean gray tunic and loose brown pants. He walks toward me, scuffing the heels of his saggy leather boots. His tattoos seem to come alive as he flexes his fingers, and I'm relieved to see they're back and his magic has strengthened after almost being depleted.

"What happened?"

"The elders know it was someone from my coven," he says, his heavy boots thudding against the floorboards as he approaches my bed. "They saw the ash, too. They know someone else killed the two Phovi."

Adrenaline rushes through my body and bile rises in my throat. "Did anyone see you?"

He shakes his head. "They were at my house. My mother told them I was hunting for our dinner."

My stomach knots. "Which of the elders was at your house?"

He mumbles from under his palms, "Everist, your father, and Dephina."

I climb out of bed. "Fuck."

We both fall silent. If Arabella is right and Everist, the infamous Sight Seeker, is with the elders, they'll quickly discover Drake's presence in the church. Unlike me, he has no one to protect him. They won't hesitate to hang him as an example. I push those thoughts aside. "There are more people here now than ever before. Anyone could have destroyed the statue."

His biceps strain against the thin fabric of his tunic as he tightly clasps his knees. "The Harvest is in five days. They know it was one of the potential sacrifices. Who else, aside from us, would try to sabotage the ritual?" He releases a quivering exhale. "There are only six of age in my coven, and someone saw the light from my illusion when they passed the church. It won't take long for them to know it was me. I'm as good as dead if I don't escape."

Absent-mindedly raking his fingers through his black hair, he adds, "They said The Offering is still going ahead."

I shake my head. "How can they still go ahead? The statue is destroyed."

His expression softens, revealing a gentler side to his rugged features. "I don't know, but it's happening."

The possibility of the words we once joked about draws closer and closer. I grip my legs under the skirt of my dress, feeling the sharp sting as my nails dig into my skin, trying to ground myself as I contemplate leaving my sisters behind.

"I'll go alone," he says, as if I'd ever allow that. "I can go to one of the human kingdoms."

I scoff. "Where they will kill you the moment they realize you have magic?"

My eyes fixate on the swirling symbols on his arms, each one depicting a different scene of him sailing away.

If he leaves Dahryst—the only sanctuary for witches and warlocks—he will be forced to seek refuge with the non-magical humans who despise our kind. They'll make a show of torturing him.

If he chooses not to leave, Drake will have no choice but to take part in The Harvest. That, or he'll be executed once they find out he was a part of destroying the statue and killing the Phovi.

None of this was supposed to happen. How in the Darklands are they planning on choosing the so-called sacrifices now? Without the statue. I knew this whole ceremony was corrupt. They don't even need Death's magic or the gods. They'll likely pick the names themselves. Bastards.

Through the open window, I hear church bells and let out a weary sigh. "They're summoning everyone."

"You should go," he replies. "If you don't, they'll suspect you."

As the final dong resounds, my body shivers and a wave of coldness washes over me. "Darklands, no. I'm not staying while you run, and who says they won't arrest me?"

"You know they won't." He pauses. "I'm sorry, Cali. I should have done this alone." He takes a step forward and wraps his arms around me in a tight hug. Despite Drake's body pressing against mine, I can't find any comfort, rendered numb to any other sensation.

My voice is barely audible as I mumble into his chest, "Like I'd have let you."

"If we both go, they'll hunt us faster. You're the daughter of an elder," he says, as if I could ever forget. "Even if they find out you were involved, they won't kill you." As he retreats, his eyes remain fixed on me, their intensity unnerving. "Don't come after me. Promise me."

An irresistible urge to lean in and kiss him consumes me, even if everything is hopeless. The desire has been building up inside me for so long, but the fear of losing our friendship keeps us from acting on any feelings we have.

But that doesn't matter now. Not if he's leaving.

I drift closer, my heart hammering against my ribcage. He leans forward and caresses his thumb over my lips, tracing them with his eyes as he inches closer. Wild-eyed, his lips brush against mine, and I hold my breath.

His grip tightens, then he squeezes his eyes shut, shaking his head. "We can't," he whispers, his voice cracking. "You need to forget me." Gulping, he pulls away, lingering his fingers over my hand for a second longer. "It's for the best."

He turns slowly, pressing his lips tight, as if he might break at any moment. I watch him leave, and step forward, desiring nothing more than to go after him. But as his footsteps fade, my bottom lip trembles, a sob quaking my chest. Shaking my head, I run to the window, grabbing the rotting ledge, battling hot tears, refusing to let them pierce through.

NIGHT OF DEATH AND FLOWERS

Gods know if I start crying, I won't stop. He will be okay. He *has* to be. As I stare through the grimy glass, my heart sinks. I watch Drake appear below, then run toward the forest. Closing my eyes, I suck in several deep breaths, attempting to ground myself. Drake must leave. It is the only choice. Yet, even with him gone, the elders know someone used decay magic.

Wasting no time, I hurry to the other room, snatching a vial of poison from the table and staring at the shimmering dark-purple liquid. Resolved to push aside the emptiness left by Drake's absence, I prepare to leave for the church.

I tighten my grip around the vial of poison. If the elders find out I'm behind the use of decay magic, even my father won't be able to protect me. But I refuse to go down without a fight.

SEVEN

Azkiel

I sink deeper into the foliage of Morcidea Forest, keeping to the shadows. My eyes focus on a willowy man in the center of the town square, tonight's entertainment on the second eve of the Night Market.

The witch's magic echoes mine as he devours the light from the torches illuminating the booths and glittering, dark items on display. The crowd gasps as they are plunged into darkness, with nothing but the reprieve of the crescent, white moon.

Flickers of orange light glow on his fine, embroidered tunic as he absorbs and weaves its essence into his clothing. In moments, every part of the fabric covering his body glows with a fiery beacon.

With a twist of his wrists, the specks of light leave his clothes, then return to their candles. My lips curve as I watch the practiced magician. He cannot be any older than thirty, yet he has mastered light absorption—one of the three powers my coven can inherit from me.

Cheers and clapping erupt throughout the market, and I take another step back, wondering where she is.

My senses reach out for my ethereal power, every part of my being aching to see the witch I plan to kill. Leaves rustle around me as shadow vipers slither closer, drawn to the magic in my veins. With a hiss, they watch the mortals alongside me, our eyes focused as one on Ennismore.

Everything has changed since I was last here, except for the church. What was once a handful of scattered small houses now includes shops and a market, transforming the area into the town square.

The festivities of The Harvest pause when the church bells ring and crows scatter from the branches. A small smile curves my lips when I spot my sigil emblazoned on tents and the cloaks of the witches and warlocks. They still worship me the most, but as I notice the symbols of my sisters and brothers, the contentment quickly fades.

I move deeper into the shadows of the forest as the crowds pour from the buildings and the square, all making their way toward the church. Excited, intelligible chatter rises amongst them as they discuss The Harvest.

Despite some of their elders' weaknesses, I swell with pride as the people celebrate the traditions I created, so they could have protection after I left. With each Harvest, a new elder is born, acquiring the powers of the fallen sacrifices, ensuring a long lineage of elders through the generations.

In return, I could return to the Darklands knowing the elders forbade anyone to go to Tenenocti, except on the night of The Harvest, on my orders and the new sacrifices join my dead in protecting the island. Although, few try. Those who do are drowned before they can arrive.

While my reapers—cloaked, skeletal beings born from darkness, and created using my sister's magic—take over my tasks of guiding the dead. Not that the dead have a destination.

NIGHT OF DEATH AND FLOWERS

Without Cyna, we drag most of them to the Darklands, deserving or not.

The crowds in the square disperse, dressed in their finery, the colors varying depending on the coven they were born into, and head toward the church.

My magic tingles as I turn my eyes to a woman who hikes up the skirt of her dress, showing worn boots stained with the inky blue blood of my Phovi.

I grit my teeth, then look up to see her long, brown hair cascading down her back, the golden and chestnut hues catching against the moonlight.

I never expected my heart to skip a beat until I lay my eyes on her for the first time.

I growl under my breath as my ethereal power—living within her—caresses my senses from afar.

Each step is graceful, every movement hypnotic and enticing, yet I can't help but notice the darkness lurking in her eyes. There's something familiar about her, perhaps because of the power we share.

My breath catches unexpectedly in my throat when she half-smiles at a woman in passing. Her cheeks dimple, her full lips slightly curved, and a deep, aching sadness drowns my thoughts.

Calista.

It takes several seconds before I move again, and my heart rate picks up, each beat a struggle. I cannot take my eyes off her, and sweat slicks my forehead, a fog clouding my mind until I cannot think. I shake my head, desperate to remove the anxiety threading my veins.

Every time I lay eyes on her amidst the crowd, observing her as she navigates through it and pondering how she acquired my magic, I am frozen.

My lips part as I track her movements. She carefully maneuvers herself, keeping a safe distance from the other people. For a moment, I contemplate whether she also shares my fate of never experiencing another's lingering touch.

Except, as she reaches the church gates, her bare shoulders rub against two others, and nothing happens.

They do not turn to ash.

Rage floods my veins. She possesses my magic, but she is not confined to a life of loneliness.

I steeple my fingers, bringing them to my lips as I watch her disappear, my magic longing to turn her to ash and end this prophecy.

EIGHT

Calista

The church is transformed by the red glow of the setting sun—the rays piercing through the stained-glass windows, scattering fragments of colors onto the stone ground.

I spot my family in the first pew, my mother dressed in an opulent silver gown embroidered with the symbols of Essentria's coven. My three sisters, each descending in height, gaze at the elders appearing on the dais.

Eliana spots me, her wide eyes shining as she waves. I shoot her a grin, then find my mother's venomous glare and sour expression.

I turn my focus away from her, knowing she won't cause a scene in front of such prominent families and the other elders. It's the one thing I can count on her for.

My eyes track the space where the statue stood now houses a large stone basin sat upon a pillar of marble. My mouth dries as I track my father across the raised wooden platform where he joins the six other elders. Long, crimson cloaks hang in contrast to their pristine white robes, a mimicry of the robes the sacrifices will wear. As I cast my gaze over each of them, I notice the absence of the eldest among them, who must be almost ninety. Standing at the back, the youngest—at only thirty and the most recent victor of The Harvest—rubs his bloodshot eyes.

Typically, their number stands at eight, though it occasionally dwindles to seven or expands to as many as nine. But as there can only be one new elder every decade, it is always a small coven.

With bated breath, I await news of Drake. I hope he's already on his way to another land, but any sliver of comfort dissolves when I consider what dangers may wait for him when he arrives.

NIGHT OF DEATH AND FLOWERS

My father steps forward, his cloak billowing around him in a ripple of red. His gravelly voice resonates throughout the building, packed with the most important people from each coven in the community. "It is a dark day for us all."

Repressing the urge to roll my eyes, I slip behind a family with two small children, slinking into a pew at the back of the church without being noticed.

He continues, his bright blue eyes matching mine as he takes a second step forward. "You may wonder why the sacred statue of the God of Death is missing."

He pauses for dramatic effect. Gasps and hushed whispers fill the air, and I blow out a tense breath as I notice a hint of disgust twisting his features.

His voice booms again, and the chatter fades into silence. "It was destroyed by traitors, hiding within our beloved community. This barbaric act stands as a reminder that we will fight against those who try to destroy our traditions. We fought against the non-magical humans, and it was Death who saved us from them," he states, enunciating each word. Finally, his pointed stare finds me in the crowd. I shift my body, positioning myself half out of view, but he doesn't look away as he preaches. "The humans will kill us all if they find any weakness amongst us. The Harvest keeps us strong. It is our honor to serve you, to hold the magic of all six covens, gifted to us by the sacrifice of our own, to keep Dahryst strong."

He averts his gaze to the rest of the congregation, and I shake my head. Gifted? I'm certain the other people who were sacrificed would disagree if they weren't dead.

His voice raises an octave, and I focus on the elders. "If we fight amongst ourselves, then we open the way for the humans, who will slaughter our sons and daughters for holding powers they envy. They call us an abomination of nature, yet we are born from it. We are only as strong as our leaders. Without us, the borders will not hold, and the humans will come," he explains, as if we haven't all heard this hundreds of times already. However, I detect a slight waver in his tone, so subtle that it could easily go unnoticed. Yet, I know my father well, and he never falters unless he's afraid.

The elders can feel their power slipping.

My father continues. "We must find these treacherous cowards and remove the poison from our society before it spreads."

I zone out as he proceeds into a historical lecture, hoping the so-called poison spreads. I want everyone in this town who disagrees with The Harvest to finally take a stand against those who practice with blind faith, like the devoted—fanatics of the gods—who aid the enforcers that protect our towns and preach to masses in our church. I spot one of them standing at the side by a wall, nodding along with everything my father spews. The man's body is covered with painted symbols of the gods, wearing nothing but a simple brown tunic and breeches. I recognize him from the sermons I attended before I stopped coming to worship.

As my decay magic seeps under my skin, I am reminded of how precarious a situation I am in. At the last Harvest, I didn't fully understand what was happening.

I tune out almost entirely as my father drones on about our origins, having memorized the entire lecture down to every word.

We were folk witches once and took our magic from nature. The humans from the other lands hunted us until our population dwindled. It was then that the gods we venerated surrendered their ethereal forms for mortal bodies to help us. With their empyreal powers, we found a haven in Dahryst—a continent protected by the Black Sea, and the Pistoren Ocean on the other side.

Except, all the Gods but Azkiel abandoned before the war finished, abandoning us to fend for ourselves. He saved us—supposedly—then vanished too, but not without a parting gift. A leader was needed, and The Harvest presented the perfect opportunity to offer blood as a tribute to him. Simultaneously, it serves to find the strongest of our age to become the next elder.

The corner of my mouth twitches as I stare at each of the elders. Their powers—siphoned through murder—give them the strength to place wards along our borders, to aid in the growth of our crops in the absence of the gods.

The elders want power, and so once every decade, they excuse murder for their own gain. After all, magic can only be absorbed by killing another on sacred ground, and Tenenocti Island is the only place where such a ritual can occur and is coincidentally within Death's domain. Why else would they allow only a man and woman—aged between sixteen and twenty-four—from each coven to participate?

Drake had it right when he once explained that our magic is still malleable at this age. The elders hide behind their gods to keep people from rioting when their children are slaughtered in The Harvest.

I gaze around the portraits of the six gods and goddesses hanging in silver, ornate frames against dark stone. Essentria, the goddess of Creation, is vibrant in a golden robe. Her golden eyes are alight with flecks of green.

Nyxara, the Goddess of Destiny, is the most striking with purple eyes and silver hair. Volan, the God of Will, looks like a warrior, with his dark, pointed stare and black tattoos covering his muscular body.

Cyna, the God of Judgment, stares out of his frame with discerning green eyes, as if he is silently looking into our hearts. Astraea, the Goddess of Dreams, has an aura of innocence with her soft indigo eyes, flowing blue hair—her entire body a tapestry of paintings, depicting our history.

And then there's *him*.

I stare at the portrait of Death. His silver eyes are tinged with black, as if the night sky is seeping into the stars.

I blink twice, the present flooding in as I hear Drake's name uttered from my father's lips.

"Drake is the culprit we seek."

Every muscle in my body tenses, the hairs on the backs of my arms standing erect. I lean forward, gripping the pew in front of me. I lean forward, eyes wide.

A small smile carves my father's lip when he looks at me. I scratch the side of my neck, suppressing a gulp, and force apathy into my expression. He steps back into line, and the only female elder takes his place at the front.

Her voice comes out raspier than I expected as she addresses the room. "We have yet to capture the criminal," she says, relieving the panic squeezing around my heart. "However," she continues, and my nails splinter into the wood, my knuckles white. "We are interrogating his family. We believe he is on the run, possibly attempting to leave Dahryst. I assure you, he will not get far."

The icy cold seems to penetrate my bones while I decipher her words. They must have blocked travel from the coastlines. We are on an island, and there is only one way off—by ship.

As for the interrogation of his family, we all know what that means.

The croakiness in her voice persists, even after she clears her throat. "Anyone seen to be aiding or abetting Drake Redding will be punished. If you see him, you must come to us immediately."

A woman calls out from the front pew. "What about the other one?"

"The accomplice is from Azkiel's Coven. We are unsure of their gender, but it is unlikely the two will separate," she says, her tone wavering. The elders exchange looks, and my father casts a glance over at me, then quickly averts his gaze. "As of now, Drake Redding is our primary culprit, and the mastermind behind the attack."

I almost laugh, but maintain my composure. If Drake were here, he would have found it amusing, too. They make it sound like some carefully thought-out battle.

NIGHT OF DEATH AND FLOWERS

Everist clears his throat, his presence commanding attention. His stoic expression reminds me of the statue we destroyed. His eyes, matte-black, sift across the room as though scanning our minds. I try to stay perfectly still as his probing gaze meets mine—the Sight Seeker.

Measuring each breath, his eyes linger on me, and I hold my defiant stance until he eventually shifts his attention elsewhere. "The Choosing will be different this year," he states, every word an echo bouncing from the stone walls. "Because The God of Death has returned."

A collective gasp fills the silence before the room erupts in chatter, and I freeze. A haze settles over my mind, and the room spins.

The God of Death is here.

Everist speaks again, hushing the room into silence. "Tomorrow, he will select the twelve to compete in The Harvest. Tonight, you will all come forward and volunteer your names again in the Offering." He points at the stone basin, but I stop listening.

Bile climbs my throat. I know he's real, but to me, he's always been comparable to a myth, like a dark, omniscient presence that looms over Dahryst, promising protection in exchange for bloodshed.

Cheering sounds in my ears, as the world falls into slow motion. Hands clasp together from the congregation in prayer, rejoicing with smiles wider than I have ever seen from the people here.

I grip the pew, closing my eyes as my mind spins. Neither Drake nor I could have ever imagined this outcome from our plan. Now he's on the run, and I am as good as dead. If Azkiel has returned to Ennismore, then he will uncover the hidden magic that dwells within me.

We were supposed to make things better, but I fear we've sealed our fates for the worst.

NINE

Calista

The elders dismiss everyone from the church, except those who will volunteer in the Offering.

I look around at all those supposedly volunteering to be chosen. Some, I recognize from Ennismore, others were brought in from other cities and towns across Dahryst by their families.

While it is supposed to be an honor to compete in the Harvest, I can't believe anyone wants to volunteer. Either their families make them, or they have no choice. It's a poorly kept secret that poorer families are indirectly threatened to have their resources taken away if they do not make their children of age put their names forth.

It is expected that we put our names in. Father wants to lead by example, although none of the others here are aware of how corrupt everything is.

Everist stands behind the basin, holding a long scroll. "Step up and announce your names as you cut your hand over the basin. Now, form a line."

I glare at the basin. The Offering is sealed with blood magic—a contract holding those who volunteered accountable. If the witch or warlock is chosen for The Harvest and refuses to go, then all those they love will die.

What *wonderful* leaders we have!

The silence is deafening. Not even a whisper carries through the church as I shuffle forward with the other so-called volunteers, crowding the stone basin as the elders watch.

"I'm nervous," Arabella whispers from behind me.

"Don't be," I say, but when her breaths settle evenly, I grab her hand. "This is just for show."

She nods, and I turn to face the front. Blood is drawn from each of the chosen, their hisses and gulps filling the church after they speak their names. Most of them don't stand a chance if they're sent to Tenenocti.

A muscular boy steps forward, his dark brown eyes glaze over those around him. When his stare meets mine, my lips form a hard line. I remind myself that none of this is real, and that he isn't someone I will need to fight.

He must be from one of the visiting families, because I haven't seen him before. "Alaric Varwic," he announces as he slices his hand over the stone basin, etched with the sigils of the gods.

My sister's whisper catches in my ear. "At the very least, we'll get to meet a god."

"I can hardly wait," I reply dryly, and place a hand over my stomach, willing the nausea away.

A girl I recognize from church sermons, Elenore, trembles in front of me as she stands over the stone basin, wincing at the sight of the blood. Shakily, she grabs the dagger by the silver handle carved into a knot, with sacred symbols on the blade, and lets out a small whimper.

"Here," I say, placing my hand over hers. "It will only hurt for a second," I promise, and she glances over her shoulder, her round brown eyes swimming with tears. "Remember, this doesn't mean you will be chosen," I add.

When she turns back, I grit my teeth, shooting a glare at my father. She can't be older than eighteen. Fucking monsters, decorating us in symbols, while preparing to send us to the slaughter. Most of the people here are still children.

Carefully, Elenore hovers the blade above her left hand, over the palm.

"No," I say and point at a finger that will hurt less.

She closes her eyes and softly whispers, "Thank you," then digs into her skin, hissing as the blood pools.

"Elenore Amenbore," she states shakily, then replaces the dagger before leaving to join the rest of her family from Astraea's coven.

My sister smiles. "That was sweet."

"It was necessary," I correct her. "She was holding up the line."

She rolls her eyes, then stands next to me. "Sure. Deep down, I know you care."

I grimace, then stand over the stone bowl, slowly lifting the dagger. Death haunts my every thought as I slide the blade across my skin, and my blood drips, merging with the rest.

"Calista Bellevue," I spit, then throw the dagger down, shooting the elders a glare.

NIGHT OF DEATH AND FLOWERS

I place my hand on my sister's shoulder as she steps up behind me, then cuts her finger with the dagger.

"Arabella Bellevue," she states. Her blood pools onto the stone while the other elders nod in approval. She brings her hand to her lips, sealing the wound and steps back.

"Arabella," my mother scolds when she reaches us, seemingly out of nowhere. I guess families of the elders are allowed in here. My other two sisters, Cecilia and Eliana, aged nine and ten, gaze at the basin, their eyes brimming.

Cecilia is the first to speak. "What happens to the sacrifices after The Harvest?"

My mother grabs her by the shoulders, moving her away from the basin. "They go to the gods," she whispers, but her eyes are trained on the other family elders, offering placid smiles as they glance our way.

My little sister pouts, her big eyes focused on the bloodied basin. "They die, Cee," I say, and my mother's glare snaps to me.

"They don't need to hear that," she hisses, covering my sister's ears.

"Why not?" I ask as Cecilia shrugs herself out of my mother's grip. "They should know, considering they will be forced to supposedly volunteer themselves at the next Harvest."

Eliana gasps. "I don't want to die."

"You won't." I lift my stare to meet my Mother's. "I will never let *anyone* hurt you."

My mother's lips tighten into a frown. "No one is dying."

Cecilia's eyes brim with tears, and she looks at me, then to Ari. "But you're both volunteering. What if you're picked?"

My mother hushes them. "That won't happen."

"It's true. She'd never let us enter the tournament," I say, with a smirk as I lower my knees to meet Cee's height. "Because if I win, then Mother would be forced to bow to me."

I wink at my little sister, and she giggles.

"Calista," Mother warns.

"Calm down," I say. "Before you give yourself another headache."

Eliana interjects this time, while playing with her long braid. "Maybe we can choose an elder without the Harvest?"

"What an intriguing thought, Eliana."

She grins while our mother rolls her eyes. I smile in return, but my stomach dips when I realize no matter what I say, their voices won't make a difference. Not now, nor in ten years when it is their turn. Children have an innocuous ability to shine a light on hidden truths. Yet, their voices, no matter how honest, are cast aside.

NIGHT OF DEATH AND FLOWERS

I sigh, then turn to look at my baby sisters, crossed between wanting them to know the truth, but also realizing how hard that will make life for them.

My mother turns her attention to me. "You, outside."

Heaving a deep sigh, I follow her out of the church. Her nose wrinkles as she gestures for me to hurry with a harsh flip of her hand.

As soon as we step out into the chilly, early evening air, she grabs my arm a little too tightly. "Smile," she hisses into my ear, "as though you're not the heathen you are. Your sisters will go with your father. You and I are going alone."

She definitely knows. I force a smile. "Oh, how *wonderful*."

"I should lock you away for what you have done," she hisses in my ear. Her grip tightens, but she plasters a smile on her lips and waves at the other esteemed members of our society as we walk home, hurrying around the horse and carriages for those who have come from the other side of town.

Men pour into the Grumpy Gurger Tavern, grabbing metal tins overflowing with ale. My eyes narrow on one of the warlock's arms, covered in the likeness of Azkiel.

News of his return buzzes through the crowds, the excitement palpable. I follow my mother down the rain-slicked narrow streets winding through small houses with slate roofs. The sound of horses clopping against the cobblestone hammers in my ears as a carriage glides past us.

Candlelight flickers from behind the netted curtains of one house, allowing me to spot the symbol of Asentrai—the moon, sun and stars—hanging from a string on their door. Probably hoping the gods will bless them.

As we continue moving, our house comes into view, its front walls adorned by clay symbols, showing that our home is the leading house in Essentria's coven because of our father's position. Our coven has one elder, Death's coven has two, but some, like Astraea's, have none. It depends on the winner of each Harvest and what coven they originated from.

While we all live as one community, our given powers separate us. Even in the academy, we were taught separately from the other covens, each of us knowing we will hold different roles once our magic showed itself around age sixteen, or earlier, if a tragedy or trauma occurred, forcing our powers to show themselves sooner.

In Essentria's coven, most became healers and those with nature enhancement magic take care of the forests and magical plants all over Dahryst. Those in Cyna's coven often became enforcers of the law, guards and chief judges sentencing those for their crimes. But all of us answer to the elders, who supposedly answer to the gods.

We reach the door, and the moment we are in the foyer, my mother's grip tightens, her fingertips sure to leave behind slight bruises. "When will you learn, Calista?"

"They'll be fine," I say, sighing. "You still have plenty of time to indoctrinate them."

"You little brat," she spits. "I am not just talking about them. You snuck back out last night."

"I don't know what you're talking about," I say calmly, then shove my mother's hand away.

She walks out of the foyer, and I begrudgingly follow. With a glance around to check for any lingering staff, she lowers her voice to a whisper. "Everist knows it was you and Drake."

I purse my lips. "Funny, I don't recall my name being mentioned in Father's speech."

I follow her past bundles of lavender piled under the stairs, carefully bundled by the maids, then emerge into the great chamber room. Breathing in the rich smell of wood and polish, I scrunch my nose.

My mother turns back to face me, her violet gaze narrowing. "No, fortunately for you, they are going to find another to place your crimes on."

My mouth dries instantly. "They can't do that…"

She bares her teeth, tears swimming in her eyes. But I know better than to think they are for me. "Do you know what would happen if anyone discovered what you are?"

I blink twice, then reorientate myself. "What do you mean, *what* I am?"

Her bottom lip trembles as she turns away, as if my magic might seep into her if she looks at me too long. "Nothing but *that* kind of *disgusting* power could have killed a Phovus."

"Decay magic?" I say aloud for the first time, an unexpected freedom ringing in my tone.

She winces, and I smile. "Keep your voice down," she whisper-shouts. "Unless you want people to hear you. Do you know what they will do if they find out?"

"Kill me?"

My mom's brows shoot halfway up her forehead, wrinkled by time. "Worse. Do you want your sisters to never find suitors? To be shunned by society."

I shake my head, as if to agree with her. "That would be a tragedy."

She points at the large window overlooking the gardens. "They will think we're all like you. I don't know how you came from me and can possess such… repulsive magic."

Her words shouldn't affect me. Yet, tears sting the corner of my eyes, but I refuse to cry. I will *never* cry for her. "I didn't ask for it," I say, my voice coming out far meeker than I'd have liked.

She sighs. "You were such a lovely girl when you were little. This is what happens when you abandon your worship of the gods. I warned you."

"I won't let Drake and an innocent die for my crimes. I killed the Phovi. It was my idea to destroy the statue," I insist.

"And the gods will see you are punished for it, but, for now, you will keep quiet and let your father take care of things."

"No!" I shout. "To the Darklands with him and the gods."

I gasp when my mother's hand lands on the side of my face. Pain shoots through my cheek and jaw, radiating into my temple. My ears ring as I touch the hot, pulsing mark branded on my skin.

My mom scowls, spitting her next words through clenched teeth. "Keep speaking like that, and it will be you who goes to the Darklands." She places her trembling hands on her hips. "You will burden us for the rest of our lives. You will never find a husband acting the way you do, and you will doom your sisters to the same fate. Your disobedience will cost this family everything." She sighs, then casts her eyes to the ceiling, painted with scenes of the gods. "You don't care about us at all."

My lips part, but I hold back the hundreds of things I want to spit back in response—about how she consistently treated me as an outsider, and blames me for every bad thing that happens in this family.

"You know what? Fuck you."

Her mouth turns in disgust, but I turn around and storm through the foyer, hurrying up the grand staircase.

Beneath my fingers, the familiar sting of decay magic pulses. Since using it the other night, it craves more death. With every step, it sparks to life, and a small part of me desires to use it on my mother.

I push away the thought, uncomfortable with how easily the idea of murder comes to mind. No. I don't want my mother dead, no matter how much pain she's caused over the years. My sisters need her, because without her, my father will send them away to academies where things are even worse than what they are here.

She's different with my sisters. Perhaps she's a good mother to them, or at least, as much as she can be.

I slip into my bedroom and light the candles. Furniture emerges from the darkness as candlelight bathes the room in warmth.

Beside my bed, Thorn stands perched on my window ledge. Arabella calls him my pet, but crows require too much freedom to be domesticated.

Thorn hops onto the floorboards, and I lean over him, stroking his silky feathers until my fingertips brush against a rough, foreign texture. He winces, and I tighten my hold, restraining him so I can get a better look.

Upon closer inspection, I notice a tinge of blood on his feathers. "What happened?" I spot a union binding ring on the ground next to him, covered with crystals. Someone must have caught him taking it, then hurt him. "I warned you to stop stealing jewelry from people's houses."

He squawks. "Pretty ring."

I roll my eyes. Quickly, I pull out my collection of dried roots, jars of venom, and other ingredients. While most of my collection is at the abandoned manor house, I keep a small supply here in case of poison related emergencies. But that isn't the only thing I can do.

I unwrap the cloth, pinching a small amount of Sanare Medicis root, then add a few drops of moon water, until it turns into a paste.

Thorn flinches when I touch the wound. I shoot him a look, and he tilts his head. "It will help," I promise, then carefully apply a thick layer of the ointment. "I'm not Arabella, but it'll speed up the healing."

He perks up on hearing my sister's name. Footsteps sound outside the door, and I tense. Listening intently, I decipher they are not heavy or forceful enough to be my father's, or if it's a maid. My chest tightens, nonetheless.

Arabella opens the door, then coos at Thorn. "Hi, sweet baby."

He preens his wings back, then ducks his head. Only Arabella sees the softer side of Thorn.

"Mother knows," I say, then turn to face my sister. "Did you tell them Drake was involved?" I say through gritted teeth, my voice growing louder with each beat.

"No, I didn't." Arabella picks at her blonde hair, sprinkled with pink wildflowers, each layer of her hair tied back under the other, creating a wave. "They already knew," she exclaims. "Everist got a vision in the church when he touched a pew. He knew you were there. He sensed decay magic too, but not who cast it, so I told them someone else was with you and Drake to throw them off your scent. They're panicking, Cali. You've got to stay unnoticed for a while."

I rub my forehead, smoothing out the lines forming as I stare back at my sister. "This is bad. They'll likely pin this on some poor innocent witch in Azkiel's coven and hang them."

Her hands cover her dainty features, hiding the brim of tears. "I… no…" she mumbles between her fingers. "They won't. Father won't let them kill an innocent."

"Don't be naïve," I look at the ground, uneasiness settling in my stomach. "Father will, but there's nothing we can do about it. I just hope at least Drake left before they stop the ships from disembarking."

I hold on to the idea that he's long gone, but not knowing whether he's safe has me feeling more anxious than ever.

She lowers herself onto my bed. "I'm going to talk to Father, make him see reason."

"Don't," I say wearily, knowing he'll only see it as an act of defiance. I can't have her be treated in the same way I am. She must always appear the dutiful daughter. How else will she ever survive this family? "He'll have no choice but to act," I explain, each word laced with years of resentment. "Even though the statue is gone, The Choosing is going ahead anyway now that Death has returned. I accomplished nothing." A frigid chill laces around the back of my neck, and my heart skips a beat. I steady myself, then briefly close my eyes.

"I can't believe it either." She pauses, then chews on her lips. "What do you think he's like?" As she leans forward, the wooden frame of the bed creaks. "The God of Death?"

Leaving my spot, I stroll over the intricately designed rug towards the tucked-away seating area, where I place my feet on the low wooden table. "I really don't care," I say, anxiety lacing my words. "But if the elders are terrible, then I can only imagine that he's even more dreadful."

She leans against the headboard, admiring the meticulous carvings that depict the goddess of creation. "The God of Death loves his people. We're safe from the humans because of him. I'm sure he will be magnificent, although, I admit, I am a little afraid of seeing him."

My eyes widen in astonishment as I turn to her, my nose scrunching up in response. "Yes, we should be. He sends people to be *sacrificed*. He is a monster!"

She changes position, crossing her legs. "I suppose. But don't you think it's for a good reason? I mean, we need the elders."

"No, we don't."

She sighs, then returns the subject to Drake. "Do you think Drake's left Dahryst yet?"

"I hope so," I reply, but the knot of fear in my chest only tightens.

"Me too. I'm sorry, Cali. I know you'll miss him. We both will."

"Yeah," I reply weakly. I can't think about the danger he's in without going out of my mind. Drake is smart, quick, and resourceful. He has a better chance of evading capture than any of us. "You should rest," I say, rubbing my forehead. "We'll talk tomorrow."

She nods and lets out a long sigh. "We'll be okay. Drake will be okay."

Gods, I wish I had her optimism.

Slowly, she climbs off the bed, and I avert my eyes. I listen to the sound of her footsteps fading away, then close my eyes once the door clicks shut.

I push aside all emotions and enter a state of dissociation as my eyes focus on the wardrobe.

Suddenly, Thorn jumps into my line of sight, startling me. I'd forgotten he was here. His small, beady eyes lock onto mine with an intense gaze. He leaps into my arms, his weight pressing against my chest, and I cradle him as I carry him to the bed.

"Sorry I didn't ask her to heal you, but look," I say, pointing at the area, "you're already on the mend." I examine the wound, which will most certainly be closed by morning.

Exhausted, I ease us onto the soft mattress, my muscles protesting with every movement. I play with the idea of running while I still have the chance before the God of Death unveils my powers. With dread slithering in my stomach, I close my eyes, ignoring the urge to flee.

As I drift off to sleep, the haunting essence of decay magic seeps into my dreams, transforming Tenenocti into a wasteland. The branches, twisted and gnarled, hang like skeletal remains. The trees wither away gradually, their branches crumbling into powder and falling onto the lifeless soil. As I reach the pebbled beach, I take in the sight of the dark waters stretching out before me. Even the wind seems to whisper as it catches dead leaves, skimming them across the ground.

Startled, I jolt awake, and the world slowly comes into focus as I sit upright. A silhouette of pink appears in my peripheral vision, and I whip my head around to see Arabella sitting by my bed, staring at me. "Good gods, Ari."

"Sorry, I know you're taking a nap, but I had to wake you."

"With a heart attack?" I ask as voices float through the floorboards. I try to decipher who they belong to, but I can't place any of them except for my father's gravelly tone. As she passes me a clay mug, wisps of steam twist through the air. I inhale the subtle hints of peppermint, then take a sip. "Who's here?"

Her fingers intertwine with a ribbon from her dress as she twirls it around repeatedly. "The elders."

"Why?" I ask, trying to keep my tone calm.

"They're having a meeting…about you," she says, tilting her head. "Where's Thorn?"

I turn my gaze to the open window. The gentle breeze carries with it the scent of blooming flowers as the sky above paints a beautiful shade of sapphire. "He probably left early."

She clenches her lips tightly. "Father's upset. But it's more than that…" she pauses.

"Spit it out, Ari."

She purses her lips, then droops her head. "They've captured Drake."

The world moves in slow motion. I stand, almost like every part of my body is moving of its own accord. I listen carefully as footsteps pound underneath my floorboards, fading out toward the front of the house. I whisper, "I'm going to find him."

She stands in front of the door, as if that would stop me, then whisper-shouts, "Are you insane?"

"I'm not leaving Drake imprisoned."

She shakes her head. "He will have a fair trial."

"Don't be delusional. They will kill him. They must."

She folds her arms over her chest. "I care about Drake. But I love you more. I won't lose you."

"You can't protect me, Ari. This is because of my choices. I won't leave him to this fate alone," I say as I pull on a gray dress so as not to draw any attention.

"What will you do?"

"I'm breaking him out."

Her muscles tense and her lips part, but she doesn't speak.

"He doesn't deserve this," I continue. "It was just a statue. We did this to stop them from murdering innocent people. What if Father dies and Cee or Eliana are chosen for the next one? What if it's me who is sent to The Harvest?"

"That won't happen."

"If it did? What would you think of it all, then?"

She drags her blond strands through her fingers, then curls several of them around one finger. "It's not just the statue. The Phovi were killed too."

"So? They're awful creatures. One tried to kill me once. Remember?"

"I know." She bites her lip. "It's just…I'm scared for you."

I swallow hard against the lump rising in my throat, then pull her into a tight hug. "Don't be," I whisper into her hair. "You have to be strong no matter what happens to me."

Her grip tightens around me. "Don't go."

I pull her at arm's length. "I have to save him, or at least try, but it has to be now, before Father comes to talk to me, and he and Mother lock me in this room."

She bites her lip. "Please be careful and try not to get into any more trouble."

I nod and grab my boots.

She sighs. "He's at the Incarcuri."

Anxiety races through my heart as I stop tying my laces midway, staring at a floorboard while stories I've been told of the Incarcuri weave through my thoughts. Each scenario of incarns accused of crimes being psychologically tortured is more horrific than the last.

"Thank you."

"There's no way the Enforcers will let you in to see him."

I climb up onto the window ledge, barely focusing. "They can't stop me. No matter how much they want to."

TEN

Calista

Someone's about to be executed, and I cannot tear my eyes away from the grim spectacle.

    I stand in the town's square, watching the sun's gentle caress on the mountains, casting a deep orange glow over the cobbled roads and brown buildings. The fading sun rays form a halo around the freshly hung noose swaying from the gallows. Wooden boards creak under the weight of the executioner, dressed in black robes and symbols marking him as one of Azkiel's coven.

As the day slowly draws to an end, The Night Market becomes a forgotten fantasy amongst the stalls of bread, fish, and fabrics. Behind them, merchants call out to passersby, hoping to make a quick sale before they are forced to pack up.

The hordes of witches and warlocks visiting our small town flood the streets, their colorful robes adding a vibrant energy to the usually quiet atmosphere. The festivities reach a crescendo of noise as they huddle closer to the gallows, drawn to the morbid sight.

Beyond them, children gather in a circle, their eyes filled with awe and anticipation, to witness an enchanting puppet performance showcasing the six deities.

Everyone is so happy, as if we're not surrounded by unjustness and death.

My heart is in my throat as a hooded man with trembling fingers is led up the five steps toward the rope. Surely, they wouldn't hang Drake without a trial. It is against our highest law. But then, when have the elders ever respected the rules they force the rest of us to adhere to?

I focus on the details and notice the man's arms are skinnier than Drake's. He couldn't have lost this much weight in the short time we've been apart. This man doesn't even have any tattoos either, and he stands at least three inches shorter than Drake. Yet, I have to make sure it's not my friend.

I wrap my navy cloak tightly around myself, navigating through the bustling crowds to get a better look. I pause at the front, my shoulders brushing with a man carrying a small child. Beside him, a girl, no older than little Cecilia, watches on with macabre fascination.

The potent smells of incense and ale permeate the air. Liquid sloshes from the tin cups of men, bubbly golden liquid slashing against where the cobblestone fades into dirt.

Covered in inked tattoos depicting the symbols of all six gods, a Devoted dressed in a purple robe steps next to the hooded prisoner. A burst of cheers erupts from the eager crowd as he unrolls a long piece of parchment.

"Jaron Hughmus Endignor has hereby been found guilty of robbery and arson and shall be hanged from the neck until dead here, in our square of Ennismore."

I'm sure the fire is what led this man to the gallows. Even though they don't elaborate on it, those who steal are thrown in the Incarcuri or have their fingers hacked off with an ax.

The prisoner's hood is torn from his head, revealing his blanched face and sullen, icy-blue eyes. He squints, steadying himself as he stands, his hands shackled behind him. Slowly, he climbs his gaze to the rope, his chapped lips parting as the sun lowers in the sky. Then, he shakes his head to himself, as if he could deny his inevitable fate.

Intelligible chattering buzzes around me, the energy of the crowd too high and vibrant for such a sickening event. Whether or not he is guilty, killing him is utterly unnecessary. It's a miracle that anyone remains alive with traditions so deeply rooted in sacrifice and punishment.

As always, a discerner climbs the scaffolds after the last charge is read. Dressed in an emerald tunic with belled sleeves and black pants, the Discerner steps in front of the accused. A few seconds tick by, and he clasps his hands together before stepping back.

It's all for show, though. From what I've heard, the actual discerning is done at the trials, but it makes me wonder if they're fair at all.

The discerner announces the accused is guilty, prompting a roar of cheers.

Tears swell in my eyes while I watch the man's bloodshot eyes, raspy breaths leaving through his open mouth. I imagine Drake standing in his place, staring at me with those big, green eyes that will silently tell me to stop worrying because he is okay, even when he is not. If he is found guilty, the show will be much worse than this. The darker the crime, the more severe the execution method. The gallows will do for robbery and arson, but it is the chopping block for murder and sacrilege.

A shiver shudders my bones, slinking down my back and spreading goosebumps along my arms.

The executioner shoves the prisoner toward the noose, but his legs buckle as he takes a step forward. The devoted man and executioner pull him up from under the arms and carry him, but it is the discerner who forces his head through the noose and holds him in place.

"You may speak your last words," the devoted declares.

Silent tears sliding down the man's face are his only reply. Bloodshot eyes land on two sobbing boys wearing caps and dirty brown clothes, and as I look around, I notice their mother is not in attendance.

The devoted clears his throat. "May Cyna conclude the fate of your soul, and Azkiel guide you to the afterlife."

The unmistakable sound of wood creaking followed by the whip of a rope sounds from the gallows, followed by a small scream.

I whip my head around as one boy fights his way through the swelling crowd. People gasp at the realization they must be his kin. Why we allow children to witness these executions is beyond me.

I slap my fingers over my mouth as the boy is dragged away by two men. The Gurger scales on their uniforms shimmer under the sun, and I realize they must be Enforcers. Our so-called muscle to keep order in our towns and villages.

Shaking my head, I make my way through the crowd. "Vile," I snap, pushing my shoulder against two smiling women as they discuss the deceased man's crimes.

I walk quickly, reaching the dwindling market. On the other side of the square, three people are lined up to enter the tent with Nyxara's symbol over the door, impatient to see the threader from the Fatius Coven—a practiced foreteller of fates.

Next to it, a bread maker's stall stands, where a tall woman with flour-dusted red waves greets me with a smile. Nodding at her, I hand her two knogs from my purse and grab a loaf of fresh bread, hoping this small gesture might bring a bit of comfort to Drake.

I must get him out. I can't bear to imagine watching his execution next. The dark thought looms over me as I walk further, surveying my surroundings.

Smells of incense fade as I move unnoticed, sliding between cobblestone streets, to the edge of town until the paths clear, and nothing but silence accompanies me to the Incarcuri.

Long, brown ferns adorn the thinning grass around the uneven path, reaching out to the dark tree line of the forest. I gaze at the building, its tall, thick gray walls encompassed by the trees of Morcidea Forest.

Weathered stones, in various colors of gray, many bleached by the sun, make up the symmetrical building.

Small, rectangular windows, some narrower than others, line either side of the central entrance, protruding from the rest of the building. Moss covers much of the exterior, and ash floats from the sky, only adding to the eeriness. As I enter through tall gates that creak open as I approach, I am greeted by two enforcers in Cyna's coven. Their dark irises penetrate my soul, as they place one hand on their poison-laced swords.

I clear my throat. "I'm here to visit Drake Redding."

The first man, with dark hair and a light stubble, pulls out a piece of parchment. "Your name."

"Calista Bellevue."

The wrinkles deepen around his eyes as he glances down, then back at me. Even here, my family name is infamous. But I am not what is expected from the daughter of an elder—pious, obedient, or powerful, well, as far as they are aware.

The second enforcer steps forward, his armored uniform absorbing all light as he wears the scales of a gurger, a sea monster that dominates the Pistoren Sea. "Turn around."

As I turn my back to them, the man's hands frisk my torso, stomach and hips, and I squirm, despising every touch. Fortunately, he doesn't linger in any spot. Finally, I face them, and the enforcer looks me up and down. "Does your father know you are here?"

"Yes," I lie. "Not that it matters. I am free to visit with whom I like."

I peer over the parchment, spotting Drake's name.

"What's that?" he asks, eyes latching onto the slab of bread. I run my finger over the glazed coating, then tilt my head.

"Bread," I state, although my tone comes out far more condescending than I would have liked it.

"I know that," he snaps back, his lips pulling into a tight line. "Why do you have it?"

"To eat," I drawl, and he rolls his eyes.

"You can't bring that in here."

"What?" I glance at the other enforcer, as if he may overrule the decision, but he shakes his head. "No food. No weapons."

"In that order?" I ask. "My father, *Vaknor*, gave it to me to give to Drake."

They pause, then one says, "You may proceed," the enforcer says, his tone laced with a frustration he attempts to conceal.

Muttering under my breath, I walk between them, then up the narrow path, towards the building with three sides casting a shadow over the courtyard. Desperate screams echo from the incarns inside—assumed criminals undergoing interrogation, and those deemed unfit for society.

I walk around a weathered fountain, the mossy waters thick with dirt, and a sense of doom washes over me. On spotting a smaller building with a chimney billowing smoke, my stomach churns. It's clear that this is where they dispose of the bodies. Then, I realize—the Incarcuri isn't a place where incarns are freed; it is where they are brought to die.

Ash floats up my nose, agitating my senses. I sneeze, then glance at the billowing chimney of the building, horrified.

Enforcers stand on either side of the black double doors, several daggers in their belts. They glance over at the enforcers behind me, and a chill creeps through the courtyard. Stepping aside, one knocks four times, pauses, then follows it with two more.

Foggy breaths leave my lips as I wring my hands, the air somehow colder here than in town.

A woman opens the door, her blue, orb-like eyes with silver flecks announcing her position within Astraea's coven. She looks at the enforcers, then turns her gaze to me. "Name."

"Calista Bellevue."

She sighs, pulling her graying, blond strands over one shoulder. "The incarns' name," she clarifies, as if I should know.

"Drake Redding."

A long wooden desk stands in the center of the bare foyer, chipped and dented with time. Flames flicker from a candelabra, illuminating the scattered papers, quills and ink. "This way," she orders, not offering me a second glance.

Undoubtedly, my father will be made aware soon that I visited here, only inducing his wrath further. Fortunately, I plan on fleeing as soon as I figure out how to set Drake free.

The woman leads me down a dark corridor, marks left behind where blood has been scrubbed from the walls. Her alarming tone echoes as she announces, "Do not touch the bars. They are infused with magic."

I sense Death's magic, harnessed from his coven, as I near the bars of the empty cells. "What will happen if I touch it?" I question, tracking each step to ensure I can find my way to Drake next time.

She doesn't answer, but beckons me to follow her down an adjacent corridor, where the floor-to-ceiling cells are filled with incarns. Walls between them are only ten inches thick. Unintelligible whispers hang in the air as I gaze inside the dark holes. The men and women inside hide in the most shadowy corners of their cells, clutching their heads. Bald spots pattern what little hair they have left. One whispers to a wall. None of their eyes focused on anything at all, as if they are lost in memories and thoughts I cannot see.

The thought of Drake being confined in a place so devoid of hope tears into my spirit, sending waves of pain through my heart.

Finally, we reach the most depressing corridor of all. A lonely torch offers little light to the seemingly endless passageway where the cells are replaced by rooms. We stop in front of one door, created from heavy iron with two bars and a slot small enough to pass a slice of bread through. The numbers hang grimy on the front: 817.

"You may speak with him through here," she explains, pointing at the slot. "Visiting hours are almost at an end."

"Thanks," I reply, failing to keep the condescension from my tone. "You have been so helpful."

She slides herself back a few steps but keeps her eyes trained on me. I shouldn't expect them to leave us alone, but none of that matters once I hear movement from inside. "Drake?"

"Wildflower?" His voice is hoarse and meeker than usual, and my heart sinks on hearing his endearment. I swallow hard as his bloodshot eyes come into view on the other side of the slot. "Don't touch the door," he warns. "How are you?"

I refrain from touching the slot, desperate to feel Drake. Within these walls, forgoing sunlight and sleep, I imagine its loneliness that breaks the incarns' spirits first. His eyelids close, then slowly open, and I notice the same far-off look as the other incarns I passed. It's as if he can't focus. I'm losing him. "Drake? What in the Darklands are they doing to you?" I ask, my tone pleading as I glance over my shoulder and shoot a death glare at the woman behind me.

"Nothing. I'm fine," he lies. I can't see the rest of him, but just from the rectangle view of his face, I know something is horribly wrong.

"I'm going to come back to visit you," I promise, enunciating each word so he knows what I mean.

"No." He moves away from the door, but his trembling voice reaches me. "Don't come back here." Regret resounds in every word. I want to scream and use my decay magic on the woman to break Drake out now.

"It's too late, but at least you're safe. That's all that matters to me," he says, but his voice is fading.

I shove the bread through the hole. "Here. I got it from the market."

The loaf disappears as he grabs it and I step back as the woman pulls me away. In response, I grab her fingers and twist. "I'm not done."

She hisses and wrenches herself from my grasp. "Visiting hours are over," she snaps, and three prisoners audibly whimper at the sound of her voice.

"Fuck you," I spit, and she growls under her breath. Her eyes are alight with an unstableness that makes me wonder if she should even manage a place like this.

Her fingers graze my arm, and the room shifts, knocking me off balance. I grapple with the stone ground, trying to steady myself as the room spins. It's as if I've walked into an illusion, but it feels so real. The stone walls turn into a forest and just like in my dream, everything is dying, and it's my fault.

After a minute, the illusion fades and I stare at the woman, unblinking. A sadistic smile curves across her thin lips and my magic pulses, sensing the evil under her skin. Unlike Drake, she doesn't possess the magic to bring art to life. Her skin is clear, there's no proof of her nefarious desires. But as I look into her eyes, I've never felt depravity like this before. It's then that I decide she must die.

Tomorrow, I will return. But this time with poison and decay. I call out to Drake, ignoring the woman who eagerly waits for my reaction. I won't give her the satisfaction. "I will come back tomorrow," I promise.

It's only after she leads me back to the front desk, then the doors, that she speaks. "He won't be here tomorrow. The God of Death himself has ordered his execution, after The Choosing."

"Wait, what?" I ask, but she closes the doors in my face with a smug grin, the slam sending a wave of panic through my body.

Everything moves in slow motion as the memory of the hanging earlier slithers into my mind, tightening around every idea of how to get Drake out.

I can't watch him die. I won't. I stand outside the doors in the darkening evening, and a heavy helplessness hovers over me. Even if I can do anything, time is running out.

The Choosing is tonight, then so is Drake's execution.

ELEVEN

Azkiel

The haunting gaze of a threader lures me toward the tent hidden in the entrance of the forest crowding the town square. The tent, emblazoned with the sigil of Nyxara, draped in deep purples, is cloaked by the gnarly, long branches of ancient graywar trees.

Night consumes the small town of Ennismore, and in the distance, the Night Market blooms to life in velvety shades of blue and silver. I turn away from the crowd, my face and hair concealed in the shadows cast by the large hood of my black cloak.

The witch's icy-gray eyes meet mine as I approach her, standing at the door of her tent. "My most gracious god, I had wondered when you would come," she intones, sinking into a courtesy.

While she cannot be any older than thirty, her voice is entrenched with the wisdom of a person far older.

"You are the one who answered the calls of my crows and reapers," I state, sensing my sister's magic sparking within the woman.

"I was honored to serve you," she says, as if she had a choice in the matter. Her eyes dart to the side as a shadow viper slithers up beside us but does not attack.

"How about a reading, Threader," I say lowly, and she sucks in a shaky breath. She was foolish enough to stay here upon hearing of my return. But I cannot deny that I enjoy the naïve ones. After all, they are the most useful. "You can tell me what else you know of this prophecy." I push past her, then walk into the tent through the fabric doors.

In the center of the tent, a round table holds three crystals and six cards, depicting each of the gods. I notice they're lined up by the order of a mortal life span—Fate, Creation, Dreams, Will, Judgment, and Death.

I take the seat across from her, placing myself on a chair carved from the wood of the graywar tree. She leans over the table, her long, dark brown waves falling around her dainty arms, covered in tight, purple material. Her dress is simpler than most, with little embellishment on the front.

My eyes remain fixed on her face as her stare plunges into the depths of my soul. Bewilderment etches on her features.

"Speak," I command, and her hands tremble over the cards, her breath hitching.

"I-I see you must not try to stop the prophecy," she warns, her long, ringed fingers sliding over my card.

I do not flinch, nor give anything away in my expression. She hesitates, and I scowl. "Speak freely, or I will loosen your tongue."

With a curt nod, she averts her eyes, lifting my card, then placing it next to Nyxara's card—fate. "The more you attempt to destroy the prophesied one, the further you will be buried by the prophecy."

I lean back in the chair. She's clearly lying, to save the witch. "Did Nyxara tell you this?"

Slowly, she shuffles her position on the chair, then glares at the cards as if they may save her from my eyes. "My goddess? No.

I didn't know that was possible." She pauses. "The vision could be wrong."

"How did you learn of the prophecy? Of the witch?"

Her thumb skirts over the gilded edges of the cards. "I saw the words, in a dream," she explains, then lets out a shaky breath. Briefly, her eyes flutter close as she recalls a memory I cannot see. Vines of violet magic seep from her eyes, the ropes of power snaking around her head until she is haloed by purple, shimmering swirls.

I lean forward, my fingers crumpling the cards, wrinkling the images of my siblings.

"I saw Tenenocti Island and the Black Sea," she admits. "The prophecy was etched into a stone. Then, when I looked up, Tenenocti Island was reduced to ash. There, screams rang out, and that is when I saw you, sailing over the Black Sea, blood on your hands, and darkness in your eyes."

My eyes widen as my mind shifts back to that period, over one-hundred and fifty years ago. Rage swallows my words as heartache claws into my chest. I suck in a deep breath and look at the threader. Her brows furrowed, and her thick lips pulled into a tight line.

"What else?" I demand, impatience lingering on the edge of my words. "Tell me."

"Nothing," she swears. "That is all I saw." Panic threads her gray irises, and I lean back in my chair, glancing down at the six crumpled cards glistening with flecks of gold and silver gilding.

Her posture stiffens as my expression changes, and an accusation escapes my lips. "You know the gods are on the island."

She shakes her head, forcing a faint, watery smile. "No... I won't tell anyone. I can try to see more."

My fingertips blacken as she first picks up Essentria's card, then Cyna's. After a few seconds of silence, her eyes trace the darkness in my hands.

"There was so much anguish." She looks over the large cards, sadness etched into her elongated features. "Your sister betrayed you."

"How?"

"It's foggy. I can't see past that. It's as if—"

"Nyxara is blocking you," I conclude, grinding my teeth as I glare at the Threader. "Tell me of the witch who will awaken my siblings."

Her lashes tremble. "She has ethereal power. Everything will end with her. That is all I know."

My nostrils flare as she confirms what I already knew. "Then you have outgrown your use for me."

"No." She presses her hands together, sliding from the chair onto her knees. "Please, I will do another reading. I will try to find out more."

Nyxara will not show her anything else. Even in her comatose state, she still tugs the threads of fate where she can. I will fucking destroy her for it. At least I found out one thing: My sister was the one who betrayed me.

I stand to full height and take a step back. The Threader's expression briefly registers my movement as a sign of mercy, but any relief fades swiftly as tendrils of darkness surge forward, coiling around her mouth to stifle her scream. Two more shadows pin her to the ground, her body quivering with sobs as tears pour from her wide, pleading eyes. Stooping down, my fingers hover just above her cheek as she fights against my shadows, to no avail.

"You cannot be allowed to live," I state. "It is a pity that even with my sister's magic in your veins, you did not see this coming."

My touch lands on her face, and she squeezes her lids shut as my decay magic throbs through her, sinking into her bones and reducing every cell into ash. Her body crumples, embers floating as her eyes dissolve, and my shadows release.

I step back, breathing in the remains of her, as she joins the rest of my dead. Her gray-tainted soul rises like a light, then morphs into an apparition of her younger self.

"I told you everything, and you killed me," she says with a faint, raspy voice only I can hear.

"You knew too much," I explain. Wind whips around us as I walk out into the frost-bitten night, her sobbing soul trailing behind. A gust billows out the tail of my cloak as we move through the foggy forest, animals scattering away at the sound of my heavy footsteps.

She cries, her tone aching. "Don't leave me here to wander this world."

"I am not," I reply dryly, and a smile curves my lips as distorted, anguished shrieks echo through the nearby trees. I turn my head as one of my reapers glides through a shadow.

The creature tilts its head toward me. Unlike the decayed arms of the dead that can be glimpsed breaking through the surface of the Black Sea, the bones of my reapers are polished and clean.

"What is that?" the Threader asks as I tighten my cloak around my torso, the whites of my nails scathing with pricks of pain from the blistering gusts of wind.

The reaper bows, its long hood sliding over its skull as its bones creak from the movement. Keeping one hand on the long scythe in its bony fingers, it rises back to full height.

NIGHT OF DEATH AND FLOWERS

I watch as the creature walks toward the Threader, sliding through a fog, appearing around it with each step. Created in the Darklands, using a combination of Essentria, Astraea, and my magic, my reapers are the most beautiful embodiment of death.

Tattered back robes cover the reaper's skeletal body, dragging pieces of rock and bramble as it drifts over the mossy carpet of the forest. A faint gasp leaves the soul's lips as the creature towers over her, swinging its scythe. Cutting right through the woman's translucent form just as she presses her hands together in prayer, they both disappear in a cloud of black lightning.

Another sound replaces the absence of the Threader's cries. Shallow breaths and pounding footsteps hammer into my ears from deep within the forest.

My powers tingle, sensing her close.

The witch.

Calista.

She is here.

TWELVE

Calista

Twisted pathways lead me deeper into the labyrinth of trees until I lose all sense of direction. Shadows cast by bare branches stretch from the forest depths I've scoured a hundred times. The eerie silence surrounding me weighs heavily, suffocating me even. Still, being here is better than returning home. I'm only surprised that my father hasn't sent a group of the devoted to hunt me down yet, although my mother will surely stop him if he tries. It would raise suspicions, and their leaving me has less to do with concern for me and everything to do with our family's reputation.

I don't complain. It is freedom, and I have no desire to return home before The Choosing.

Leaves crunch under the soles of boots as I walk, the moon my only light as I venture deeper. Nightbor spiders hang from intricate webs, like a grotesque ballet as they twist and turn from threads hanging from dying twigs.

A hiss drags my attention to the underbrush. A pair of gleaming, red eyes peer through the blackness, its body coiled tightly, ready to strike should I come too close.

An icy breeze circles my body, carrying the pungent smell of decaying vegetation and damp wood with it. I tighten my cloak around me, keeping north, hoping I will soon find my way to the shoreline.

Once the God of Death discovers I hold his ethereal power, and Drake's escape is discovered, we are as good as dead. Fleeing to Tenenocti is the only way we can elude persecution. Nobody will dare go there, and we can cross on the night of the Harvest with the chosen sacrifices.

I scan the area, searching for places Drake and I can hideout until The Harvest. Later in the night, when everyone is busy with the Choosing, I will break him out. Poison will take care of the enforcers and that awful woman who runs the Incarcuri.

I look up as I slow my run into a walk, glimpsing the moon, its pale light filtering through the dense foliage overhead. The moment I reach the forest's edge, I am greeted by the pungent, ashy aroma of the sacred ground lingering in the air. Vines hang like the skeletal fingers of the reaper and tenderly brush my shoulders as I turn to face the island.

My eyes fixate on the shadowy outline of the island less than a half a mile from shore as I near the water's edge. The entire place is a dangerous thicket of overgrown weeds, dense trees, and poisonous plants.

Mesmerized by the melodic symphony of the distant forest, I almost fail to notice the subtle shuffling of footsteps. Goosebumps spread over my arms and around the nape of my neck as a tendril of dread slides down my spine.

Slowly, I turn, shadows dancing in my peripheral vision. I gaze at the tree line, my fingers darkening as my magic seeps to the surface.

A man materializes from the shadows, as if he belongs to them. As our eyes lock, my lips form a tight line, mirroring the intensity of his silver gaze.

NIGHT OF DEATH AND FLOWERS

His hair, as white as the moon, floats around his ears when he draws near. Everything about him has an ethereal quality, like he has been molded from the brilliance of stars, yet there's something dangerous about him behind the beauty.

His lips curve, and the moonlight captures the chiseled edges of his features. My breath hitches as I catch myself staring at the fabric of his tunic clinging to his muscles. The closer he gets, the more he towers over me. I've never seen anyone like him before.

Gods, he is incredibly handsome.

I try to avert my gaze, but I can't look away, especially not when he's gazing at me like that. He appears just as surprised as me, as we stand in silence, the night falling around us.

My heart palpitates, my jaw slacking as I recall where I'd seen his likeness before. His portrait did not do him justice.

I stand under the piercing stare of the God of Death, suddenly nervous, yet there's something utterly magnetic about him, a strange recognition I can't quite understand.

He rolls up the sleeves of his unbuttoned tunic, revealing a series of tattoos that adorn his muscular arms, resembling those from Astraea's Coven. But unlike them, his tattoos remain unmoving.

My cheeks heat as I trail my gaze over his torso. I take a cautious step back, and he follows my movements.

His eyes darken as he looks me up and down with a discerning stare, his fingers flexing when he looks at my throat, and I inhale deeply.

My nose scrunches, my lip twitching as decay magic shifts under my skin, clearly aware of Death's closeness. I hide my hands behind my back, forcing apathy into my expression. What am I supposed to call him? I settle on his name. "You're Azkiel."

"You didn't bow," he says, more intrigued than angry.

"No."

His lip curves. "Interesting."

Gods, that smile is devastating. I close my eyes briefly. What in the Darklands am I thinking, and why do I want to see him smile again?

His lips fall back into a hardline, but as he gazes at me, he seems to mirror my expression. Shadows slide over his face as clouds roll over the moon, and in the flashes of gray, I notice sadness cloaking every shift in his stunning features.

"Why are you sad?" I ask. I can't breathe under the energy, so palpable I can taste it.

His shoulders tense, shifting his gaze towards the island, as if he's trying to figure something out. Something I cannot see. After a brief pause, his brow creases, and he exhales a clipped sigh. "I am not."

My eyes glaze over the bulging contours of his muscles, and I wonder how long he has been back, in his mortal body. I've read enough to know the gods are supposed to exist in their ethereal form.

He closes his eyes, the sea spray brandishing us both as a dark wave crashes to shore.

"The dead are angry," he states, and I look out over the Black Sea.

"If you're talking about the souls you've damned from The Harvests, then yes, I can imagine they are furious. I know I would be."

"What's your name?" he asks.

"My friends call me Cali." I pause. "You can call me Calista."

Anger flashes in his eyes, and just like that, all the sadness in his expression vanishes. "Calista," he says, as if he's tasting my name on his tongue. "Then you may call me your God of Death," he states, and I clench my jaw so hard I'm surprised my teeth don't break.

Fucking egomaniac.

"My most gracious God of Death," I drawl, hoping I can use it to my advantage. Because I need to get out of here before he finds out about the magic beneath my skin. I can't help but wonder if mine calls to him, too.

He casts a glance toward Tenenocti. "Why did you come here? What drew you to the island?" he asks, impatience lacing his words.

"Nothing. I came out here to think," I lie, venom oozing from every word. I wanted to say that it's none of his concern, but the rational part of my brain is working today.

My gaze is drawn to his fingertips as they blacken at the ends, and I notice a large silver band around his index finger. As his magic runs under his skin, the skull carved from the metal glimmers. I examine his every movement, fully aware of the historical records detailing the consequences of his touch. "I really must be leaving."

Dimples curve his cruel, handsome face, smirking as if I have missed some kind of joke.

The muscle in my jaw feathers, and I let out a sharp, scant breath. "What's so humorous?"

"That you believe you're leaving."

My next breath catches in my throat, and I edge away from him. "My family is waiting for me."

"No," he says nonchalantly, and I swallow thickly. He closes the distance between us, and I flinch, annoyed that I showed any fear. "You are a wondrous little creature, aren't you?" He tilts his head, curiosity threading in those ancient eyes. "How is it a mere mortal like yourself came to possess my magic?"

"Your magic?" I ask, feigning cluelessness. He inches forward, my breaths growing uneven as he closes the distance between us.

"The decay magic," he bites out.

I hold my breath for several seconds, just staring at him, praying this is a dream. Drake is alone now, awaiting a certain execution if I don't get to him soon.

"Speak, mortal. What is it you know?" He presses.

I straighten my posture, despising the way I feel under his gaze. Refusing to cower, I instead shrug my shoulders. "I don't know anything. It's just… bad luck, I guess."

His gaze drops to my hands, likely drawn to the magic under my fingertips. "I do not believe you."

"I already told you," I say, stumbling over my words, eager to get away from the arrogant god who treats mortals like vermin. "I have no idea how I came to possess your magic, but I swear I want nothing to do with it. In fact, I'd be glad to be rid of it."

And you. I think the last part in my head.

Hurt pinches his features, so swiftly I may have missed it if I wasn't watching him so carefully. His expression quickly shifts back into a stoniness that reminds me of his statue—the one I destroyed.

"Calista." My name falls from his lips as if it belongs to his voice. Everything about him is utterly captivating, like a predator built to lure me in. "Goodbye, mortal."

My heart thumps, almost to a stop. With quivering fingers, he slowly lifts his hand to my face, eyes alight with both promise and fear. The air thickens, and I struggle in a breath. His fingertips graze my cheek, and I'm paralyzed under his touch.

He holds his breath, flinching when his icy fingertips meet the warmth of my skin. Shadows unfurl from his body, swirling around us in an uncontrollable tornado of darkness. I feel tiny under his height, his chin almost resting on my forehead. I glance up as he closes his eyes, seemingly savoring the moment.

My mind races to process what's happening. He's trying to kill me.

Wild-eyed, I glance down at his hand, the blackness at his tips seeping into my skin. Yet, instead of harming me, his magic—the very magic I've despised all this time—melds with mine, almost as if it's trying to protect me.

He opens his eyes, the orbs of silver darkening as the realization that I'm not dying dawns on us both.

I grab his fingers when my heart thuds normally again, then lift my boot, slamming it into his leg, but he doesn't move, or even flinch. Instead, he stares at me, his lips slightly parted.

"Get away from me!" I stumble backwards, looking at my hands, quickly checking that I am, in fact, not crumbling to ash, just as the Phovus had done under my touch.

The night darkens into a deep indigo, and I lift my gaze to Death, watching him cautiously. I shudder as a glimmer of darkness sweeps over his silver eyes. His brows pull together in the middle, and I take another step back.

His jaw slacks, and he opens his mouth to speak, but no words come out. My heart pounds while I wait for him to react. He turns his stare to his blackened fingertips, then inhales sharply. Slowly, he looks back at me, anger sweeping those handsome, sharp curves of his face, revealing the monster hiding just beneath the surface.

His nostrils flare. "You should be ash! Why are you not dead?" he asks, as if I know the answer.

"I—" I pause, then exhale shakily at the audacity of his question. "Why didn't I die?" I shoot him an incredulous look. "*Why* are you trying to *kill* me?"

His jaw clenches, and dark wisps, like glittering shadows made from the night, dance around his fingers in swirls. "You are not supposed to possess my magic," he insists, his tone dripping with venom. "Yet you do, and without the curse attached to it. You can still feel the embrace of other mortals," he continues, his voice growing louder with each beat. "Now I find you are also immune to my power."

"I didn't know you were such a jealous god."

Shadows envelop us as he lunges at me without warning, and within a second, his hands are on my wrists, his eyes ablaze with uncertainty. I grip his arms as he knocks me off my feet, then pushes me back. My back thuds against a tree trunk as we fall into the forest.

"Let me go!" I shout, kicking his legs as he holds me firmly, his body pressed against mine. "You fucking monster."

Silence hangs in the air as his expression falters, his hold loosening. Gradually, his fingers slide over my wrist and along my arm, his intense gaze tracing every movement, as if the experience of touching another is foreign to him.

Maybe it is.

He brings his unblinking eyes to meet mine, remaining frozen in place while his fingers continue their path up to my throat. I had expected his movements to be guided by anger, but they are gentle, slow, and building in intensity instead.

Short, rugged breaths leave him as he presses me against the tree, his fingers coiling around my throat. His other hand is on my hip, carefully gliding me up the trunk of the tree as he lifts me effortlessly, his puzzled gaze fixed on me the entire time.

My thighs clench together, my body willfully oblivious to the precarious situation I'm in—or perhaps the danger is heightening my desire.

There's something so hungry in his eyes, a need to devour, and my stomach knots at the thought of him, against me, looking at me like he wants to… kiss me.

What the fuck am I doing? He tried to kill me.

I wrestle against his impossible hold. His brows furrow, and he inches away, his eyes focused on my lips. Seizing the opportunity, I drive my knee into his groin with all the force I can muster. He elicits an anguished scream as he stumbles back, and before he can get up, I launch my boot into his dick again, and he drops to his knees.

Shaking, I run into the darkness of the forest, my calves burning as I weave around the trees, praying I can be fast enough to escape into Ennismore.

I jolt as a gut-wrenching roar scatters through the trees. While birds flock from treetops caw into the sky, I realize I'm utterly doomed.

THIRTEEN

Azkiel

My skin tingles from where my fingers met her skin. Usually, such moments are reserved for when I take a life, one final touch before their hearts stop beating. A time I savor, for it's all I have. But this time it lingers, and the pounding of her racing heart taunts me as I chase her.

Her beating heart.

She's alive, and she kicked me.

NIGHT OF DEATH AND FLOWERS

A growl erupts from my chest as the muscles around my eyes and lips twitch. I sprint toward her, the hunter in me focused only on its prey, acute senses picking up on every trace of her. The words from the prophecy echo through my mind, throbbing in my temples like an ache I cannot escape.

The witch's labored breaths wisp in my ears, alerting me to her whereabouts. I breathe in the scent of rain-soaked soil, detecting a hint of vanilla that was captured in the air from the perfume that lingers around her throat.

That smell.

I bite my nails into my palms, gritting my teeth.

I let her best me, allowing a touch to distract me enough to let her get away. I will not let my siblings win. I will not let her win.

The wind is my chorus as it howls through the tall, narrow trunks. I tear a branch from a tree, roaring as it turns to ash under my fingers. I stare at the cinders in a trance, my eye twitching, before I take off again, tearing through the forest with reckless abandon, laying death to everything in my path.

I catch her scent again, hear her panicked breaths, and my eyes widen. I growl under my breath as I quicken my pace, stretching through time with ease, then slide out of the trees ahead of her.

She's close, her footsteps loud against the mossy mattress beneath our feet. Twigs snap, branches crackle—it's as if she wants to be caught.

Beneath the moonlit branches, her silhouette draws closer until she runs into the clearing where I stand, concealed by the shadows. Her striking blue eyes widen as she stares into the abysmal darkness below, clearly sensing something. I enter the clearing while she places her hands on her knees, sucking in long, deep inhales.

The moment she spots me, she takes off running in the opposite direction. Such a foolish girl.

Shadows whip through the air, lashing around her throat and pulling her back so she lands with a thud on the moss-covered ground.

Her scream is music to my ears as the inky ribbons bind her hands and legs, until she's splayed out in front of me, writhing against my darkness. I crouch next to her, smirking as her blue glare latches onto me. Her nostrils flare, and before I realize what she's doing, a splatter of saliva lands on my cheek.

I chuckle darkly. "You kick me and spit at me."

"Don't feel bad," she says and glances at my groin. "Greater men have fallen because of their cocks."

"Such a poisonous little mortal," I state.

"Then maybe you shouldn't get too close."

Flexing my fingers, I bring my hand inches from her sweat-slicked neck and press the tips against her collarbone. "Tell me what you know of the prophecy."

"Prophecy?" she echoes, confusion clouding her expression as she struggles to break free. "I don't know what you're talking about."

I gaze into her intrusive, hardened stare in silence as she continues her defiance.

"I'm telling you the truth!" she hisses out through clenched teeth when my shadows squeeze her throat further. "Is-Is that why you're trying to kill me?" She forces apathy into her expression, attempting to conceal any hint of the pain I cause her, but the beads of slicking her forehead tell a different story.

I angle my arms between my knees, crouching lower. What a brave little witch.

"Do not feign ignorance. Tell me what you know," I demand, "or I will snap that pretty neck of yours."

"So, you think I'm pretty?" she taunts, and I stand to full height.

"Enough!" I bark, but my heartbeat stammers. "I will not ask you twice."

"You already have," she points out with a breathless laugh. "And you will get the same answer because I know nothing!"

"Fine," I growl. "Have it your way."

I command my shadows to constrict around her windpipe until the veins in her eyes darken into rivers of scarlet. She writhes under the pressure, her lips pressed into a hard line as she attempts to stifle her screams.

Bringing her close to the edge of death is not unlike what I've witnessed thousands of times. Death is peace. It is the end and the beginning of a cycle, yet this time, it feels… sad, knowing I am about to take the only mortal I have been able to touch from this world.

"What the—" Weakness creeps into my hands, my heavy arms dropping to my sides. I peer over at the witch, my eyes trained on my inky tendrils uncoiling from her wrists.

Impossible.

My heart hammers in my chest as I will my shadows to restrain her once again. To my dismay, they remain unresponsive to my command, optioning to caress her skin instead, as if they long only for her touch.

I watch her slowly crawl onto her knees, strands of hair clinging to her forehead, speckled with bits of twig and leaves.

NIGHT OF DEATH AND FLOWERS

Shallow breaths leave her mouth as her hand grasps her neck, now free from my shadowy hold as they curl back into my hands.

Shock roots me to the spot as my eyes dart to the red marks kissing her smooth skin, then to her wrists. How is she still alive?

She staggers to her feet, chin lifted in defiance, the top of her head reaching level to my chest.

My jaw slacks a little, but I quickly swallow my pride, then stand closer. "Nice trick," I say, hovering my hand close to hers, sensing the powerful magic emanating from her skin—an electrifying sensation that shields her against me. Our eyes lock for a moment, then she looks away. "But you must know," I continue, sliding my thumb under her chin to force her reluctant gaze to meet mine. "I do not need my magic to kill you."

"You don't need to kill me," she exclaims hoarsely, her throat bobbing as she struggles to swallow. I glide my fingers over the angry, crimson marks encircling her throat. "I do not know, so unless you tell me—"

"You do not command me," I snarl as her defiance crawls through my veins.

She steps back, holding my gaze. "Why are you so threatened by me? I'm a *mere mortal*, as you put it. Besides, prophecies are usually made by someone else." She pauses, her expression shifting as realization dawns, and she utters her conclusion. "Who predicted I would be your downfall?"

I grab her wrist, then tug her close to me. "Mock me again, Poison, and I will show you that there are far worse fates than death."

She smirks upon hearing the name I have given her, as if it is a victory. Playfulness dances in her blue eyes as she bites her lip to conceal a smile. She glances at my fingers and brushes her own over my skin, making me flinch. "I'm the first person you've touched that hasn't died, aren't I?"

I swallow hard as my words jumble in my mind, rendering me speechless. The truth is that every time we touch, I'm torn by the irresistible urge to both strangle her and hold her close, while the longing for that elusive human connection I've heard so much about deepens.

When I don't respond, she purses her lips and lifts her chin as her hand rests against my chest. "How long have you been alone?"

I growl, but she doesn't relent.

"I'm alone too," she admits, her voice cracking. "My parents don't care for me. All I have are my sisters and my best friend, Drake. And he is imprisoned in the Incarcuri," she divulges, as if our shared lack of love will evoke my pity. But she still has people who love her; I have no one. Yet, I can't bring myself to snap her delicate neck to end her life, and as her fingers press deeper into my chest, I find myself immobilized.

"Let me leave. I won't use my powers again," she promises.

"Where would you go?"

Her eyes narrow with curiosity that teeters on dangerous.

"Away from Dahryst."

Her breaths are uneven as her fingers slide down my arm to graze over mine, leaving a trail of goosebumps in their wake. I can't fucking think properly with her touching me like this.

"You will never see me again," she insists, probably sensing my growing hesitation.

I heave out a heavy sigh, then close my eyes. There is only one way I will agree to this, one where she can't defy me, and I can humiliate Nyxara, showing her that some fates can, in fact, be changed.

The Threader's words come back to haunt me: *"The more you attempt to destroy the prophesied one, the further you will be buried by the prophecy."*

"You will leave Dahryst and never return." Suspicion crowns her angular features. "I agree, not out of sentiment, but because I believe this will benefit me," I remark.

"I will never return." She nods, then removes her hands from me. "You said this will benefit you. I won't ask why, but you should know I cannot leave knowing Drake is imprisoned."

My muscles tense. "You want me to allow a traitor to be freed?"

She taps her fingers against her hip in a rhythmic motion, guiding my attention to her body. "It was my fault. Besides, it was only a statue."

My jaw tightens, irritated by the power this mortal wields over me—a god, who she should be worshiping. The witch deserves to be punished for her impertinence. "I will free him," I say, delighting in her naïve, grateful expression. "But first, we must seal this deal in blood."

"A blood oath," she whispers, mulling over the implications. She mentioned her sisters, who I assume she wants to protect. "When must I leave? Do I have time to say goodbye to my family?"

"The family you say does not love you?"

"My sisters," she clarifies.

She slides her long, brown locks over her shoulders with a graceful, hypnotic motion. Whenever she leans forward or touches her neck, I inexplicably gravitate towards her, which only deepens my aggravation.

I clear my throat. "You have until The Harvest, and you can attend The Choosing ceremony."

Loud dongs sound in the distance, echoing throughout the town, signaling that The Choosing rites have begun.

In less than three hours, the sacrifices will be selected.

"Okay, then, I agree," she says as the anticipation of time staggers around us.

She grabs her dagger, then presses the blade into her hand before extending it to me. I arch my brow, as if such things like contact are normal. I slice my hand, then intertwine my fingers with hers, closing my eyes as she tightens her grip.

"With this oath, I swear you will not die by my hand, or by my order. I agree to free your friend, Drake, from the Incarcuri tonight. And in return, you promise to leave Dahryst before The Harvest, or your sisters will suffer the consequences."

She gulps, her fingers twitching, before she finally whispers, "I promise."

A glittering, red swirl materializes around our fingers as our blood unites, sealing the deal. I close my eyes briefly, catching my breath as the magic dissipates.

When I open my eyes, my attention is drawn to a set of half-moon scars peeking from under the sleeve of Calista's dress. I let go of her hand and grab her arm, turning it so I can examine it more closely. She attempts to slip free, but my firm hold prevents her from retreating and concealing the healed wounds. "What happened here?"

"A mother's love," she says quickly, then tears her hand from me. "When will you free Drake?"

"At The Choosing."

After several seconds, she heaves a deep sigh. "Thank you." She steps back slowly and turns away from me. Glancing once over her shoulder as she walks between the trees, she lifts the skirts of her brown dress before disappearing into the night.

Once she is out of sight, I stare at my hands, tracing my fingertips over the spot where her touch had been only moments before.

Her words stay with me, and I look at the stars, despising how effortlessly my heart raced when she touched me. Especially when she challenged me. She knows nothing of this world, or of the wars and pain it holds. She demands from me, even though she has my magic and isn't forced into an eternity living in the shadows, without touch or love.

Tonight, she will learn the cost of such recklessness.

FOURTEEN

Calista

My heart is in my throat as I walk through the decorated front door of my home, knowing it will be one of the last times I see it.

I trace my fingers over the markings on the door frame where I measured Cecilia and Eliana's height every year since they were five and six, despite my mother's grumbling about it ruining the décor. A selfish part of me wishes I could take my sisters with me, but I know their lives will be far better here than on the run with me and Drake.

That is if Death keeps his promise. I am nervous I was not careful enough when completing the deal. Adrenaline and panic had me rushing things. Words are everything in a blood oath, and I agreed too quickly, without meticulously considering the details of what I was committing to. Although, now that I think about it, Death made a similar mistake. I am to leave Dahryst, but he said nothing of Tenenocti.

"Cali!" Cecilia exclaims, running down the corridor from the drawing room and I quickly cover the marks on my throat with my cloak.

She leaps into my arms, and I hold her tighter than usual, breathing in the smell of rose petals on her hair.

"Hey, Cee." My eyelids clamp against the building tears as she rests her head on my shoulder. I brush a hand over her dark-brown braid, then place her back on the ground.

She looks up at me with the same, wide violet eyes as Ari. "Mama's upset you're not ready. Really, I think she was worried you weren't coming." She leans in, then whispers, "I heard her arguing with Father."

I squeeze her shoulders gently and force a smile. "I wouldn't let you all go alone."

Her lips spread into a smile. "I knew you'd come. Arabella's upstairs. I can distract Mama while you get ready, so she doesn't bother you."

I chortle, then shake my head. "You've always been my favorite."

She rolls her eyes, placing her hands on her hips. "You say that to all of us."

"Well, you're all my favorites."

She turns her head to the corridor, then glances up the stairs. "You should go before they see you." Her smile fades into a frown. "I don't want you to be in trouble."

I place my finger over my lips, then creep up the stairs, watching from my ascending height as she runs back to the drawing room. Gods, I'm going to miss her. My stomach knots, forcing the panic over leaving down. I can't think about that now.

I hurry into my room and pull on the red silk robes hanging on the back of my wardrobe. Bile rises in my throat as I realize how close I'd come to dying tonight. I always knew Azkiel was a monster after learning he was the creator of The Harvest. Now I've been proven right, not that it makes a difference. No one will listen to me, and even if the elders and townspeople believed me, what can they do about it?

I roll my aching shoulders back until I feel a pop, and relief loosens my muscles. However, Azkiel's touch still lingers, the iciness etched into my skin. I inch closer to the mirror and my eyes gravitate toward my neck. My fingers graze under the fabric of the robes, over where the crimson marks imprinted around my throat are hidden by the silk, a testament to my encounter with Death. I have no idea how the fuck I survived him, or what was that prophecy he talked about. I can only imagine it was made by the goddess Nyxara, but I doubt he'd have listened to me.

"You're here," Ari exclaims from behind me, and I turn as she crosses the threshold into my room.

Inhaling sharply, I hold her at arm's length, furrowing my brows as tears glisten from the golden specks in her violet irises. "Red doesn't suit you," I say, despising her in the color branded for sacrifices.

She laughs, a tear trickling down her cheek. "I don't know why I'm nervous. Did you see Drake? Is he alive?"

"Yes, he is." I sigh, staring at Ari, knowing after the Choosing I won't see her again.

"Do you think they'll execute Drake?" Ari asks, her eyes widening and shoulders dropping.

"No," I assure her, then plaster a smile on my lips. "Don't think about this tonight."

"We will find a way to help him," she promises, and I just nod. "Let us get you ready."

After several minutes of her grabbing various items and working on my hair and face, I turn to face the window.

My heart skips a beat when I stare back at my reflection through the black veil obscuring half my face, revealing only my blood-red lips. My long hair is now pulled back into a half-crown, adorned with red berries and daggered leaves.

My gaze shifts towards Arabella's smiling reflection on the night-blue backdrop of the clear glass, and I turn to her, unable to bear another moment of gazing at myself wearing this outfit. Otherwise, I will pluck every berry from my strands until the crown falls along with the rest, then tear the dress into shreds until I deem myself suitable for such a vile ceremony.

My chest grows heavier as I glance at the pastes she made. The color perfectly matches our robes. "You're so talented, Ari," I say, and her eyes widen as my tone softens. "Please do something with it. Don't let Mother convince you into believing you're meant for nothing more than to be a wife to some man."

"Why does this feel like a goodbye?" she asks, her voice cracking.

"It's not," I reply hastily.

She arches her brow, then fumbles with her fingers. "What else happened tonight?"

"Nothing," I reply.

I straighten my posture, remembering why I'm doing this. Drake will be free, and together we will escape this forsaken place. "Let's get this over and done with."

We walk down the wooden stairs, Arabella careful not to mark her robes. As I glide my fingers over the polished banister, I pause mid-step, hearing my father's voice wisp from the adjoining room.

"You have to face him," Arabella whispers, and my stomach churns. I'd rather not, but she's right. If this is going to be the last time I see him, then I should say goodbye in my own way. Maybe I'll hug him. It'll be a first, but I prefer him to our mother.

Even if he stands for everything wrong with our society.

Mother opens the door to the great chamber, her expression twisting when she sees me. "We've been looking for you."

I push past her, then walk inside the opulent room adorned with velvet curtains and portraits of our family, painting an image of a closeness we didn't share in reality. Father rises from his green armchair, a glass filled with dark, purple liquid in his hand. "Daughters," he states, nodding as his scrutinizing gaze examines our robes. "Calista."

My chest heaves, but I step forward, nonetheless. He peers behind me to Arabella. "Go with your mother, darling."

I wet my lips as she hovers a glance at me. "I'll see you there."

I nod, turning to meet my father's gaze as the sound of footsteps behind me fades, swiftly replaced by the door closing. At last, I'm alone with him and he knows everything.

"I suppose there's no point in lying," I say, rubbing my arm. "Yes, I hold decay magic, and yes, I destroyed the statue."

I wait for him to say something, anything, but instead, his heavy sigh breaks the silence, and he stands to pace the large room for what feels like a lifetime.

Eventually, he stops by the window, staring out into the darkness, the lines on his forehead and around his mouth deepening.

Unlike my mother, he doesn't hover over details. When he finally speaks, his tone echoes that of preaching a sermon—except this time, I am the congregation. "You're going to die," he says simply, then turns, his face ashen. "The God of Death is after you."

"Oh," I reply, trying to act surprised, but failing miserably.

"Oh?" he questions. "Are your ears plugged, child? The God of Death is hunting you for your crimes. If you had returned to speak with me sooner, I would have gotten you out of Ennismore."

Holding my breath, my lips part as I stare at the man I was certain would have handed me over to Death himself after what I did to his church. To his reputation. "Wha…" I can't even finish my sentence, and glance up. "How?"

"There's a convent in the south. The elders agreed that dedicating your life in service of the church is penance enough."

My eyes widen. "You want me to become one of the devoted?"

"I *did*. Not even the God of Death would have found you there."

Chewing on the inside of my lip, I mull over my choices while processing my father's sudden care for a daughter he barely acknowledged before this. As tempting as it might sound, I can't imagine a life where I'd be tasked with enforcing the laws of our society, administering punishments and executions to those merely striving to survive or daring to rebel against the elders. Not to mention overseeing blood sacrifices. There's nothing more dreadful than that. Besides, I promised Death I would leave Dahryst, and a blood oath cannot be broken.

"It's too late now," I say.

NIGHT OF DEATH AND FLOWERS

"Why would you do this?" he barks unexpectedly, and I wince. Wild-eyed, he tracks me from across from the room, tears brimming in the corners of his eyes. "You had everything to look forward to. Your rebellious act will cost me my daughter."

I find my voice, a small, buried thing in the back of my throat that I'd suppressed for years. Talking back to my mother was nothing, but I could never do it with him. "Since when do you care about me?" It was a childish question that sounded even worse once it left my lips. But I need to know.

"Care?" his brows furrow, his expression softening in a way I'd only seen when he looks at Arabella. A tear falls, splashing against his cheek, and I hold my breath. "I love you, Calista," he says, his brows creasing. "You're my eldest daughter. I know I've been stricter with you than the others," he admits, while my skin breaks out into goosebumps and my heart balloons—a sensation I hate. The vulnerability is going to crack me, and I try to block him out, squeezing my eyes closed. He continues, his words piercing through my every defense. "You have the same fire I do. I worried it would burn you too, and now it has." The disappointment in his voice is deafening. "I tried to tame you when your mother couldn't. If you did this just because you thought I didn't love you, then maybe I have failed you."

I open my eyes, tears hazing my vision. "That's not why I did this," I admit, my tone growing harsher as the truth spills out. "I destroyed the statue because The Harvest is barbaric. These are people's lives and the fact that Arabella and I cannot be chosen shows how corrupt The Choosing really is."

His dark brows furrow. "What makes you think you or your sister won't be chosen?"

The conversation with our mother floats back, assuring us we won't be picked. That elder's children never get chosen, but then, I remember that only two of them have children. My father included. "Mother told us countless times."

I watch carefully as his fists ball, his knuckles turning white. The air between us is dense, and every breath is laborious when I realize Arabella may be in danger. He sits back in his chair, rubbing his forehead. "Your mother likes to believe that I have power over everything, but I do not. Especially not The Harvest," he says, his tired eyes meeting mine. "Death is choosing the sacrifices in person, and it is his decision who is chosen. I can only pray for mercy for my family." He pauses, then presses his hands together, his eyes glossing. "However, if you are at the church tonight, Death will kill you after. Your demise outweighs any resentment I might harbor toward you right now. You must run."

"How can you say that?" I ask. "You're an elder."

"I'm a father first. You must go, before it's too late. Flee to the winter courts in the mountains," he says, each word strained, as he goes against everything he preaches. I almost want to pinch myself to ensure this isn't a dream. "You will be safe there."

As I gaze at my father, perhaps for what may be the last time, I see the person behind the elder, and I want to hug him.

I'm old enough not to need parents, and until now, I didn't think I did. But standing before him, as he shows he cares, evokes a vulnerability I've spent years fighting against.

"I must go," he states. "Do not come to The Choosing. For both our sakes." He rises once more, and as he makes his way to the door, our arms briefly touch. Neither of us is known for showing affection, but when his hand lands on my shoulder. I remember the tenderness he'd shown me when I was a child, something I'd forgotten existed. "Don't come back and stay hidden. Gods be with you," he says after a brief pause, and leaves before I can respond.

As I close my eyes, processing what just happened, one thought forces me into action: Arabella. She could be chosen, and there's no way I can allow that to happen.

Because if what father said is true, and he has no influence over the decision, my sister could be picked, and she'll have no choice but to go. Because magic bound in blood is permanent, and once selected, there is no escaping The Harvest.

FIFTEEN

Azkiel

I silently watch a female guard—a weaver—slip into the boy's mind, sliding through each intrusive thought and shadowy, dark corner, unaware of my presence. She sits across from him on the floor of the Incarcuri cell, eyes closed, a sinister smile enhancing her sharp features.

Astraea would weep if she saw her magic being used for such suppression. My sister created the subconscious, a place where mortals can hide their fears and darker base urges, then slowly discover them throughout life, learning lessons in guidance with Nyxara's destiny.

I crouch and place my hands on my knees as I watch the one Calista calls Drake, grind his teeth, repressing a scream. His tattoos come to life against his bare, sweat-slicked chest, painting vivid images of what's happening in his mind. I'm captivated by the magic the woman uses to manipulate Drake's subconscious, not only altering his memories, but twisting his dreams to relentlessly torment him.

I tilt my head, my brows furrowing. In one inky scene, Drake's greatest fear becomes an illusion for all to see on his body. Calista, painted in blacks and grays, sports a terrifying, hollow smile as she peers around at the piles of ash, her fingertips tinged with darkness. As Drake's whimper rings in my ears, I inched closer to watching the tattoo version of her leaning over a living person. Without missing a beat, she grasps his throat and witnesses his body disintegrate under her touch.

He cares for her deeply.

Another tattoo forms a scene. This time, Calista's beautiful hands are on his chest, her deep, blue eyes staring into his as if he's the only person in the world that matters.

My jaw clenches. Does she love him romantically?

The ink swirls into a more nefarious scenario, and Calista's eyes grow hungrier, darkness leaking from her pores as she threatens to consume him. The weaver's magic shifts every memory, every dream and desire into a nightmare.

"That's enough," I say, my gravely tone jolting the woman. Her eyes snap open and she releases Drake's temples, the tendrils of blue magic hastily curling back into her body.

She stands, then steps back against the wall, her green eyes narrowing. "Y-you're the God of Death," she shakes her head, fumbling for words, and I lean over the boy so lost in torture he can't see or hear us.

A growl rumbles in my chest, knowing Astraea's magic has been tainted like this. She is the only one I still hold even a harbor of feeling toward.

"This is where you bow," I command.

She drops to the floor, her hands pressed together in prayer. As I grit my teeth, the room submits to my darkness, shadows encroaching on every corner, stealing the woman's sense.

Shadows ripple out from my core alongside my brother's magic. "You insult your goddess by twisting her magic," I state, Cyna's powers pulling back against my will, but I harness it, my shadows choking the green sparks until they're forced to obey.

"No, please. I've not done anything wrong," she cries, scrambling in the darkness, her fingers gliding over the stone floor in search of grounding.

A smirk carves my expression as I lean closer, desperate for a release of the anger building ever since the witch. Even thinking about her makes me want to choke someone. "You cannot escape me," I say, as she finds my silver gaze in the darkness. "Do you enjoy making others suffer?"

Her words come out broken in places, fragments of who she is. "They deserve it."

"As do you," I say with a tilt of my head, savoring her blanching face. "There is so much suffering in the Darklands, and my Phovi are always so hungry."

"No!" She yells, then attempts to run out the door, but my shadows are coiled around her before she can escape.

Cyna's powers of judgment spark to life, burning through my chest as I drag the woman before me.

My brother's discernment magic moves inside of me, then arrows from my eyes. Wisps of green smoke leaves me, then slither under the eyelids, blinding her. I feel her emotions alongside my own, and flashes of her past, and the truths she keeps hidden in her heart, are undressed for me to witness.

Sadism lingers on every act of torture she had been ordered to do, harbored by the pain of being beaten as a child. There is a fork in her path, after she underwent such heinous abuse, where she may have turned such hurt into empathy. She chose to walk into the darkness instead, wielding her sorrow into a weapon to ensure everyone else feels the same emptiness she does.

Seeing it resonates with something far too deep for me to acknowledge. I bring my fingers to her throat, placing them against her skin. Usually, I would elate in these moments, but as I close my eyes, feeling her touch under my palms, I realize it is no comparison to Calista's.

Digging my nails in harder than needed, I squeeze so tight that her windpipe crushes under my grip before my touch consumes her. She's on her knees as the ash steals the first inches of her limbs and she grasps her torso, as if she can stop the spread of decay. Gray leaks under her skin, her skin tumbling into a pile of ash, her blood and bones now cinders.

Her spirit leaves her in a tidal wave of black. After several seconds, the shadows take the mortal form of her body, and she opens her inky mouth, staring at the mound of ash with disbelief.

My eyes narrow as a cruel grin curls my lips, as the shadowy version of the woman attempts to touch her body, then realizing she has no physical form. The rooms grow darker as she runs out the door, and I let her go. She can haunt the walls until my reapers come for her.

Despite enacting my control over the weaver's death, my anger is not quenched. I'm still left wanting for more, desperate even.

I turn my attention to Drake. My nose scrunches as I hear his incoherent whispers. "Calista freed you," I inform him, and her name seems to reach him. His green eyes refocus, and a pang of envy shoots through my chest.

Slowly, he rises, his fingers gripping the stone walls for support. "She… where is…"

"She's at The Choosing, and we are late."

"You," he says, his voice raspy and weak. "You are Death."

"Move," I order when he stumbles, struggling to stand upright. "Or my shadows will drag you from here."

"Why are you helping me? Is Calista okay?"

"I am not doing this to help you," I spit as we walk. "Now shut your mouth."

His jaw slacks in argument, but he swiftly swallows his words and obeys. My fingers ache to end the traitor's pitiful existence, but if I do, then I won't get to see Poison's face when I take him away from her.

No, this will be far worse.

NIGHT OF DEATH AND FLOWERS

The night has dropped several degrees when we leave the Incarcuri. The enforcers scatter, but the few who are caught in my line of sight sink into low bows as I walk with the boy struggling to keep up behind me.

I quicken my pace, if only to hear the struggle in his breath increase. He's slumped over, his heart beats uneven by the time we arrive at the town.

Countless candles line the cobblestone paths, warding off the midnight hour. Accompanied by a magnificence only the organ can provide, a melancholic, deep sound resonates from the church as we walk through the empty town square and down the path. The heavy tune grows louder as we near a sea of silver-cloaked townspeople, illuminated by the orange glow of their candles.

Either out of fear or respect, their hundreds of eyes stay focused on the path as I approach, but most young children give in to their curiosity and gaze up at me in wonder before their parents force them to look away.

We hit a wall of incense, mixed with smoke from inside as we reach the arched entrance. Whispers sound behind me, as I assume the people finally stole a glimpse after I had passed. I stride through the gold-bricked, protruding entrance, under the spires of a gate, and into the large room, filled with the elder coven, volunteers, and the esteemed members of society.

The organ sings its last note as I enter, and only the shuffling as the rows of people drop to one knee, their heads bowed in reverence, breaks the silence.

As I glide up the center, between the pews of mahogany, footsteps pound through the entrance, followed by heavy breaths. Clenching my jaw, I turn, and Calista stands beside a blonde-haired girl, with the rest of the volunteers at the back of the church.

I stare too long at the sacrifices, consumed by thoughts of prophecy and death, and Calista is the only one glaring back. She slides her gaze to Drake, her expression softening, and one of my shadows shoves him in her direction.

Gasps sound as the traitor is released, but under my stare, they silence.

I cast one last look at Calista before striding up the center to the elders and toward the stone basin. Despite the binding pact between us, the intense desire to punish her only heightens when I sense my magic coursing through her veins. It's as if it calls out to me, taunting me with the power bestowed upon a mortal from my brothers and sisters.

A fucking mortal.

NIGHT OF DEATH AND FLOWERS

Snarling, I reach the witch's father amongst the seven, his face paling upon seeing his daughter.

Taking my place at the altar, high above the rest, I touch the stone basin, where the blood of the sacrifices is cold. "Rise, my subjects," I command, my deep voice echoing throughout the church. Once more, I spot Calista amongst the gathered, unable to look away as she dismisses my order with a roll of her eyes, and I white-knuckle the basin.

Her arrogance showed the moment she accepted the deal without adding the boys his continued protection as a part of it. Knowing I beat her, if only a minor victory, keeps my anger at bay.

Tearing myself away from her, I focus on the crowd of those devoted to me, hoping to calm the beast inside, clawing to escape and destroy her. "Tonight, I return to Dahryst to present you with your chosen sacrifices. Being a sacrifice is an honor, a tradition that has protected Dahryst from our enemies. From those chosen this night, one will serve as your next elder."

Calista's scoff draws me back to her again, the stone crumbling under my grip as she holds onto Drake, her hands gliding over his arm.

Swallowing hard, I release the basin before I unintentionally pulverize the stone and cast my gaze to the other sacrifices. Now, their eyes are on me, some filled with awe and admiration, others quivering with fear. I continue, avoiding noticing her, even as her blue eyes shine with determination behind the thin, black veil. I exhale a tense breath as she moves in the corner of my vision, plucking a berry from her hair, then bringing it to Drake's lips.

"Enough!" I shout, and the atmosphere changes, several candles blowing out in rapid succession as I struggle to contain my shadows and darkness. Quickly, I close my eyes, attempting to collect myself, then place my hands over the basin. "Enough of hiding from the humans," I say, correcting my outburst, but my heart pounds.

I can't think of anything but her, hatred consuming every thought. Her actions shouldn't bother me, but they do. Everything about her infuriates me. "Tonight, you shall take back your power, harvesting our magic for the next generation."

I place my fingers over the dried blood in the basin, and I channel Nyxara's magic to weave the names from the essence of those who offered themselves.

Sight magic consumes me as the crimson stains my fingertips. The faces of those lined up, slicing their fingers, appear in my mind. Including Calista.

The names appear in smoke in my head as Nyxara's magic presents them to me, but I force the vision away.

My stare clashes with Calista's, and I smirk at the flicker of fear threading her eyes. "Drake Redding."

A gasp slips from her parted lips, and she holds Drake tighter, her cheeks drained of color.

The traitor is freed, but I refuse to allow him to continue to breathe.

I lift my chin as she glares at me. *Checkmate.*

Her eyes remained glued to me, her chest heaving, until Drake turns to her, breaking our eye contact, and whispers words I cannot hear. After a few seconds, he steps forward. His fists ball at his side as I prepare to call the other names. I hope he dies first in The Harvest.

I list the others chosen from Nyxara's magic, masquerading it as my own, as they appear to me in a mist.

"Alaric Varwarn."

A muscular man, appearing to be around my age, steps forward and Drake stands up beside him. Alaric's willingness is a pleasant surprise as he nods in my direction, then bows his head. When I notice the subtle black in his eyes, showing his powers to the God of Will, I almost smile. Drake stands little chance against him.

"Elenore Amenbore," I announce as the second name presents itself to me.

A young girl joins them, tears sliding from under her veil, her chest heaving in sobs. It's quite clear that she will be at a disadvantage, and we are supposed to only choose the strong to compete.

I call the rest of the names as they are presented in my mind, each one stepping into the line until there are eleven. Then, the image of Calista standing by the stone basin, next to a blonde girl, appears in my mind. I shove away the vision before it can finish. Despite being dormant, my sister's magic urges me to summon a name in the mist, but I resist and instead concentrate on the girl beside Calista in the vision. My eyes close briefly, and I attempt to recall her name. Surprisingly, her name materializes in my mind, in the same mist the others were chosen from.

"Arabella Bellevue."

"No!" A scream tears from Calista's throat, and an unexpected ache knots in my stomach. I had expected this, only more with my announcement of Drake, not over the blonde.

Vaknor leaves the platform, flying through the center of the church, his robes flapping behind him.

Calista grits her teeth, her chest still as she holds her breath. When I blink, she's running toward me. "You fucking monster!"

NIGHT OF DEATH AND FLOWERS

Drake grabs her arm, pulling her back, while Vaknor runs and grabs her other arm. She wrestles against them both as they barely contain her.

"I'm going to kill you," she yells, and I chuckle darkly.

She really is intriguing, attempting this in the middle of a church filled with those who worship me, but she's dragged through the vestibule before she can try.

SIXTEEN

Calista

"I'm going to murder him," I shout at my father as he restrains me in the outer building of the church. "Let me go!"

His hands hold me in place on a chair, pinning me against the wood. Baring my teeth, I try to kick forward, mustering all my strength, but it is nothing against the mighty strength of the God of Will my father harnesses.

NIGHT OF DEATH AND FLOWERS

It is like fighting a bear. For the first time, I wonder how my father killed whoever wielded Volan's incredible strength and speed and took their power. I've seldom seen him use his powers in person.

"Stop fighting me," he orders, but I shake my head, wrestling against him despite knowing it is futile. I refuse to be restrained, not when that asshole has condemned the two people I love most to death.

"I will kill him," I shout.

My father's brows crease, his lips parting as a flash, or concern melts the hardness in his expression. "Are you delusional, girl? You cannot kill the God of *Death*. He is the *embodiment* of it."

"Then I will hurt him another way," I say, as anger clouds my logic.

His emotions shift, much like the magic he wields, and it is Astraea's power that takes over. Her magic seeps into my skin from my father's fingers, soothing my aura against my will. "We can't save Arabella from this fate," he admits. "We can only prepare her."

I bare my teeth as the tranquility, woven from Astraea's dream magic, softens my movements, hazing my thoughts. "If I destroy Death, then I can stop this. I will stop this," I say, my voice waning.

Wild-eyed, he watches me with caution, as if I were a wild viper that may strike him at any moment. "You are as likely to destroy him as you are to sink Tenenocti into the depths of the Black Sea."

"Then I shall sink the island and everyone on it," I scream, tears flowing down my cheeks.

"Enough with this foolishness," he warns.

We both whip our heads when the door slams open, and Azkiel enters, his silver eyes focused on me.

My father falls to his knees, hands pressed together while any resemblance of the man I grew up fearing—that this community still fears—is gone.

"Please don't kill my daughter," he begs, and Azkiel's lips warp into a frown. "My other daughter is already going to die in the tournament."

So much for preparing Arabella to win. She is far more competent than he realizes. My sister's biggest downfall will be her kindness.

Azkiel circles my father, his shadows morphing around him. "Pathetic."

The dream magic weaves through my core, suppressing every monstrous desire to lash out and turn this entire town to ash. My father has hazed my abilities, taken away the anger that guides my strength, right when the predator has come to taunt me.

My father's pleading only deepens my rage. "We beg for your mercy."

"He doesn't have any," I say, and Azkiel snarls, the muscles in his arms bulging as he brings his touch dangerously close to my father's throat. "Leave," he shouts. "Or I will lay waste to your *entire* family."

My father does not move. He's really willing to die to protect me.

"You should go," I say, struggling to push any fight into my words. "Azkiel can't kill me."

A sense of victory washes through me as I watch him flinch.

"Cali?" my dad whispers, his lips parting, confusion weaving through his expression.

"Please, leave." I try to stand from the chair, but I'm forced back down by the sedative effect of dream magic.

"I will not kill her," Death growls, his fingers blackening..

He would if he could.

My father hesitates between me and Azkiel and then finally leaves with a quick bow to the God, casting one final worried glance back at me.

Once the door shuts, Azkiel walks to me, standing over me in the dark, damp room, a cold draft seeping through the old bricks.

"You told him you're immune to my power," he states, each word dripping a venom that matches my own.

"I plan on telling everyone who will fucking hear me, you bastard!" I retort.

His shadows steal the light from the lone candle, and he leans over, the silver in his stare turning into a matte, smoky gray—the kind that comes from the chimneys of infirmaries where they burn the dead. "I should have broken your fucking neck."

"Now you can't," I snark and lift my chin, fighting the trance-like effects. "A person with nothing left to lose is the most dangerous of all."

His growl rumbles in his chest, thunderous to match the brewing storm outside. "Then you should fear me."

I scoff a laugh. "If you really have nothing to lose, why are you here? Nobody fights this hard without something to fight for."

"You know nothing of what you speak."

"We both know that is simply not true. You desperately want me away from Dahryst and you," I say, leaning forward, any fear I once had of him vanishing as I think about Arabella and Drake fighting to the death on Tenenocti. "I swear, I will find out what that prophecy says and ensure it comes to pass."

"Our deal was sealed in blood. Do you know what happens if you break it?"

"That all those you love, die," I whisper as images of my two younger sisters and father flood my mind.. "I guess you had me fooled. You don't have anyone you love, do you?" I was so focused on saving Drake that I didn't even think about that possibility. "You chose my friend *and* my sister."

"I did not break our deal," he spits. "I freed the boy. You said nothing of what will happen to him after. I am a man of my word."

As the dream magic heightens, I struggle to keep my eyes open. It weaves through my mind, calming everything into an ignorant bliss. I murmur one last promise to him. "As am I a woman of mine. And I swear, I will find a way to destroy you."

He leans closer, our noses almost touching. "Leave before The Harvest, or lose the rest of your family," he hisses his threat before storming out, leaving me alone with my thoughts.

I struggle against the relentless drowsiness enveloping me, resisting the urge to close my eyes. But eventually, my eyelids surrender, eclipsing the dim light of the room as I succumb to the embrace of slumber.

As I fall into a light sleep, I am transported into a dream of a memory.

We're back in my house, as children, watching as Cecilia chokes, slowly turning blue. Wide-eyed, Cee, only a toddler then, clutches her tiny hands to her throat. Something from her dinner blocks her airway, and no matter how much my mother shoves her fingers down her throat, it doesn't dislodge—only pushing it deeper.

I'm thrown back as my mother forces me into a cabinet, the porcelain clinking above my head.

My little sister is going to die. "Do something," I scream, although they're trying. My powers haven't come in yet, and my mother's healing magic—the most common of Essentria's magic to be inherited—doesn't help.

My father joins in, this time holding my sister's small body from behind, his hands linked over her stomach. With each hard abdominal thrust, I fear her bones will break under the pressure. But no breath enters through her blue-tinged lips. Even her nails have a sapphire hue as time passes on, her bloodshot, teary eyes closing.

My mother's scream evokes my own, and I crawl against the cabinet, helpless, and ball my legs to my chest.

When I glance over at them again, my father's hands are over the center of her chest, pushing deep into her ribcage. But it is Arabella, still too young for her powers, that hurries to Cecilia's side first. They say trauma can activate a person's magic at a younger age, and as Arabella stares at our dead sister, a bright glow emulates under her fingertips, moving like liquid gold, seeping into Cecilia's body.

Magic I've never seen anyone use before dissipates, and Cecilia's eyes snap open, her small body encompassed by a perfect yellow aura.

My eyes fling open. The dream plays out in my mind, where events, once hazy, I can now recall with vivid detail.

I blink twice as parts of the room come into view. Arabella sits in front of me, still in her crimson robes, but the berries in her hair have sunken. "How are you?"

I inhale deeply, still disoriented from the lingering effects of dream magic. I look around, and as early morning light seeps under the door, I realize I must have been asleep for hours. "Ari, we have to run."

She shakes her head, placing her hands in her lap. "So Cecilia and Eliana can die along with Mother and Father?" she questions. "The Harvest sacrifices are chosen using blood magic."

Dragging my fingers over my eyelids, then down my face, I try to figure out a way to stop this. To save both her and Drake, but the ancient magic ties every possibility into a dead end. "I'm so sorry."

"Why?"

"If Drake and I hadn't destroyed the statue, then none of this would have happened."

Weaving blonde strands through her fingers, she plucks out a leaf, then sighs. "The God of Death would have chosen me, regardless."

I close my eyes. "I don't think so."

"Why do you say that?"

"He's done this to punish me," I admit, my chest heaving.

His brows knit together. "Why would he want to punish you?"

"Father didn't tell you," I realize and lean forward. "I met him yesterday out on the shoreline. He's a fucking monster, but we made a deal. I must leave Dahryst, or you won't be the only one in danger," I explain, as my thoughts turn to our two younger sisters.

"I don't understand. What did you do to offend him so?"

I wiggle my fingers, the decay magic darkening the tips. "He found out."

She blows out a soft sigh. "I see. Where will you go?"

"Don't worry about that. We have little time left."

"For what?" she asks.

Goosebumps spread over my arms, as the icy reality of what's about to happen washes over me. "To prepare you, Ari, for The Harvest."

"How? We leave at midnight."

Nausea climbs through my stomach, knotting itself into a ball. "Listen to me, when you brought Cecilia back from the dead—"

"Shush," she whispers, wide-eyed. "I did no such thing. I healed her, that's all."

"I know what I saw. Until now, I didn't want to think about it. Because we know the dangers of possessing such forbidden ethereal magic." I pause and she lets out a shaky breath. "But this is life or death, and you have to use everything you have to win this."

She leans forward, fingers gripping into the silk crimson of her dress. "If I win, then Drake loses."

"No," I say, then clamp my eyes shut and try to think of a way to save them both. "I won't let that happen." I lift my fingers to my temples, attempting to massage the throbbing ache from my mind, then stand. "Leave that problem up to me, okay? You *must* win. For our parents, our sisters… and for me."

Slowly, she lifts her bloodshot gaze to meet mine. "We both know I don't stand a chance."

"You have Creations' power," I state, and she winces. "No, listen, you must embrace it. What if you can bring yourself back from the dead?" I ask, but the theory falls as quick as it formed. If she's already dead, then she can't perform the magic. And my decay magic doesn't work on myself.

"What happened when you saved Cecilia?" I ask, choosing my words carefully. "How did you feel?"

"Tired," she says, "well, actually, the most exhausted I've ever been in my life. I couldn't stay awake after."

Biting my lip, scenarios of my sister being who she is and saving people's lives, flit through my mind. "That's a problem. You moved on instinct that day, correct?" She nods and I continue. "You can't do the same on Tenenocti. It's a game of survival and bringing anyone back just means killing them later. Besides, if you were as drained as you say you were, you won't have the energy to defend yourself after using that power."

Silence hands around us for several seconds. Slowly, she lifts her eyes to meet mine, then whispers, "I'm afraid."

I pull her into my arms and hold her tight, closing my eyes as I breathe in her jasmine scent, committing it to memory. "Don't be. I'm going to teach you how to survive. "

"I've never thought much about death," she admits as I withdraw, her eyes flicking to the ceiling as if she can somehow glimpse the Everlands from here. "Now that it is so close, that's all I can think about. I don't want to die." Her soft, violet gaze lands back on mine. "What if I go to the Darklands? Or worse, what if the abyss some speak of is actually true? What if our souls wander, lost in darkness, forever? I don't like the dark, and I…" her breaths quicken, her chest quaking, and I stand, grabbing her arms.

"Breathe, Ari. Slowly. You're not going to die. I won't let that happen. I've always made good on my promises, no?"

She nods, pressing her lips together in an attempt to suppress the building tears.

"Right," I say. "Then trust me when I tell you I will get you out of this."

She falls into my arms, and I stroke her hair as she rests her head on my shoulder. Her whisper sounds in my ear. "I wish I was like you. You're never afraid."

"Not true," I admit. "I'm terrified of losing you, our sisters, and Drake." I grip her tighter, feeling everything I love slipping away. How the fuck am I going to get us all out of this alive?

SEVENTEEN

Calista

I'm undone by Drake's embrace, and the tears I'd held back throughout the day fall down my cheeks. Pulling back, I peer into the foyer of the house through the open door, and then sigh.

"It's going to be okay," he says. I watch as he drags his fingers through his dark, tousled strands. My eyes widen as his tattoos morph from the horrors that could happen during The Harvest to various images of the Incarcuri and the woman who tortured him.

"I won't let you die," I promise.

He curls a finger under my chin and lifts my eyes to meet his. "It is not up to you to save me, but I will protect Ari."

I swallow thickly, wiping away my tears. "Have you seen your mom yet? Your sisters?"

He nods, then averts his eyes. "They're beside themselves because they think I can win." He pauses and glances at the front door of my house. "We both know the elders will never allow me to become one of them."

"Death freed you," I state.

"At your request, although he didn't seem pleased about it."

"No." I lower my eyes to the ground. "He did that to punish me."

"What did you say to him?"

"Nothing." He arches a brow, and I roll my eyes. "Fine, I did, but I had no choice. He tried to kill me."

"What?"

"He didn't succeed, obviously," I reply dryly as his eyes bulge.

He shakes his head. "So, he discovered you hold his ethereal power."

I nod, but it isn't the entire truth. I'm in no mood to discuss prophecies now. Tonight, they'll leave for Tenenocti, and we're running out of time.

"My point was that the elders don't know why he freed you. They may be our leaders, but they answer to the gods. That's what our government is built upon. If you win, they'll be forced to accept you."

"If I win, that means Ari loses."

"No." I swallow hard. "I mean, I know, but I'm not going to let that happen." I pause. "I hate Death for doing this. I'm going to make him pay for it."

"I don't doubt it, Wildflower." He rubs his fingers over mine. "But for my sanity, please don't. I'd rather not go to Tenenocti imagining you in a fight with the God of Death."

"I can destroy him," I whisper, thinking about the mysterious prophecy. "It cannot be an accident that I hold his ethereal power."

He lifts my hand over his chest, his heart racing to my touch. My heart jolts when Arabella clears her throat.

I didn't even see her coming. I pull my hand away from Drake and turn to face her.

She sighs. "I'm going to lie down."

I purse my lips when I notice the dark circles under her eyes and red blotches on her cheeks. "You can't. There's not much time before you leave."

Drake chimes in. "Cali's right. We need to come up with a plan."

"Okay," she says, her voice waning.

I notice her peach-colored dress, embroidered with gold flowers up the sides. I'm only glad to see the red robes gone, although she'll be back in them in a few hours.

"Let's go." They follow me into the house. As we pass a maid, who bows her head respectfully at us, we hurry through the door and into the library. Tomes of yellowing books spill from the tall shelves encompassing the large room. I glide my fingers over the grains in the ash wood, then across the leather spines of a collection envied by most, filled with our history, religion and fables.

I'm drawn toward the crackling of a fire, burning the logs to embers in the stone fireplace, taking up the only free space of the wall. We sit around a short table, and I lean over the stack of parchment on it to breathe in the comforting scent of old books mixed with the smoked woody aroma from the fire. Grounding myself is easier than I expect, but I am reminded that the effects of the calming magic still linger in my veins.

I grab a quill and sink its nib into the black ink. My wrist flicks as I write the names of the Chosen down onto the parchment, counting them all in my head.

Arabella, Drake, Edwardo, Elenore, Alaric, Isolda, Marsilia, Rourne, Cain, Tulia, Briar, and Cordelia.

"There. That's the twelve," I breathe out. "Do we know who belongs to which coven?"

Arabella nods. "Edwardo is in our coven and Elenore is in Astraea's. Cordelia and Briar are in Azkiel's coven. They had his sigil tattooed on them at the Choosing."

Ink veins through the paper around Azkiel's name, and I almost break the nib of the quill on writing it.

Arabella and Drake peer over the table. My sister shakes her head, then turns away, her footsteps pacing to the other side of the library, then leans against a rolling ladder.

Drake's low voice carries into my ears. "Marsilia is a threader," he states, then pauses. But I already knew that. We all attended the same academy. "And I heard rumors that Alaric has compulsion magic," he explains. "They'll be the biggest threats. Marsilia can see attacks coming. Then there's Rourne. He's rumored to be a Sight Seeker. He will know where anyone was and what they discussed just by touching the abandoned buildings on the island."

I nod, then hover my finger over Briar's name. "What about him?"

"I'm not sure, but from what I saw at the Choosing, I think he's a Shadow Manipulator. If he is, then he'll be deadly in the dark, but vulnerable in the daytime."

"You can hunt him in the day," I state.

He nods. "Edwardo could be a healer or possess nature enhancement. Let's hope he's a healer, so he's not a threat." Arabella clears her throat, and Drake licks his lips, then says, "That's not to say healing magic isn't important. If he is, then he can heal himself from non-fatal wounds. Then there's Cordelia. I don't know what power she has. Possible shadow manipulation too, or fear induction. I doubt she has light absorption."

I nod. "It is rare. If she has absorption, then she won't pose a threat. She can't absorb sunlight."

Arabella paces her way back to us. "But if she is, then she can absorb candlelight and firelight. What if we make a fire and she puts it out so we can't see?"

My stomach knots as Drake and I glance at each other, then at Arabella. Drake explains before I can. "We won't be lighting any fires, Ari. We can't do anything that'll attract attention to us."

I agree, then stand and grab a map of Tenenocti. One I used to study, when I was younger and more daring, to figure out where the rare plants would be for my poisons if I ever attempted such a trip. But now, as I roll it out and place weights on each corner, my greatest fear is realized—we're planning the route to survive The Harvest.

I suppress my thoughts away from the possibility of losing them and instead channel all my focus into what matters right now: their survival.

They lean over as I circle the area around the collection of abandoned buildings near the shoreline, where they'll disembark. "Stay away from here. It's the first hiding spot, and the other chosen will expect you to go there." Slowly, I guide my fingertip up over the forest to the narrow river separating the island with two small bridges. "If you can get to this side of the island first, Drake can destroy this bridge," I explain, pointing to the first bridge at the south of the island. I look at Arabella. "He'll be weak after, so you will need to guide him here." I land over a temple. "It's Azkiel's temple."

Ari nods. "A temple of the Gods," she states, her eyes widening.

Drake shakes his head, pointing at the bridges. "How do we know someone hasn't destroyed the bridge already? How old is this map?"

I chew on the inside of my cheek. "I don't know, but you know how rare animation magic is. It's the only thing that can create chains strong enough to destroy them." I point and the bridges. "They're made of stone."

Arabella brings her fingers to a steeple, as if in prayer, then rests her chin on her fingertips when she looks at Drake. "What if I can't carry you?"

He gives her a half-smile. "You won't need to. I'll be able to walk, but I might just need a little help, okay?"

She nods, then glances back at the map. "What about the other bridge?"

I shake my head. "You won't have time to destroy both. By the time you reach the ruins, it'll be morning. You'll rest there, then hope it rains," I say, thankful that we're in the rainiest part of the world. "Collect water with leaves from the trees and drink nothing from that river. It runs from the Black Sea and the dead will be waiting in those waters too."

We both turn as Ari sucks in a deep breath, shaking her head as she steps backward.

"I can't do this," she says, her voice raising an octave. "I'm going to die. I am. There's twelve of us, and I can't ask Drake to die, not for me. This can't be happening. Father was supposed to protect us. It wasn't meant to be me." Tears squeeze through her closed lids, and my heart heavies as the reality of The Harvest crashes down on her. "I can't kill anyone. I won't do it."

Swallowing hard, I stand, then hurry over to her, the carpet muffling my heavy steps. I hold her tight and whisper, "You're not doing anything wrong by doing this. It's for the gods, right?" I say, holding the disdain back from my tone as I withdraw enough to wipe her tears with the back of my hand, just like I did when we were children. "They want this to happen, so it's not murder. Not really. We need the tournament so we can find our next elder," I say, repeating words my father has spoken many times, but now I need her to believe them, even if I don't. "And Drake…" I say and slowly turn my head, bile biting up my throat, "he can take care of himself."

"I'm not strong enough," she croaks. "Everyone knows it. Alaric smiled when my name was called."

Drake steps forward, placing a hand on her shoulder. "He's arrogant and that will only help us. Remember, with each person we kill, we'll inherit their powers, too." He glances from her to me, determination threading those green eyes. "If we can pick off the weakest ones first, those powers combined will give us enough magic to take down Alaric and Marsilia."

"No." Arabella pulls away, distancing herself from us, her eyes tracking us as if we're the monsters. "I can't kill anyone."

"Drake?" I croak, turning to him. We both know Arabella will keep to her word. Even in life and death situations, she won't kill, and I'm fucking terrified for her.

His pained expression matches my own, and we look in time to watch her leave the room, her sobs echoing as she closes the door, her sobs quaking from the corridor.

He lets out a heavy sigh. "I won't let her die."

"I know," I respond, but we both know what my worry is. Because even if they somehow survive and Drake kills them all, she won't take his life. The only way to win is siphon all the powers of the covens, and murder is the only way to do it.

Drake's hands are around my waist in a heartbeat, pulling my head against his shoulder. His grip tightens as he lowers his head to rest against the top of mine, and everything inside of me falls apart.

"I should go say goodbye to my family," Drake whispers, and my heart pounds. "If I don't see you again—"

"You will," I promise, as the idea I've been forming since The Choosing grows with increasing clarity. "Somehow," I add, as suspicion crumples his forehead.

I watch him leave, then close my eyes. There is no way I am letting them die. Even if it kills me.

EIGHTEEN

Azkiel

Dephina is the first to approach me on the shore of the Black Sea. Vaknor, Everist, and two other elders follow her through the tree line of Morcidea Forest.

"Azkiel, God of Death." Dephina's raspy tone sounds from behind as she steps into my view, standing in front of one of the twelve boats tied to stakes hammered into the ground. Beyond her, and across the sea, the island is a silhouette against the setting sun.

"What do you want?" I ask, impatience lacing my tone.

She clears her throat, running a hand over her long, blonde braid. "The traitor, Drake Redding—"

"What about him?" I cut her off with a snarl.

"We do not wish for him to win."

I stare at her, fingers flexing at my side. "You dare question me? Your god!" I shout, and Dephina takes a hesitant step back.

Vaknor joins her, carefully gliding into my line of sight, adorned in white robes. "Please, we do not care about the boy," the elder chimes in, and Dephina shoots him an incredulous glare. "I only ask for mercy, for Arabella, my daughter." He blinks twice, his eyes the same shade of blue as Calista's.

I step forward, the fabric of my tunic straining against my muscles as I close the few feet between us, desperate to rid myself of them all. "You have been gifted with the powers of all the gods. You have overseen Harvests and sent sacrifices to their deaths. When you won your Harvest, you took an oath to me, and to Dahryst. Your daughter's sacrifice is an *honor*!"

"She will not survive it," he splutters, bowing his head so as not to look at me, but as I recall our earlier meeting, humiliation shoots into my chest. He knows Calista cannot die by my touch.

"Then she will die," I spit.

"Vaknor's daughter may die, but we cannot allow the traitor to win," the youngest elder speaks *to my back*. "You must eliminate him from the tournament and choose another."

Dephina shakes her head at the youngest. "Melevin, don't."

I spin to face him, then tilt my head. "Must I?" I ask, and his brown eyes narrow, sweat beading on his tanned forehead. "You have forgotten," I yell, my tone thunderous, causing crows to fly from the treetops, "that I command you!"

Shadows dance from Melevin's fingers as he stumbles back. They flurry across the space between us, poised to attack. Gasps erupt from the other elders, and a maniacal laugh leaves my lips. I slice my hand through the air, and the shadows dissolve.

The other elders back away from Melevin quickly, averting their eyes.

"You attack me with my own magic?" I hiss through clenched teeth. "I am a god, and you are *nothing*."

His breath hitches as he crumples the white fabric over his chest in his fingers, then drops to his knees. "Please, you were going to kill me. I—I'm an elder. Dahryst needs me."

"You are what I *decide* you are," I shout, then glance from him to the others. "Look at him!" I order. Their gazes return to Melevin, who is slumped on the ground, his heart racing so fast I wonder if it may stop before I can destroy him. "This is what happens when you question me."

Ribbons of glittering darkness shoot from my fingers and the elder pushes himself backwards in a futile attempt to escape me. He scrambles to his feet, and my shadows snatch around his body like vicious vipers, constricting him until he is unable to move. He begs the others elders for help, but his pleas fall upon deaf ears. Twin wisps of darkness leap through the air, striking and sinking into his eyes. Urine veins through his robes as his scream rattles the beach. Crimson seeps from his sockets while I push my magic deeper, slicing through bone and muscle alike until he's choking on his blood. His body collapses onto the sandy ground unceremoniously the moment my shadows release him.

I catch Dephina's vengeful glare in my peripheral vision, but it quickly fades when I face them. "Clean this up," I command, not staying long enough to watch his soul leave his broken body. One of my reapers will take over from here.

I walk into the forest, the sound of Vaknor's sobs quaking from the shoreline. *Pathetic.* I should have ended them all, but to do so before The Harvest would be counterproductive. Dahryst still needs them, as useless as they might be.

They act as if I am the villain, yet they have overseen these tournaments, murdered countless people, then speak of mercy as soon as it is an inconvenience to them.

I halt on my tracks, goosebumps spreading over my neck as the familiar call of my magic emanates from deep within the forest.

Calista still hasn't left. Her defiance crawls over my skin.

I descend into the maze of trees, veering off the beaten path and toward the abandoned house. I reach the house, then throw open the rotting door. Our eyes clash across the large room, hers alight with vengeance.

"You disobey me," I state, my eyes narrowing on her satchel. "And you have enough poison to kill an army."

"Or a god." Challenge threads her blue stare.

I stride over to the formal dining table, stopping a few feet from her. "Such things cannot kill me, Poison, although I would find it amusing to see you try."

"Perhaps I'll go to Tenenocti with them," she baits, and my eyes widen.

Swallowing hard, I force apathy into my expression, despite my racing heart. I stare at her, as if I'm watching the prophecy unfold in front of my eyes. "Your threat is without base," I retort.

"The sacrifices were chosen, and only *they* can cross the Black Sea."

"Such lies." She laughs, and my jaw clenches. "Anyone can cross over tonight."

"I'm the only one who can dictate who does," I remind her. "Did you forget that The Black Sea and island are in my domain?"

"I don't believe you. You're just trying to stop me from going because you are *afraid*."

"You are so very arrogant," I drawl. "Magic is unique, even in those who hold the same powers as another. Do you not wonder why, when there are three powers that can be inherited within a coven, a witch or warlock only possesses one? The magic chooses them and adapts to who they are. That is why every healer or shadow wielder is different. Our powers bend to their personalities."

She shrugs, and my nostrils flare. "What does magic have to do with letting the sacrifices cross?"

"Have I rendered you speechless?" she asks, taunting me with a grim smile. "You have no arguments because I am right. I can cross the Black Sea, and I will."

She is arrogant and reckless, thinking she can easily accomplish this when hundreds before her have failed.

"You must not." While a part of me wants to watch her drown, panic squeezes in my heart at the thought of Calista trapped in the barriers of my domain, so close to the other gods. "Magic has everything to do with who may pass. The dead will not touch those who possess the sacrifices' particular trace of magic. Anyone absent from their essence and power will drown." She doesn't flinch when I shorten the distance between us, gazing into her eyes. "It is a fool's errand to attempt to follow them."

"I hate you," she growls.

"Good," I state, because the opposite would be much worse.

"They're going to be slaughtered. You forced them into this. You care not for mortals like history pretends."

"I did no such thing. Your sister volunteered for The Choosing, and Drake is a traitor. This punishment is far better than he would have had at the hands of the elders. You should be thanking me."

She grits her teeth, the scent of Nightmor clinging to her dress. It tickles my nose, and I draw an inch closer. The deadly plants in her satchel, likely worked into each vial, are as beautiful and poisonous as Calista.

"Ari didn't volunteer," she states, then takes a step back. "She had no choice. None of us did. If we don't put our names forth, then we will be outcasts, thrown in Incarcuris for crimes against the church. Against *you*." Slowly, she walks toward the front of the house as the afternoon darkens into evening, filtering orange light through the grimy windows. "I never understood why anyone worships you. You send those who praise you to their deaths, then enact some sick revenge on me for having a power I *never* wanted, and that is as disgusting as you," she hisses as she opens the door.

Hurt pinches my chest, the words jabbing into me like a knife. The room is a blur as I speed over to her, placing myself between her and the door. Her breaths quicken when I grab her by her throat, squeezing her windpipe. "It is a part of you for a reason," I spit. "If my magic is so disgusting, then you are rotten, too."

Her fist connects with my jaw in slow motion, the impact clashing my teeth against my lip. She stumbles out of my grip, smirking. "Fuck you, Azkiel."

My heart quickens as I drag my thumb across my bloodied lip, then stare at the crimson staining my skin. Pressing my tongue inside my cheek, forming a ball against the skin, a sadistic laugh escapes.

Little by little, I lift my stare to meet hers. "I'm going to kill you."

She scoffs, her fingertips blackening at the tips. "Oh, make a new threat already."

A growl resonates as I storm over to her, gripping her arms. "There are other ways I can hurt you," I promise, my nails digging into her skin. "Your sister, for example," I say, smiling as fear lights her eyes. "I can always ensure she never makes make it to the island."

"The people will hate you for it," she retorts but hesitance wavers in her voice. "I suppose they will finally see their so-called savior of a god for what he truly is—a villain."

"I do not care what they think of me," I growl, the taste of blood intensifying every feeling. She is under my skin, like an itch I cannot scratch. I need to be rid of her before her presence drives me to insanity. "You will pay for this."

"I'm not afraid of you," she shouts. "Threatening my sister is cowardice. Your fight is with *me*. So, do your worst."

"Stupid girl," I snap, and her shoulders tense. "You threaten me when your family could die because of your actions."

"I am leaving," she shouts, her watery stare fixed on mine. "Also, I don't regret tearing down your statue. Knowing what I do now, I wish I had burned the entire fucking church down."

She wrestles against me, our bodies clashing together with the movement. I close my eyes, wanting to savor the contact and her warmth, but my anger is far stronger than any desire of touch—even if being in close proximity with the witch weakens me.

"I saved you," I say, the final word catching in my throat as I gaze down at her, my breath hitching, and an unexplained sense of grief washes over me. "I let you live."

"That was beneficial to you, although you won't tell me why," she says through gritted teeth, "Do not pretend you have any caring part of you. You are evil. We can have leaders without the elders possessing the powers of all the covens. Things have changed since the last time you were here one hundred and fifty years ago. Humans know better now than to challenge us. Yet this continues, because of you."

I shake my head, stepping back. "Your generation has been softened by the absence of war, but just because you cannot see the threats, does not mean they are not there. The other kingdoms know of the elders, of us gods, and they fear the witches of Dahryst. If your people show any weakness, they will attack again. I lived through the war," I shout, my fingers flexing. "Thousands died until there were almost none of you left. This is nothing compared to the loss of life if The Harvest is not completed. The tournament is for your people's benefit, not my own."

She scoffs, her nostrils flaring. "You get something from it, otherwise you wouldn't be here. I do not believe you are doing anything out of the goodness of your heart."

"Enough!" We both pause, my heart pounding as the sun slowly sets. "You will find out how terrible the humans in the other kingdoms are soon enough. You will understand why everything is the way it should be. Now leave," I command with a growl, "before more of the people who love you die for your recklessness."

"You are so desperate for me to go, and so threatened by my magic," she says, then laughs, the sound causing my eye to twitch. "It is amusing to me that a God has such a fragile ego. I was *no* threat to you, but I am now."

Swallowing hard, I close the distance between us, her breaths against my chest as her stony stare penetrates mine. "I disagree. You do not understand."

"I understand more than you realize." Slowly, she brings her hand to my chest, and my heart races under her touch, my breath catching before I step away. "See? You wear your desires so glaringly. The need for me to leave, and all this punishment. You say it is because of a prophecy, but I know the truth." Her lips curve. "It is also jealousy. Because you can't touch, and I can." Her fingers blacken at the tips as I feel my magic seep through her veins. "I may be alone now, and perhaps I will lose the people I love," she says, "but you will always be starved of love and affection."

Clutching her satchel, she heads for the door, pausing before stepping outside. "You did not have to send my sister or Drake into The Harvest. We both know they were not fated to go." Glancing over her shoulder, her alluring blue eyes meet mine with fierce determination as she says, "You haven't seen the last of me, Azkiel. Whether it is in life or death, I will make you pay."

NINETEEN

Calista

Midnight falls in a haze of crimson as I reach the edge of Sacrifice Road.

My gaze travels the path of the dirt winding through the forest, ladened with the purple petals of Night Blossom, the silver veins in the flowers sparkling under the red moonlight.

As I move through this part of the forest, the chilling realization of how many chosen ones have traversed these very footsteps toward their potential deaths. Now, Ari and Drake will join that number, and unbeknownst to them, so will I.

Even though Azkiel's words haunt me, nothing will sway me from participating in the Harvest. I refuse to let my sister and Drake face the horrors that will unleash on Tenenocti alone.

I recall the spark of vulnerability in Death's eyes from when I mentioned going to the Island.

I do not need a discerner to know Azkiel was nervous, and I'm going to find out why. Even if it means embracing the worst parts of myself.

I always knew I was destined for the Darklands, anyway. That fate lingers in me, a constant reminder of my greatest sin—existing. I am rotten from the core, and death touches every breath of my body and soul. It is not just the decay magic that darkens me, but even now, as I watch the chosen ones enter the forest, I am strategizing how to murder all, except two of them.

The group treads carefully over roots and branches, knotted like contorted bones, while the blood moon casts an eerie glow upon them. As they pass, the light from their torches falls upon vipers waiting in the thickets of weeds.

Cloaked in the darkness, I scan each veiled face amongst the crimson-robed chosen in search of Ari and Drake. Yet, I'm unable to distinguish them. When they approach, followed by the elders draped in their finest white robes, I turn away and veer into the blackness that leads to the shore.

Twigs snag against my skirt as I race closer. Because Death is correct. My time is almost up, and if I don't leave now, the rest of my family will pay the price.

I pause, taking a moment to catch my breath as I reach a familiar narrow tree. As I trace my finger over the carvings of mine and Drake's names, memories of our childhood come flooding back. My lips curve into a smile as warmth spreads through my heart, recalling times when we would play in the forest and pretend we had magic before our powers surfaced. We would pretend to be esteemed potioneers, dress painters like those who weave with shadow magic, then build shelters from the dead branches. I would imagine living in my own house, finally being rid of my mother, and being able to do what I want.

However, being an adult is not as free as I'd been led to believe. In fact, it's awful.

I shake my head, allowing the memories to fade back to the past where they belong. I can't let sentiment have such a grasp on my emotions, not when I am about to become the monster my mother thinks I am.

Ghostly whispers carry in the wind as I climb higher, careful not to bang the leather satchel filled with clinking vials of potions.

A hiss sounds through my teeth as thorns from the vines strangling the gray trunk scrape my palms, drawing blood. I unsheathe the dagger from its casing on my thigh, cut through the thorns blocking my next climb, then replace it.

Squawks sound as I settle on a branch, under a murder of crows sitting upon the higher branches. "It's Calista," I say, hoping some of them remember me. They tilt their heads when they see me, curiosity threading in their black eyes. I recognize a few of their distinct features, such as the scar over one of their eyes in the shape of a hook, or the discolored feathers of another.

My heart skips a beat when I find Thorn amongst them. He jumps down two branches, then lands on my shoulder. "Hey, old friend," I whisper, ruffling his feathers. "I have to go," I tell my frequent visitor. "So does Arabella. You must not go to our house anymore," I warn, hoping Thorn understands. "No house," I reiterate. He has learned some words over the years, picking up the most important ones, like treasure and food.

He caws, then points his beak at Tenenocti. I glance toward the silhouette of the sacred island and take a deep breath as I brace myself for doing something I would've never imagined—willingly entering The Harvest.

Slowly, I cast my gaze onto the cloaked chosen ones as they near the end of the path. Two of them emerge out onto the shoreline, and through the maze of branches, I watch Arabella and Drake, the reds of their robes shining under the moonlight.

The rose-pink skirt of Ari's dress peeks out from the slit in her red robe, a reminder of the girl underneath the sacrifice. Not that the elders care. Most of the town doesn't. Their cheers are sickening as they rejoice in watching the chosen prepare to set sail.

"Stay here," I tell Thorn. Carefully, I slide down the side of the tree. A twig snaps underfoot as the group reaches the end of the path, their torches lighting the way. My heart pounds as the reality of what I am about to do settles through my bones.

I follow the group to the shore, hiding within the crowd as they reach the edge of the water. Twelve boats, made from ancient oak—carved with intricate symbols—sit on the bay. Cobwebs glisten under the red hue of the sky, adorning the insides. I can tell they have been sitting in the boathouse for the past ten years. A sense of panic washes over me as I gaze at their tall, bare masts.

I exhale shakily, goosebumps plucking over my arms. I close my eyes briefly, then step out into the gathered crowd.

Keeping my head low and my hood up, I walk toward one boat where one of the veiled women awaits, then stand at the edge of the waters, the waves lapping at my feet.

My heart skips a beat when I spot Arabella next to Drake, tightening her cloak around her body, attempting to hide her shaking. She lifts her veil, tears shining on her cheeks as she looks at the boat, shaking her head. "I can't," she says, her voice breaking in parts.

Drake throws back the hood of his cloak, then unveils. "It's okay," he promises, but she gulps, then steps back.

Her body wrenches with a sob, her waves poking out under her hood. The beautiful flowers interwoven in the strands are withered, and the symbols painted on her hands in an intricate gold, are smudged. She rubs her eyes, wiping away her tears. I get closer, hiding myself behind three men discussing the tournament, and discern Ari and Drake's conversation, focusing only on their voices.

"I can't do it. I don't want to kill anyone. Nor do I want to die."

I swallow thickly, looking around for our parents, who are several feet away from Ari and Drake. My father stands just a few paces from my mother. Next to them, Everist stands, his sharp stare fixated on Arabella.

Drake snarls at the elders as the elder attempts to move through the crowds. The crowd disperses around them, and

NIGHT OF DEATH AND FLOWERS

Everist takes one step forward. "Don't," he warns as they get closer. "She'll get on the boat."

They pause, mid-step, then hover nearby. My fingers tremble with the need to touch each of them, to let my powers seep through their bodies until they are nothing but ash.

The rest of the chosen embrace their families one last time until the watchful eyes of the elders force them to separate.

One of the veiled girls crosses her arms, then glares at Drake and my sister. "She's ruining this for all of us!"

"Shut your fucking mouth, Isolda," Drake warns. He glances at the elders, his nostrils flaring as he leads Arabella to the boat. She climbs inside with his help, her eyes widening at the surrounding sea waters we have been told to stay away from ever since I can remember.

"Where's Cali?" Ari asks as Drake gets into his own boat.

"She'll come," he promises, casting his gaze around.

I close my eyes, unable to listen to them for another moment.

Isolda climbs into the boat in front of me. The crowd roars as the dongs sound from the ancient bell, one for each of the chosen. Half the group glances around frantically, as the elders walk to the shore.

I shift from Everist's view, who stands behind Isolda's boat. I notice my father is behind Arabella, tears in his eyes as he holds her hands in his, shaking his head at a question I cannot hear.

On the second dong, they push the boats out to sea, and one of the chosen grips the sides, shaking his head and removing his veil. "I don't want to go," he shouts in a chorus of cheering, his panicked pleas lost in the crowd. "Please, Mother!"

A man, woman, and two children turn their backs on the boy in the boat. I assume they are the boy's family, from the parents' tears. The boy who called out looks over the side of his boat, but recoils deeper into his seat upon spotting a ghostly hand breaking the surface of the waters.

There is no escaping now. To abandon the tournament means braving the dead in the sea, and if he survives, then he'd have to face the wrath of the elders and Azkiel, as well as breaking the tournament's blood oath, resulting in the death of his family.

My mind fogs as I remove my hood, racing into the waters, my mouth drying as I push myself forward.

"Stop her!"

Yells sound behind me as people grasp the air behind me, all too afraid to touch the dark waters.

The energy shifts the instant I enter Azkiel's domain, the only place where magic can be siphoned. Holding my satchel to my chest, I reach out for the guiding light of Isolda's torch as the inky waves swallow my torso.

The icy waters prick against my feet, and seaweed slides around my ankles as I delve deeper, until I'm kicking my legs, treading water. I have only seconds before the dead find me and drag me to their depths. I swim a few feet to Isolda's boat, grabbing its side just as I spot ghostly fingers breaking the sea's surface.

The boat tips sideways as I swiftly push myself up and climb aboard, water sloshing inside. With the boat still rocking and my heart beating wildly, I sit myself up and draw in a deep breath, trembling from head to toe.

My father screams my name into the night, but I refuse to meet his frightened gaze. Instead, I turn to Isolda. Even though I know it's too late to turn back now, that doesn't stop the tears from stinging my eyes.

I hesitate as she stares at me. "What in the Darklands are you doing?" She shouts as gray-blue arms rise from the waves, followed by the heads of the moving corpses.

My heart pounds as I glance over the edge.

"Get off my boat, you lunatic," she screams, pushing me to the side. I grimace and fall against the wood.

Glancing into the water, I gasp as the dead draw closer, their white, sunken eyes as terrifying as the stretched skin over their mouths. I always believed it was only souls in these waters, but they still have physical, decaying forms.

Hands reach inside, toward me, and I close my eyes, willing the decay magic to come. Death said they only will allow those with the chosen one's magic in their veins to pass, but as the decay magic slips into my fingers, bile climbs my throat.

She shoves me harder this time, her weight slamming against mine.

I grab her wrist, and my fingers darken at the ends. "I'm sorry," I say as the townspeople's yells fill the night, but it is Isolda's blood-curdling scream that runs me cold.

Under my touch, her fingers turn to ash, and as the rot swiftly climbs through her veins, her skin adopts a sickening gray color. She grasps at her chest as it caves inward, her jaw slacked as her screams dry into silence. I avert my eyes, unable to watch as I will the magic to consume every inch of her.

Her family's cries ring into the night, following me to Tenenocti as they watch their daughter crumble to ash, dead before she even had a chance to fight.

A tear slides down my cheek, and my stomach knots. Isolda's magic leaves her body, and siphoning becomes as easy as breathing. Her mental resistance seeps unfamiliarly into my mind, melding with the decay magic until they are forced to coexist.

In my peripheral vision, I spot Drake and Ari, horror mixed with disappointment in their expressions. Tears fall, thick and fast, but as the dead rest back within the waters, sensing Isolda's magic inside of me, I accept my inevitable fate.

I am a murderer, a monster just like Death, and as Tenenocti draws closer, I know I am about to become so much worse.

TWENTY

Azkiel

I have never seen such destruction at the hands of a mortal. It is wondrous, like watching an echo of myself.

If she wasn't heading to my sisters and brothers—bringing the prophecy to the precipice of fruition—I would be proud of her bravery. However, the sentiment is overshadowed by the panic shuddering in my bones.

She cannot die there. I must stop her.

I run cold as the reality of what I must do sinks in.

NIGHT OF DEATH AND FLOWERS

Fuck.

I watch from the empty stretch of shoreline, away from the crowd. Calista's every movement demands attention. Flames flicker from inside the boats, and the pale, rotting fingers of the corpses caress the symbols etched into the wood.

They long for the souls of the sacrifices to join them, to quench the loneliness. But no matter how many they drown to join them in the Black Sea, they will always feel empty. Or perhaps some of the dead, foolishly, believe if they obey my commands, I will one day free them.

Under my command, through the power of my Skhola ring, they leave the boats alone.

Their spirits cry out in distorted screams, a reminder of the danger of what is in the waters in case any of the sacrifice's families get the urge to aid their loved ones.

The chosen one's wince under the shrill shrieks of the dead, but not Calista. She wears murder and death so well that I cannot help but wonder if she somehow belongs to it—to me.

My breath hitches as Calista's eyes widen under the hue of her torch.

My heart hammers as she grabs the oar, navigating away from the others and toward the shipwreck. "Clever girl," I admit aloud. She waves for her sister and the boy to follow her, but they do not and instead sail with the others to the docks.

Idiots.

I watch as Calista stands, knees bent, extending her arms to steady the boat. Her eyes fixate on the island, the magic we share darkening, weakened only by her own guilt. Her long, brown hair glows under the light of the torch, cascading in waves down her back, stopping at her waist. She runs her hands through her strands, pushing some from her face, then slides her hand over her waist. My eyes follow the trail of her fingers, and I lick my lips, some desperate ache in me wishing they were my hands, gliding over the contours of her body.

What am I thinking? This must be our shared power drawing me to her and nothing more.

Fate has bound the witch to me, and as I reflect on every step I took that brought me here recently, I know I have only aided the prophecy. I should have taken her to the coast and watched her get on a ship.

Yet, I am certain destiny would have weaved another path to reach this very moment. So far, I have been unable to kill her, and my blood oath prevents me from doing so. Because Calista was wrong. I love someone—my sister, Astraea. I cannot understand what led me to trap her with the rest of them when she wasn't like them. She was kind and always there for me, but she must've betrayed me.

I simply cannot remember.

Gritting my teeth, I focus only on the witch, panic stifling me as the dead near her boat. Seeing her get closer to the island instills a dread in me I have seldom felt.

To awaken my siblings, she must die in a sacrificial ritual. Once her blood is spilled, it will undo the magic I used to bind them into a sleeping spell. However, it's more than that. The thought that I may lose her pains me. The sentiment makes no sense, yet it feels so raw, it could be real.

Snapping myself out of my thoughts, refusing to linger in my mind for any longer than needed, I turn my attention to my dead, who await my orders as they allow the sacrifices to pass. I flex my fingers at my sides, the powers from the gods siphoning through my Skhola, a reminder of what I am about to give up.

The ring will not work the moment I step foot through the veil separating the world from my domain. Not only will I lose my siblings' magic, but the strength I siphon from the dormant monsters and spirits of the dead.

With a scowl, I pivot to the forest, then walk inside. The distant roar of the crowd accompanies me as I meticulously gather only dead or inanimate objects that will not disintegrate under my touch—carcasses of dead logs, the skeletal remains of fallen leaves, dry and brittle twigs and branches, tiny skulls of animals long perished, and crow feathers. I place them into a pile on the shore, then close my eyes, rooting deeper into the recesses of my core, seeking my sister's magic, residing unwantedly beside mine.

Essentria's power of creation seeps into fingertips only meant for death with a subtle tinge of light. The ability to manipulate nature has always been a source of envy, and as I guide delicate golden swirls around the pile of foraged items, I ache with the soon-to-be loss of the magic.

The objects combine and take the shape of a boat, clashing together in a flurry of power as I evoke my shadows to choke my sister's swirls into submission.

Feathers bind, creating a sail of shimmery blue and black. Skull fragments levitate from the ground, fusing to form the hull. My sigil etches into the side of the boat, next to Essentria's, a stamp of anything formed from our combined power.

With a push, the boat glides out onto the calm waters. I step through the shallow waves, my dead sensing my presence as soon as the water laps around my black boots. The faint smell of sulfur tingles inside my nostrils, and my spine tingles as they grow closer, always angry, but under my control.

NIGHT OF DEATH AND FLOWERS

The boat rocks as I grip the sides, then climb inside, sliding myself into a seat carved from dead wood. A silent command leaves my mind as I instruct the souls to pull my boat toward the island.

Rotting hands emerge from the dark depths, forming a crown of decayed fingers around the bottom of my boat as the dead push me further out to sea.

Whispers grow louder, calling me home, as I grow closer to Tenenocti. I cloak myself in darkness, absorbing any light that falls upon me until I am nothing but a shadow sailing around the other side of the island, and away from the sacrifices.

A raging storm brews on the horizon once I am firmly within my domain. Pain spears through my skull, my eyes rolling into the back of my head as the powers I've held within me for one hundred and fifty years stretch out from my core.

"Agh," I shout into the sky, dropping to my knees, clenching my fists as I desperately try to hold on to my sibling's magic. But my family beckons their powers from their sleeping states, and as I near the shore, I am powerless to prevent it.

I clamp my eyes shut as my control over the dead slips away. Wisps of gray smoke curl around me, creating a misty haze as the boat glides over the inky waters. A sudden bolt of bright, blue lightning illuminates the sea, breaking through the thick, black storm clouds shrouding the glowing crimson moon.

The sky rumbles with thunder as dark clouds gather in swirling shades of purple, blue and silver, unleashing torrential rain, each drop resembling tiny needles piercing my body.

My silver strands slick around my face and jaw, and I clutch the thick fabric of my tunic, a primal roar ripping from my chest.

Astraea's dream magic evaporates through my pores, in a swarm of radiant, glittering light. My mouth falls open as her power gracefully creeps over the dark waters and into Tenenocti. Hunched over and breathless, my chest aches with the absence.

The sky splits in a vibrant green flash with rain transforming into heavy droplets that pelt against my skin while thunder grumbles overhead..

My boat crashes onto the deserted shore of the island, far from the sacrifices, the bone-fused hull grueling over pebbles, a wave forcing me onto the island, but I do not leave the boat. Instead, I grip my knees as guilt pierces my heart, forced into me by Cyna's powers. Before I can stop it, a lone tear slides down my cheek, pausing at my lips as the desire to speak my truth hangs on my tongue.

Each guilt-laced tear aches my heart, and as they fall in a haze of green, regret twists in my core.

NIGHT OF DEATH AND FLOWERS

My nails pierce the sides of the boat, splintering the boat as a guttural sob quakes my body.

My shoulders tense as the last remnants of my brother's strength drains from me with a powerful sting. Struggling to catch my breath, I lift my head and fix my gaze beyond the forest, on a familiar, small tower strangled with vines.

"No!" I yell, desperately seeking a respite from this torment, as a third bolt of lightning shatters the clouds, dyeing the sky purple.

There is no reprieve with Nyxara. Her magic courses through me like poison, pulsing as if it may burst through my veins. My vision blurs, and the world around me dissolves into a myriad of memories, each more fragmented than the last. I grip my temples as memories of the past and potential futures collide in my mind, every scene transitioning into the next in rapid succession, disorienting me.

A mystery woman is in each of them, her fingers on my chest, and in one, her lips are pressed against mine. The memories are tinged in bloodshed, vignetted in darkness, and my heart aches with each flash. I shake my head as the visions of the past carousel too quickly for me to focus on anyone in particular.

The boat tilts sideways and I topple over, landing on the wet pebbles, the rain soaking my tunic.

A final surge of energy leaves through my eyes, and Nyxara's magic dances away from me, sweeping through the trees in shimmering purple ribbons.

I crawl toward the forest and collapse against damp mud and entwined vines as I reach the tree line, every breath a labor. Volan's powers climb through my veins like liquid fire, boiling my blood until I scream through clenched teeth. The sea roars, and I turn my head in time to see a tall, black wave slam against the hull, shattering the wood and bone. More furious waves drag the remains of my boat away and into the merciless, hungry depths of the Black Sea. I lift my fingers, weaker than I've ever been, and hiss as bruises appear on my body. With each punch of Volan's magic erupting from me, pain shoots through me, rendering me immobile.

The rain does nothing to relieve the searing heat, but an icy blast frees me of the gut-wrenching anguish the moment his power, darker than the night itself, darts through the trees like an arrow shot from a bow.

Essentria's magic is the last, and it is the most vicious. I gag, grasping my throat as I choke against the power creeping up in a nauseating, cloying liquid until light emanates from my mouth. The surrounding vines curl around my ankles and wrists, binding me to the dirt that quickly crumbles under my body, sinking me deeper into the island.

My heart beats erratically as I gasp for air. The sky clears slightly, clouds retreating into the horizon as her magic pulls me further. The liquid pours over my lips like honey, sticky, then turns to dirt, clogging my airways.

As I wrestle against the vines, a root snakes along my shoulder, then moves up to my throat, tightening around it until my vision is filled with stars.

The sky flashes with a bright yellow like an arrow of sunlight that has somehow reached through the Everlands, and the roots and vines instantly fall lifeless. Her magic seeps into the mud as a heaviness settles in every one of my limbs. I extend my arms and tear through the vines around my wrists, then rip the root coiled around my neck.

I suck in a deep breath, staring out from the now six-feet deep hole. The decay magic in my veins is depleted temporarily, and I think about Calista and how it will affect her ability to defend herself.

Tiredness claims me, unable to keep my eyelids open.

I shudder, and I wonder if this is what mortality feels like. Dread slides into my stomach as I sense *their* energized auras for the first time in over a century—my family.

TWENTY-ONE

Calista

It's as if time has ceased to exist as we reach Tenenocti Island, the forest vibrant under the sudden terrain of rain. My eyes fixate on the trees, their outlines slowly emerging from the dense blanket of fog shrouding the island.

The unintelligible screams from the townspeople on the shore fade as a silence consumes the surrounding waters. Eleven torches flicker around me, illuminating the group as the docks appear before us. Wind whips around my ears, my rain-soaked, gray cloak weighing me down. Wringing out the gray skirt of my dress, I search for them through the curtain of rain.

"Ari. Drake," I whisper-shout as I sink my oar deeper into the water, but they don't hear me. Using the last remnants of my waning strength, I propel my boat toward them. Unlike before, when I killed the Phovus with decay magic, I am completely drained. Perhaps it's because this time I used it on a person instead.

Every push of the oar against the thick waters aches my shoulders to the point of exhaustion. Despite the stillness of the Black Sea, I can sense the dead waiting just below the surface.

The island is a labyrinth of towering trees, their branches intertwining like a natural canopy over the ruins of an ancient civilization. A collective gasp sounds as the others lay their eyes on the first skeleton of many, tangled under the grip of vines covering the docks.

Sweat beads against my forehead as I use every ounce of my energy to stand and climb out of the boat. My satchel slips down my body with the movement, the vials clinking inside.

Footsteps pound over the docks, vibrating through the ground as two people run past me, not noticing me in their haste.

My eyes glide over my competitors, Elenore at the back, her veil lifted, tears shining under the light of the torch.

I turn my head from the sight, and I breathe out a clipped breath while Arabella and Drake wade through the shallow waters, torches in her hand, but drops of heavy rain extinguish the flames. They both look around, wild-eyed.

I quickly scan the area, my gaze sifting over the waves of ivy spilling onto the stretches of dirt where I find Alaric, his veil discarded on the ground, his robes already torn. He slips into a mountain of vines, a gleaming silver reflecting the moonlight as he produces a dagger. Fighting against the instinct to disappear under the docks, I instead reach for my onyx one, unsheathing it from my thigh. The blade, laced with poison, is etched with ancient symbols of sacrifice. Running into a bloodbath is foolish, so I plan on picking the competition off, one by one, until only Drake and Ari remain.

My heart pounds in my ears as I run, attempting to locate the seven others not accounted for. A shadow moves from within an abandoned building, barely visible under the overgrowth.

"Cali!" I whip my head around at the sound of Arabella's voice, my eyes widening as the shadowy silhouette behind her emerges from the forest.

Rourne steps into the light, and my raspy scream breaks the silence. "Run!"

NIGHT OF DEATH AND FLOWERS

My boots hammer against the wet ground, splashing mud around my ankles while I race in their direction, my heart pounding in my ears. The scene becomes a blur, and I strain to focus on their movements. Drake steps into view, pushing Ari back, and I pause for half a second as she loses her footing, falling to the ground. Ari sits up as Drake's arms wrap around Rourne as they wrestle. Grunts and growls fill the air until Drake lifts Rourne a few inches off the ground and hurls him down with a skull-crunching thud.

I can barely breathe as I finally reach them, my fingers sore from clutching the dagger with all my might in case of any sudden attack. For it is dark, and prey quickly becomes predator once we're away from society, with only ourselves to depend on for survival.

Desperation clings to Rourne's features as he continues to fight back against Drake, despite the blood leaking from the back of his head.

I hold a hand out to my sister, and she takes it without hesitation, hoisting herself up with my help. "Stay close to me, Ari," I command when I hear footsteps nearby. Adrenaline courses through my veins, and I struggle to catch my breath as I glance around us, keen to find any other potential threats.

I can barely think.

"Stop fighting," Drake shouts, his voice broken in parts. Rourne groans, attempting to push Drake away as he lies on his back, but being unable to, and I realize he must be paralyzed.

I fall to my knees at Rourne's side, and Drake takes a step back.

"Tell my mom I love her." Rourne's voice cracks, tears slipping down his cheeks. "Tell her—Tell her I didn't suffer. She won't survive it otherwise," he splutters, the haunting emptiness setting in his brown eyes as the fight leaves him altogether. "Please."

Ari's hands clap over her mouth, tears shining under the red moonlight. "Oh, my gods. What have we done?"

I swallow hard against the lump forming in my throat. "He attacked us first," I point out, although he had no choice. Any of us would have done the same. Yet, it doesn't make this any easier.

His pleading gaze finds me, and I nod slowly, seeing the boy in front of me clearly for the first time. He can't be any older than Ari, and he has a mother in Ennismore who's probably praying for him right now.

Drake squeezes my arm and I flinch. Rourne splutters a cough, blood foaming at his lips. His chest quakes, and a gurgling choke leaves his throat.

NIGHT OF DEATH AND FLOWERS

"I can save him," Ari whispers, leaning forward, but I shake my head.

Drake glances at me, and I press my fingers against Rourne's forehead.

He winces under my touch, then closes his eyes as he waits for my magic to consume him. Except nothing happens. The more I try to will the magic, the more exhausted I feel.

"What's wrong?" Drake asks when I stare at my fingers as they refusing to darken.

"I—it's not working." My jaw slacks as I try again, to no avail. Rourne's cries fly from his lips in short wails, and after a moment, I lift the hand holding my dagger.

Drake's brusque voice disrupts the silence. "Cali, *no*."

The mild, sweet aroma burns in my nose as I bring the poisoned onyx blade down and swiftly drag it across Rourne's throat, spilling his blood in a splatter of crimson. I hold my breath as his eyes fling open, panicked gurgles sounding as his bloodshot stare widens.

Seconds feel like minutes as I watch him die, but it is unlike the stories I have been told. He is still alive, but suffering.

Ari covers her mouth and looks away with a quaking sob. I exhale shakily, the anticipation crawling through me, swirling the building nausea in my stomach. I press the dagger to his throat once more, this time applying enough pressure to hack through his vocal cords, each thrust straining the muscles in my arms, the motion spattering more blood over my face and chest.

Rourne's eyes shut, his chest caving as he goes limp at last, his breaths falling silent.

"Good gods," Drake states. The horrified edge in his voice only makes this harder.

"He's dead now," I whisper, closing my eyes briefly, refusing to stop and think of Rourne as a person. I shake my head, strengthening my resolve, aware that people may be closer than we know, hidden in the trees. "We need to go. Now."

Ari stands over Rourne, her legs wobbly as she holds her trembling fingers over her lips. She lifts her gaze to my face, her eyes bulging as she takes in the blood. I look down at my feet, then crouch, replacing the dagger into the holder strapped to my thigh.

The moment I stand straight, my legs suddenly buckle, and I collapse to my knees.

"Cali!" Drake's hands are on my shoulders as I struggle for breath. A suffocating darkness engulfs my vision, plunging into blindness.

Rourne's essence lingers on the fringes of his magic, and I clutch the sides of my head, squeezing as my brain throbs against my skull. I wince as a sharp pain pulsates through my temples, intensifying with each beat of my heart.

A small shriek escapes Arabella's lips, but it is hastily smothered by Drake's hand.

Time stretches into what feels like an eternity until the tight band of his powers dissipates, and my sight returns. I take in my surroundings through a blurred haze, and slowly, as if a veil has been lifted, the world comes into focus, materializing clearly before my eyes.

I inhale sharply, and Drake removes his hand from Arabella's mouth, his eyes locked onto mine. "Rourne's magic?"

I nod, and Ari's expression shifts, a quiver over her lips. "Your eyes turned dark green. Even the white parts. Then the blood…"

"Thanks for that horrifying image."

Shame consumes me as we stand, evaluating the perimeter.

Drake's expression is unreadable, but we have no time to ponder on things that cannot be undone. All that matters now is their survival. Otherwise, everything I did was for nothing.

I take off into the cover of trees, and they follow. My thoughts turn to Death as we race over the uneven, vine-stricken ground, wondering if he somehow took my powers away, now that I am in his domain.

I flex my fingers as we hurry through the eerily quiet forest, knowing that without my powers, I cannot save them. Perhaps this was Death's plan all along. He's probably laughing at my fate wherever he may be.

TWENTY-TWO

Azkiel

This is not the first time I have been buried alive. Essentria has a penchant for dragging her siblings into the ground and covering us with fucking soil and insects.

Slowly, I peel back my eyelids as the frosty breath of night caresses my face. Above the high walls of dirt, the crimson moon hangs low in the sky.

I lie still for a moment, the sound of worms burrowing in the mud beneath me scratches deep in my ears, enhancing my agitation. When I get my sister's body out of her tomb, I'm going to drag her to the deepest part of the Black Sea, where my dead can torture her in the darkness until the vibrance left in her soul is extinguished. Despite her comatose state, Essentria's spirit remains strong. Her magic pulsates in every damaged leaf and twig around me, still fighting.

"Fuck." I splutter and push my palm against the vines covering the ground.

My fingers carve into the hard mud as I force myself to sit upright. I cast my gaze up the inside of the large, rectangular hole. It has to be at least six feet deep. Cursing Essentria's name under my breath, I climb up and grip the edge, hoisting myself out of the hole, then landing on my stomach.

I should have expected this, but I deceived myself into believing that the physical consequences would not be so severe once my siblings' powers abandoned me.

Once I am back on solid ground, I spit out the remaining leaves and dirt from my mouth and examine my arms and hands.

My skin is marred with bruises, the blues, blacks and browns covering most of my exposed flesh. *Fantastic.* Not only do I feel weak, but I also bear the evidence that my mortal body can take a beating, or at least, only at the hands of the other gods, or their magic.

NIGHT OF DEATH AND FLOWERS

I cast my eyes to the sky. The horizon ombres from the inky depths of night, into a deep, ocean green. Down below, broken branches litter the shore, reclaimed by the forest creeping closer to the edge of the Black Sea. Vines that made it to where the tide meets the pebbles lay withered and browned at their tips. Although the storm is fading, dark gray clouds shield the edges of the crimson moon that will only last one night.

Calista.

I must know if she is still alive.

My power reaches out from me in tendrils of invisible smoke as I search for the energy of her soul and the decay magic in her veins.

Only two have joined my dead this evening. I can taste their sadness as they join the rest of the souls in my domain. Neither of them are Calista.

I breathe out a sigh of relief, then glance at the sky as the sound of flapping wings grabs my attention. I tilt my head back further to witness a crow gracefully flying overhead, its caw echoing through the air as it vanishes into the forest. I close my eyes, and the scent of damp moss and rain-soaked pine penetrates my nose.

I focus on the small, winged creature, observing its boldness as it fearlessly enters my domain. Merging my mind with the bird's is seamless, and when I close my eyes, I am transported into its perspective. The wind rushes through its feathers as it soars above the treetops, lifting us to greater heights.

He caws, and I reach into his thoughts. The crow is trying to find Calista.

My eyes fling open, and I am back in my body.

Of course she has a crow. If I had known, I would have used him to spy on her.

With a deep exhale, I use my fingers to remove the last traces of dirt from my hands, the gritty sensation clinging to my nails. As I cast one last look at the grave, a heavy sigh escapes my lips. I cannot waste any more time. I must regain possession of my sibling's mortal bodies before Calista can die.

I head toward the tree line. The weight of exhaustion deepens with each step, each breath accompanied by a rattling within my lungs.

As I walk into the confines of the forest, I glimpse a girl's spirit, lingering close, and my eyes flick towards her.

I press my palms against the jagged bark of a graywar tree trunk, the rough texture grounding me as I pause to catch my breath. Using her energy as a guide, I turn my head to face the approaching girl. Unlike spirits outside of my domain, these remain in a space between life and death, her figure transitions between being almost transparent, to appearing like a walking corpse.

Red robes cling to her body, the fabric ripped and soaked with old, brown blood. As she stands at the edge of the tree line, the glow of the moon dances on the sea behind her, shining through the gaping hole in her chest.

I avert my gaze, attempting to distance myself from the overwhelming waves of sadness rolling off her.

There are countless individuals who resist accepting the finality of things, and it is only humans, not animals or any other creatures, who become trapped in a state of denial.

But this spirit is different. She wants to leave. As her black hair hangs around her shoulders, strands slathered to her face from the blood, I can feel her ache. Whoever butchered her was violent. This was no merciful, quick death.

Her heart was ripped out.

She must have been one of the initial contenders in The Harvest. They were skilled warriors filled with fierce determination and raw strength, unlike the ones now.

I blink twice as inky tears spill from her empty eye sockets, an illusion of pain manifested by her memories of crying. Her sorrow pierces through my emotional barriers, leaving a lasting imprint.

"Leave me," I command, my voice hoarse as my vocal cords slowly heal from the earlier attack.

But she remains nearby, still as a statue, and a heaviness settles in my chest, churning my stomach.

"Get out of here!" I yell as she floods my aura with her emotions. I turn away, heading toward the center of the forest, every muscle screaming in protest. My heart skips erratically, then stops for a few seconds, as if it has forgotten how to beat. While I cannot die, my mortal body can be destroyed. Fortunately, despite its limitations, my flesh vessel can withstand more than the other mortals.

"Cyna," I growl as I sense his hand in this. They must be already regaining some form of consciousness. My family knows I am here, and they are sending the restless spirits here to torture me. Why else do I feel such guilt?

I turn to move again, but I am forced onto my knees by my weakened body and the shrouding magic of my siblings.

With a groan, I lean against a tree trunk, then close my eyes as I fall into a forced slumber.

My mind spins as I am pulled deeper into a dream, landing at the entrance to the Darklands.

"I know you're here," I call, sensing my family's presence. "Come out."

My eyes flit to the narrowing passage of walls, lit by the faint blue flames from flickering torches. Echoes of distant cries and anguished moans reverberate around me as I walk around a curve, then stop at a cross between seven tunnels connecting to the different levels of the Darklands.

Fleeting glimpses of spirits wander the tunnels, then evaporate as they try to free themselves of this place. My gaze focuses on the seventh and darkest tunnel. A slow, icy fog crawls from within its depths, and a shudder shakes my body. Why does this place bother me so much when it is mine to rule over?

"The seventh tunnel haunts you." Cyna's voice booms throughout the cave's entrance. "It should. You are foolish to return to Tenenocti."

A smirk curls over my lips as I slowly turn, sensing my brother' magic. Cyna holds his bow, with a green arrow poised at my heart. My tongue balls in my cheek as I laugh, stepping forward. "Are you going to shoot me, Brother?" I ask. "Has your long sleep affected your brain? Arrows will not work on me here."

His emerald stare is colder than the frigidity of his heart. "No, but it will *hurt* you."

Cyna releases his finger from the bow's string, sending the arrow whistling through the air, but I snatch it without effort before it can pierce my chest.

Our eyes meet and I snap the wood in my hand. "Is that all you've got?" I taunt, discarding the pieces on the ground.

"It's been a long time since I practiced."

"Centuries," I remark as if we aren't mortal enemies.

He lowers the bow, then tosses it aside before brushing the wrinkles from his ocean-green tunic and black pants.

My brother, always immaculately dressed, without a single blemish or imperfection. As a mortal, he is insufferable, always seeking perfection. I recall even in his ethereal form, he prided himself on keeping his energy free of darkness.

"I have never been afraid of you."

He drags a thumb to his lip, then clicks his tongue, smirking. "You cannot stop the prophecy, little brother. The girl is already here."

"Calista will fail," I snap back.

His groomed, dark brows pinch together, an unnerving smile claiming his mouth. "Come now," he taunts. "We both know why you did all of this. You betrayed us for your heart."

My lips close, my breath held as I stare at him through blurry eyes. "Then why you don't you fucking tell me what happened? I know Nyxara tampered with my memories."

He laughs, and I lunge at him, but before I can hit the smirk off his face, I'm slammed back into consciousness.

My eyes fling open to the dark forest. "Bastard," I groan. "Fucking prick!"

Cyna stands so high on his pedestal of judgment, telling me I fear the seventh level of the Darklands when I rule it. A place reserved for the most damaged people, where souls are obliterated, fractured, and then scattered across the Ether.

My heart skips a beat, then races erratically. I slam my fist against my chest, and the pain rattles my rib cage. Ignoring the dead, lingering in the trees, I continue, moving until I reach a clearing.

The forest's edge beckons me as I get closer to the graveyard containing their crypts. As I walk, memories unveil, like a long-forgotten dream resurfacing.

With each stride, the ground beneath me pulses with my sibling's magic, as if anticipating my return.

I find the path, concealed by a labyrinth of brambles, and push through them, the thorns scraping against my skin.

The gate creaks as I push it open, then carefully trudge through the once-meticulously tended graves of the witches who lived here, now hidden beneath tangled vines and ivy, the names on the tombs now faded.

Silence shrouds the graveyard, occasionally interrupted by the soft rustling of leaves. As I approach my sibling's tombs, my forehead creases as I observe the scene—the five pale crypts, lined up next to each other, are open, their lids laying shattered on the ground.

Wide-eyed, I kneel by the lid from Astraea's crypt and glide my fingers over her symbol—the moon and stars. A sharp, musky scent claims my senses, and as I peer down into the darkness, my stomach knots.

No.

I hurry to each crypt, my fingers gripping their sides, my heart pounds in my ears as realization sinks in.

They are all empty.

TWENTY-THREE

Calista

"Watch your step," I whisper, putting an arm out to stop Ari from walking ahead as I peer into the darkness for any sign of movement. "Here," I point at a collection of trees, then grab Ari's hand and pull her over the uneven, root-stricken ground. I stumble, and she steadies me as ivy catches around my ankles like nets, as if the island is trying to capture me too.

Twigs whip my arms and vines glide over my cheeks as we enter through the trees. A cobweb clings to my face, and I wipe it away, biting my tongue as we fight nature to allow us through.

There is an abandoned village this way. We can find shelter. I'm not sure how I know. I've never set foot in this place, but perhaps I've been here before in a dream.

We walk quietly, but I cannot shake the feeling that we are being followed. I listen for footsteps, but only the sounds of waves crawling over the pebbly shore permeate the area.

The damp, musty scent of decaying wood hits my nostrils, and I stop. "Do you hear that?" I ask.

Drake holds his breath for a few seconds, then shakes his head. "I don't hear anything."

"Exactly," I reply, my voice barely a whisper. "It's far too quiet," I add, and look around. It's as if every animal and insect escaped this place long ago. Even the leaves, in various stages of decay, seem trapped in time.

Blackness envelopes us as we delve deeper under the canopy, robbing us of our sight. The silhouette of the trunks is slightly darker than the rest of the background, and I narrowly dodge a graywar tree as I feel around us.

I halt, whipping my head around as a loud crack echoes from the branches behind us, and my muscles tense. I gesture at

Arabella as we step into a clearing. The light from the moon filters through the canopy, lighting the feathery moss hanging from low branches in an ominous red.

Drake steps beside me, his posture poised to fight. He keeps one arm out, as he waves Arabella over as a second crack sounds. My sister's arm brushes mine when she reaches us, and we form a circle, standing back-to-back as we peer into the darkness.

Drake points toward the trees he is facing as footsteps sound, twigs snapping a moment after. I hold my breath, carefully following his lead as he walks back into the blackness.

Leaves lightly crunch under his heavy boots, and my heart hammers in my ears, each exhale shaky as I try to control the sound of my breathing.

A loud caw sounds from the branches overhead, and my eyes flick to the canopy. The air whooshes from my lungs as my boot snags on a stray root. Grunting, my palms hit the ground first, the impact shooting needles into my wrists. I hiss through my teeth, then turn.

I try to muffle my raspy breaths, desperately covering my mouth with my hand.

Arabella's panicked voice carries through the trees.

"What happened?"

"Brace yourselves," I snap as I narrowly avoid a vine thrashing in my direction, before coiling back into the ground.

Every nerve in my body screams danger as I stand. After a few seconds, a thud booms from behind us.

"Grab Ari," I yell as the time-chiseled trees shed their foliage, the skeletal corpses of leaves drifting around us like snow.

I glance around, sensing a familiar tingling in my fingers when my magic pours into my hands, like it never has before.

Relief floods me as my power fills me up. It was only temporarily depleted, but the desire to feel another turn to ash under my touch is suddenly an itch I wish to scratch. I know it is wrong to answer the call to death and destruction, but the more I use it, the farther it embeds into who I am. Madness fringes my mind. What in the Darklands is happening to me?

I shiver as cold air shoots down my spine. Power surges through my veins, coursing alongside adrenaline, and I squint, my nostrils flaring.

It must be Edwardo. He's the only one who could have nature enhancement and manipulation.

Our eyes are instantly drawn to the treetops by a chorus of deep groans, accompanied by cracking, as the fibers of the branches come crashing down.

"Run!"

NIGHT OF DEATH AND FLOWERS

Drake's shout is drowned out by snapping and loud cracks arrowing into the night as branches cascade down upon us from high above, tearing through thickets of leaves, revealing the light of the moon.

I take off running toward Ari when the deep moan of a tree branch fills my ears. Splinters fall like a hundred pins onto my face.

I squeeze my lids shut, my throat drying as sharp pain lances into my skull. "Fuck!"

I run blindly, my arms outstretched.

A second thud reverberates behind us.

"Drake," I yell, but another thud thunders ahead, shaking the ground. I try to steady myself as my boots slide over slick algae, coating the forest floor.

I push myself faster, pulsating behind my temples as I race between the trees, my palms eventually landing against the rough bark of a tree trunk. Coming to a halt, I listen for any indication of where Ari and Drake might be. Then a tickle curls in the depths of my nose, and I take a sudden breath in, the potent, musty scent agitating my senses.

An explosion of air forces itself out of my nostrils, my eyes rolling up, mouth opening as I sneeze, once, then twice. I fall to my knees, my sister and Drake's panicked yells combined with the occasional scream, race my heart. I sneeze again, tears streaming from my eyes as the splinters etch deeper, and my fingernails carve into the dirt.

I don't have time to think, to react, before another sneezing fit consumes me. That's when I hear theirs, too. The musty odor, laced with a deadly, fruity scent tugs at my memory, and then I realize, I've created poisons using this plant.

"Don't breathe!" I shout into the chaos, unaware of how far I've traveled from them. "It's Lumonice Lux pollen."

Holding my breath, I grab handfuls of the fabric from my dress, then tear as hard as I can. I grit my teeth, letting out a guttural scream as I force the fabric away, until I hear the satisfying rip of silk. I bring the crumpled fabric over my nose and mouth and wince as the fabric touches my shredded skin. I breathe through the spores, holding back another sneeze as the pollen clouds the air.

I breathe slowly, my heart strained with each beat.

Without warning, tendrils of vines swiftly snake out under my dress, coiling around my ankles, restraining me to the ground.

"Cali!"

Ari's scream pierces my soul. She's close, but I can't see anything. "Breathe into your dress. Now."

Her loud sneeze sounds a few feet behind me. I lower my head as twigs shower me, landing in my hair, whipping against the exposed skin at the top of my back. The tree before me groans, and I reach my hand out for Ari. "He's destroying the fucking forest."

The air is knocked from my lungs, a thud landing on my back, winding me. I fight for breath, grasping desperately around me. My eyes fling open to a vision filled with stars, as the splinters destroy my sight. It takes me a few seconds for me to realize it was a large branch that had hit me.

Edwardo is going to kill us. I shouldn't have underestimated him.

I tense when icy fingers grip my arms until Ari's rushed tone fills my senses. "Don't move," she states, and I freeze, knowing she can see whatever I cannot.

Despite the dropping temperature and the chilling blasts in the winds, warmth seeps into my shivering body. The heat of Ari's touch starts in my arm and travels up to my face, tingling with a building heat.

"It will hurt," she says, heaving. "Only for a minute," she finally splutters.

I scream as her healing magic turns to liquid fire, somehow hot and cold at the same time.

Every inch of my being is engulfed in excruciating pain, forcing me to lie on my back, my body convulsing violently, and as the fabric shielding my airways from pollen slips off, I struggle to breathe.

As I inhale, the scent of pollen fills my nostrils, its cloying sweetness overpowering my other senses.

The vines tighten around me, and my muscles twitch as I wrestle against the constraints. Ari's hands slip away from my arms, and I lie back the algae, moisture seeping through my dress.

Footsteps pound as someone reaches us. At first, I think it's Drake, but as my eyesight is restored and the fiery sensation trickles out of my body, I turn my head to see Edwardo.

The color drains from Ari's face as she collapses in front of me, and I scramble to get on my knees, my adrenaline fighting against weariness.

"You."

He glances at my torched fingertips. Under the crimson moon, his big, brown eyes seem even darker, and as the canopy above us unravels, revealing the sky, I notice how much he has changed since The Choosing.

His confident stance and hungry stare are accentuated by the gray bark he wears as armor, splattered with blood that suggests his victory over another witch or warlock rather than his own injuries.

"I'm going to kill you," I promise as I shakily rise to my feet, poising myself to attack.

The pain and exhaustion lessen, but as I lunge at Edwardo, he reveals a handful of purple seeds, then hurls them at my arms.

My brows furrow, and I glance at my arms and hands, horrified as the tiny seeds penetrate my pores, dotting blood around the areas like a large rash.

I move forward, only to be forced back down on my knees by a sharp pain that cuts through my muscles, while a growing pressure builds beneath my skin.

My jaw slacks when I realize he's forcing the plants to bloom from within.

Every fiber of my being is alight with a vibrant, all-consuming pain.

Waves of anguish pulse through me, any thoughts of survival and fighting back suddenly eclipsed by unrelenting suffering.

A guttural cry quakes from my chest, my fingers curling into the slimy moss.

Delicate stems emerge from my arms, tearing through flesh, as the green sprouts become drenched in my blood. My eyes well up with tears as I unleash another scream, the sound reverberating in the air, while unbearable agony mercilessly tears through me, as if my very cells are being ripped apart.

Buds form at the ends, bringing forth a garden of crimson, lethal blooms that cover my exposed arms, shoulders and hands. As I hold out my trembling hand, thorns spiral from my skin, chunks of flesh catching against the thick spears of the flower, transforming into a crimson rose.

Stars fill my vision, my head throbbing as each breath becomes a labor, the slices of agony shredding through my upper body, my senses distorted by Edwardo's relentless attacks.

Screams tear through my lips until my throat is raw, my body curled up on the ground, every tiny motion enhancing the excruciating pain radiating through my muscles.

My racing heart pounds in my ears, drowning out all other sounds, while I desperately long for death to hurry me and take the pain away.

"Stop," I beg between agonizing sobs, my limbs convulsing. "Please, stop, please."

A shaky groan leaves my lips as I hold my breath, my eyes rolling to the back of my head.

I close my eyes, dizziness consuming me, and I welcome oblivion, the sensation of falling, of passing out, folding me into the edge of blackness.

I linger on the fringes of unconsciousness, the sharp stings needling my sticky, blood coated arms while the roots of the plants uncurl around my bones, etching closer to my heart. The vines move alongside my veins, meeting my magic. The moment that happens, my hungry darkness devours everything in its path, necrosing what is left of my shredded skin.

I refuse to lose my senses, turning my head in time to watch Drake launch himself at Edwardo. My heart stammers when Ari runs up behind him, then grabs his neck.

In no time, the whites of Edwardo's eyes shine with unshed tears as his lips part, blood frothing through them, crimson bubbles trailing down his chin.

That's when I realize that she's infusing a tremendous amount of her healing powers into his body to overwhelm his system.

Vines thrash around them while Drake takes the brunt of their whips, seeds sowing into his arms to turn him into a grotesque human garden.

Edwardo's shrieks taint the edges of my hazy mind as I watch Ari sink the claws of her powers deeper, and his abdomen swells to ten times its size before exploding.

"Ari," I whisper just before I fall into nothingness.

TWENTY-FOUR

Calista

It is a most beautiful place, a dream found between life and death.

The golden petals of the sun stretch into the horizon above me, the sky alight with the most captivating purple and pinks. Misty clouds settle together, as if the sky is dancing, welcoming a new day. Orange hues peek into the sky, its rays arrowing around me, spreading warmth over my desperate, aching body.

I blink twice, enjoying the heat, and as the colors touch me, I am as vibrant as this brilliant morning. Tall grass tickles my sides, brushing up against my cheeks as a gentle breeze caresses me. Bees buzz in a symphony with the crickets, and a smile settles over my lips.

Wait. *Ari. Drake.*

The torture floods back to me, cutting through the fog in my mind. The memory of the plants erupting through my skin throbs anguish into my skull. I sit up, folding myself forward, inhaling sharply as I stretch my arms out in front of me. I note the bracelet around my wrist, woven with silky wildflowers and threads of roots. "What the—"

"You are awake," a woman's low, hearty voice exclaims behind me.

I scramble onto my knees, my fingers running over the grass. I gaze around at the meadow, and after a quick glance around, my eyes land on a stunning woman. Shimmering gold covers her skin like glitter, catching the sun's rays as if she belongs to it.

Her round, deep gold eyes are pools of familiarity drawing me in. A sense of home washes over me as her full lips curve into a genuine smile, dousing the flames of hatred that have always burned inside of me.

Daggered leaves bursting with life are perfectly placed within her crown of dark brown curls. She strides closer, her arms outstretched, ready to embrace me, her emerald dress gliding silky over the grass. Flowers bloom in her presence, and behind her, a trail of pink and red flowers becomes her path.

My lips part, and a whoosh of air circles to the back of my throat as I stare at the woman I've seen in hundreds of portraits and paintings depicted in books—Essentria.

Her arms are around me, and my muscles relax as I breathe in the familiar bouquet of smooth honeysuckle, floral fragrance. My heart balloons as I recognize the mixed notes the longer she holds me—an evocative smell, laced with the energizing smell of grass after a light rainfall.

I don't know her, yet I can't help but squeeze her back, curling my arms around her, a tear dancing from my eye. My soul recognizes her, even if my mind doesn't.

"My goodness," she says, once I'm at arm's length. Her finger hooks under my chin, and she raises my eyes to meet hers. "You're really here."

I purse my lips, searching for the words to speak, yet my brain struggles to catch up with my unexpected rush of emotions. "Am I dead?" I ask slowly.

Her thumb glides down my cheek, brushing over the escaped tear. "No. This is a memory, inside of your mind as you cling to life," she explains as the meadow fades in my peripheral vision.

Essentria lifts my hands in hers, a flash or red crossing her dangerous stare. It lasts only a second, but the effect remains on my emotions. "Decay magic." Her expression warps. "Such a pity."

"I wanted your power," I admit quickly, recalling when the God of Death's powers appeared alongside hers. I felt her magic, before it slipped away, but now I sense it, something alive, blooming deep, but it's so repressed by the decay I cannot access it.

"You had it, once." She drops my hand as if it was made of poison, her lips twisting. "This magic was your choice."

I inhale sharply, but do not look away from her. "What? I didn't choose this magic."

"Where is Azkiel?" she asks.

"I don't know."

Her eyes alight with menace. "Good."

Before I can inquire any further, I'm grasping at thin air, and she dissolves along with the meadow. The darkness threatens to steal me again, and I'm slammed back into my body with such force that I jolt forward.

The first breath is painful, and I'm breathing daggers of air into my lungs, the deep pockets of tissue objecting to the sudden, sharp breaths.

I peel back my eyelids to reveal what is left of the fog-haloed trees, towering to form a thinned canopy above. I squint as my eyes become accustomed to the harsh red light of the moon, reminding me I am still in The Harvest.

Arabella is over me, her blonde strands falling around her face. Blood splatters carve into her delicate features, her lashes flicking away the last remnants of crimson drops dripping from her forehead.

"Thank the gods," a deep voice announces, followed by a sigh of relief. Ari whips her head around to who I assume is Drake, his footsteps growing louder as they scuffle closer.

"Ari," I croak, my voice strained as it climbs out of my mouth. I struggle up, pushing my arms into the thick of the moss and scattered bark, but my head is too heavy. I heave out a breath as I drop back down, my head hitting the soft ground, the forest floor a blanket for my aching body.

Drake comes into view, and I've never been so glad to see that relieved, lazy smile settled over his lips. I notice the blood against his tanned arms, and my chest pangs.

Ari shushes me as I open my mouth, bringing her finger to my lips. "Edwardo is dead."

The scene floats back to me. "I saw," I whisper, nodding slowly. "He exploded."

"Yes," she says, her eyes veiling over. "You saved me. I thought I was as good as dead."

Drake presses his lips together, glancing from my sister to me as they both crouch over me, their knees on either side of my torso.

Ari's sigh sends a fresh wave of anxiety through me. "Yes, I saved you."

I attempt to sit up again, my elbows holding my weight.

I wrinkle my nose as a putrid, rotting smell of feces mixed with iron confuses my senses. The cloying undertones of the smell seep down, as bile rises in my throat, settling like oil against my tongue. My mouth waters and my stomach churns until I forcibly gag.

I slowly turn my head to the left, twigs pushing against my skull as I strain my neck. My gaze climbs the broken branches and trunks around us. Chunks of flesh and muscle cling to the leaves, bodily liquids slicking to every surface.

Drake clears his throat, trying to force back a gag, too, but my sister doesn't seem to care. She doesn't even look at him.

I focus back on her, forcing apathy into my expression as I notice her observing me. "You died," she admits, her words temporarily freezing my mind.

I gasp, a bad idea, as the death rot clings to my throat, and I taste the particles of Edwardo's insides.

Do not think about it.

I breathe out a steady breath, not wanting to freak my sister out, whose eyes are already rounder than normal, a madness circling her irises.

"Dead," I repeat, then close my eyes. Maybe this is a nightmare. I hope it is. But I'm never so lucky.

The dream with Essentria floats back. She acted as if we had met before, then said I chose Death's magic over hers when I did not. *I had no choice.*

Memories flit through my mind, each thought scattered as I try to hold on to a shred of anything that may reveal the truth.

I turn to Ari, wheezing. "You brought me back," I state, assessing her paling face as she hovers over me. She's drained, yet somehow kneeling. If she can do it, despite being exhausted of her powers and having somehow killed Edwardo, then so can I.

Ouch.

My bones crack in a way that should be concerning as I force myself up.

I tilt my head, straining my neck until I hear a pop, and an ache dissipates from my shoulders. I hunch forward, my next breath accompanied by a stab of pain in my ribs.

I sit upright, my hands pressed against my stomach as I breathe again. Once. Then twice. It is easier this time, but my heart continues struggling with each pump. I listen quietly as it thumps in my ears, and every few beats, it palpitates.

"You shouldn't have brought me back," I splutter as I stare at her golden hair, the ends coated with drying blood.

"Why not?" she asks, her lips mostly drained of color. "You would have done the same for me."

"We both know I'm not capable of anything more than killing you."

"But you would have, if you could," she argues.

Inhaling deeply, I suppress the wince when my ribs grind with pain and shuffle myself to face her straight on. "That's different. I'm your older sister. It's my job, but this could have…" I trail off as her pupils narrow as she slips closer to the ground. "Ari?"

"I'm fine," she lies, barely holding herself up. She huffs, puffing out her cheeks. "I'm not as fragile as you think. So, stop treating me like I may break."

Drake shoots me a suspicious glance, and I nod.

He curls his arm around Ari, who shrugs him away. But then, she quickly falls onto the ground, groaning as she turns from her side onto her back, her eyes closing against the night sky.

Her lashes flutter as she tries to reopen her eyes, then lets out a mumble before finally falling asleep.

After a couple of light snores, Drake whispers, "We need to talk."

My stomach knots. "Yes." I glance at his arms, the tattoos fading. He must have used his magic when I was blind or passed out. "First, let's find shelter. Before another one of them finds us while we're weak."

He nods, pushing an arm under Ari's back, then one under her knees. Before lifting her, he sighs. "I'm glad she saved you. Seeing you like that… it was hard."

I force a watery smile because I have no idea what to say in response. I was entirely useless at fending off the attack. Incompetence haunts me as I struggle to my feet, using the tree to steady myself.

Drake grunts as he scoops Ari up in his arms.

"How did she do that?" I whisper. "It's like she… over-healed him."

He shakes his head, his lips twisting as he looks at Edwardo's mangled corpse.

Bones protrude from the hole in his stomach, their jagged edges covered in a thick, sticky layer of blood. A swarm of flies circles him, their buzzing growing louder, and the putrid smell of death stifles the air, making the harsh reality of death impossible to ignore.

"I think that's exactly what she did," he agrees, his voice barely a whisper. "It happened so fast. She healed me because you were already dead, but she didn't seem upset over it. Then, when she brought you back to life, I realized why." His eyes meet mine. "Ari knew she could revive you."

I knew something was off when I woke up, as if she was in complete denial of what surrounded us.

My sister will never forgive herself.

"Right," I breathe, knowing I will need to reveal the truth of my sister's secret—how she possesses Essentria's ethereal magic; how she is the mirror version of me. Sisters. One light, one dark. Two sides of the same coin.

Although that may have changed after today. I didn't even know healing magic could be used offensively until now.

"We will talk," he promises, then grunts as he treads over the uneven, branch-covered ground, carefully navigating the thickets of vines. He groans, holding my sleeping sister, his bulging muscles straining the fabric of his shirt, poking out from under his red robes.

After ten minutes of trekking through the forest in silence, each step is lighter than ever before. My calves would normally burn, the aches lasting for days. But now it is easier—as if being touched by Ari's creation magic has changed something in me.

The remaining raindrops descend from the tall branches, creating a gentle pitter-patter around us as the storm from earlier moves further away from the island. As we reach an abandoned house nestled within the heart of the forest, I let out a sigh of relief. The stone statues by the door are saturated with the remnants of rain, giving them a shimmering, wax-like appearance.

Swinging loosely on its hinges, the front door creaks with each movement. As I journey ahead, the unmistakable sign that my ancestors who inhabited this place worshiped Death peeks out from the surrounding outline: the twisted stone faces of Phovi with empty eyes that follow my every step.

I'm grateful they are just statues. I can't fight anymore, not for at least a few hours.

I peer into the darkness of what was once a window, now just an empty frame where shards of shattered glass remain, their grimy, jagged edges pointed out in warning.

Cracks in the structure are filled by roots, their tips curling out over the gray-brick like fingers, strangling it into submission.

Drake climbs the two steps to the door, then lowers Arabella onto the doorstep. His hands rest on the black railing by the entryway as he leans over, his exposed skin glistening with sweat. "We need water," he says after a minute, and I nod in agreement, my eyes already searching the area for long leaves that might have caught the earlier raindrops.

"I'll find some. You get her inside and rest."

"I'm not leaving you out here alone," he retorts.

"I'll stay close. Just get her inside."

I pace toward a towering plant with oversized, luscious green leaves, and kneel. Small pools of water have formed in the sunken areas. It's not a lot, but it's something. I lick my dry lips, then drain a leaf, the water doing little to remove the taste of death in my throat.

Plucking the leaf from the plant, I scrape together more raindrops, scooping them into it before slowly rising. I pause for a moment and stare at the forest as the intensity of our first few hours of The Harvest sinks in.

Three are dead. Two by my hand, one by my sister's. Gods know how many else are gone. Seeing Ari being forced to do something dark, pulls on my heartstrings. I shake the feeling away, focusing instead on the one thing I cannot be distracted from: survival.

A twig sounds from within the trees, and I crane my neck, surveying the darkness. Decay magic readies in my fingers, its energy thrumming through my body with unparalleled intensity ever since I woke up.

I ready myself for another attack. Someone must have followed us. I won't lead them to the house, not with Ari unconscious.

Another twig snaps, then footsteps pound behind me.

TWENTY-FIVE

Calista

Leaves crunch under the heavy thumps of my boots as I race over the uneven ground and through the maze of shadowy trees, sensing whoever is chasing me approaching swiftly.

An arm wraps around my waist from behind, tugging me against a hard body. The person's icy fingers are around my mouth. Decay magic sizzles, then seeps into the person's arm, and I smile under their hand before I notice they do not turn to ash.

"Are you trying to get yourself killed?" a voice whispers against the top of my ear, and I freeze.

My heart pounds as Death's hand lifts from my mouth, and I push against his biceps until he releases my body. I spin to face him, teeth chattering as my eyes bulge.

"You!"

"Me," he mocks, his silver stare matching my intensity.

My hand darts to my hip, gripping the hilt of the dagger. "What are you doing here?"

He stills, his brows creasing as he stares at me with a chilling pointedness. "What did you do with them?"

"With whom?"

He closes the gap between us until I am shrouded in his shadow. "Do not play with me again. I will break our oath. I do not care."

I look up, my chin grazing his hard chest. "Still threatening to kill me?" I laugh, then bring the blade to his throat because I have little to lose.

He leans into the blade, smirking. "Go ahead, Poison."

"You're fucking insane," I say, half-laughing, pressing the blade deeper until droplets of blood form.

After a few moments of silence, he pushes the dagger away from his neck as if he is swatting a fly. "You need to leave," he states.

"We're not in Dahryst," I point out. "It seems I was not the only one who wasn't paying attention to the details during our deal."

"You distracted me," he growls. A vein in his temple throbs, and I trace my gaze over his chiseled features.

I watch him closely as he flexes his fingers, his untapped power swirling in those eyes, as if it may explode at any moment. "You look flustered."

"I've had a bad night," I spit, tightening my grip around the dagger.

He steps closer, swallowing any distance between us. Our fingers brush together, and his intense stare latches onto mine. "You will leave here now. I will take you to shore."

"Why do you care if I am here?" I ask and take a step back, my heart pounding. "Just tell me about this damn prophecy. Does it have to do with The Harvest?"

He lowers his chin, glaring down at me, and for the first time, I see the ancient darkness in his silvery eyes, an evil so pointed and deadly that sends a chill to my bones. "Fine." His tongue darts between his lips, wetting them. "Do you think me a monster, Poison?" he drawls.

"Yes."

"Then the last thing you want is for the other gods to awaken."

I blink twice, the statement throwing me back "Awaken?"

He casts a glance at the sky, then snaps back to me. "Yes. That is why your presence here is dangerous. Not just for me, but for you, too."

My brows knit together as I stare at Death, my lips slowly parting, barely a breath passing through them as I mull over his words.

I glance around the unforgiving forest of gray, and the frost-bitten skeletal leaves hanging from knotted branches. "So the gods are here," I conclude.

He leans forward, the warmth of his body so close to mine, just inches away... His eyes are alight with flecks of black and shadow as he whispers a truth that runs my blood cold. "Yes."

My mind fuzzes as I gaze upward at Azkiel, searching his stoic expression and finding no evidence of a lie. "How are they here? Why are they asleep? What does the prophecy have anything to do with me? Is my name explicitly used?"

"No, but—"

"Then it describes me?"

"Yes," he growls, impatience threading the twitches over his face. "It is said a witch, a daughter of creation, doomed by death, will awaken my siblings."

An incredulous laugh leaves my lips. "You're telling me you sent Drake and Ari here, and almost killed me over *that*? What makes you think it is me when it's so vague and unclear?"

He lets out a tense breath, then clenches his chiseled jaw, the sharp lines of his features giving the impression that they were carved from marble. "You are doomed with death magic."

I shake my head, averting my eyes from Azkiel. "Let's suppose it's true, and it's me. Then why wouldn't I want the gods to awaken?"

I was never a fan of them, nor their theocratic government, but how can they be any worse than Death?

"You should fear them," he snaps. "For them to awaken, the chosen witch must die. They are freed by the blood of an innocent, a daughter of creation."

Historically, according to the few recorded texts left of the times when the gods were here, a few of the deities would take mortals under their care and treat them like offspring because they could not have children of their own.

So, the prophesied one can't be an actual daughter, but a witch in her coven. I was born into it, but so was Arabella. Doomed with death doesn't specify that it is a witch who harbors decay magic; it can also mean anyone sent to Tenenocti to compete in The Harvest, and I'm not officially a part of the tournament. However, if the prophecy states a witch born into Essentria's coven, that only leaves... Ari.

It's her, I realize, my heart fluttering.

Tingles pass through my shoulder, down my arm, and into my wrist. A wave of numbness captures me as an icy gust of wind carries between us, sweeping strands of hair.

Azkiel draws closer. Slowly, he lifts a finger to my face, then touches the loosen locks. We both hold our breath as he tucks the hair behind my ear, and the butterflies in my chest intensify. "What is it, Poison?"

"Nothing," I say breathily. "Earlier, you asked me where they were. Did you mean the gods?"

His shoulders tense as he pulls his hand away from my face, but his gaze lingers where his fingertips had grazed my cheek. "Their bodies are gone."

A shiver tingles my spine, and I shudder. "Well, it wasn't us."

His face contorts. "Then someone else is working against me."

I nod quickly, my throat tightening as I reach out for him, my fingers connecting with his biceps. I squeeze his arms, drawing him nearer, and the madness flecking his gaze is quickly satiated.

Wait. Why am I holding onto him? I drop my arms to my side and clear my throat. "Do you think it's one of the other chosen ones?"

"It could be."

I am paralyzed under his intense stare, the magic in my veins throbbing with newfound strength. It's only when his brows straighten, and he averts his gaze that I shake my head. "Why are the gods trapped here in the first place?"

He paces a few steps away from me, as if I am suddenly venomous, then says, "Because they are dangerous."

A wave of numbness rolls through my body, and small shivers snake over my arms and torso like currents. I can't let him know Ari is the prophesied one. He tried to kill me when he thought *I* was. Yet, my sister will die if the prophecy is fulfilled. "I'll help you find them," I blurt out, realizing he may be our best ally against this new threat.

His eyes grow larger under the moonlight. "Why would you do that?"

"It can't hurt to have the God of Death at our side." I shrug.

"I will not help your sister or the boy win. I won't interfere with the competition." He grabs my fingers, then grits his teeth, lifting his glare to meet mine. "You're tied up in this. Even if you are not the prophesied one, which I have not ruled out, there is a reason you have my ethereal magic, and I just know Nyxara is behind it."

"Or Essentria. She came to me in my dream. She was angry that I hold your power instead of hers."

"What else did she say?"

"Just that."

His expression warps between anger and confusion. "Why would she go to you?"

I shrug. "I don't know, but she didn't say anything to me about the prophecy." I pause briefly, then lick my dry lips. "So, are you coming?"

Death wrenches his hand away. "I don't trust your words."

"Good. I don't trust you either."

"If I find out that you are lying to me, I will tear the boy and your sister's spines through their throats," he warns, and goosebumps prick over the back of my neck.

"I'm not lying," I assure him. *I've only evaded the truth about Ari*, I finish in my head.

He grits his teeth, then turns his back to me. "Then we have another deal, Poison."

"I always knew the gods were monsters," I say. "Although I had always believed Essentria was good."

A low growl emanates from his chest. "No, that was Astraea."

"Is she here as well?"

"They all are. How do you think Essentria could reach you in your dream? She borrowed Astraea's magic."

"Why did you trap Astraea, if she's good?" I ask.

Guilt carves his expression as he remains in silence.

"Why allow this tournament here if you're afraid of someone awakening the gods?" I continue when he doesn't speak.

"Because," he spits, "when they die, their souls join the rest that guard this island, haunt my sea, and stop trespassers. I need more dead, so no one stumbles across my siblings. The sacrifices were too busy trying to kill each other to ever find them."

"You are revolting. Hundreds have died so you could have some ghost barrier?"

"Yes," he says simply, and it takes every ounce of self-control I have not to punch him in the face. "The elders wanted this. I only seized an opportunity. Now, let us go before the morning comes."

I grit my teeth, glaring at him before reluctantly saying, "Drake and Ari are in an abandoned house, up there."

He tsks. "Such an obvious hiding place."

"With your help, we won't have to worry about being attacked."

"*You* won't," he hisses through his teeth. "I already told you, Poison, I won't interfere with The Harvest. You are not an active participant. You never made the oath, even when you killed the girl in the boat. You are my only concern and, until I know for certain you are not the prophesied one, I am not leaving your side."

TWENTY-SIX

Azkiel

The creeping sense of Essentria's power lingers around me, choking the island with life.

I glance at the witch as we walk, my heart palpitating. Essentria spoke to her, which can only mean she is the chosen one, despite what Calista believes.

She's quiet, lines forming between her brows. Her magic thrums, growing louder and my shadows swirl inside of me in response. She has no idea how haywire her power is, and what it does to me.

I clear my throat, breaking the silence, hoping a distraction will slow her damn mind. "There was a crow searching for you. Is he a pet of yours?"

"Thorn," she gasps, and I roll my eyes. "Where is he?"

Thorn. What a fucking name. "I'm not sure."

"He'll find me." The spirit of a girl with shoulder length wisps of hair runs in front of us, her body disappearing through a tree's weathered trunk. Calista's eyes track her movements, and she slows her pace. "She looked like a walking corpse," she whispers, then halts. "Yet she passed through a tree."

My brows furrow as I watch her gaze around, then sigh heavily. "You are not shaken by the dead."

"Not really. The living are far worse."

"You're proof of that, Poison."

She clears her throat. "I suppose. So, do the dead here have physical bodies?"

"Both," I explain. "Their forms are malleable."

She lifts her chin. "So the people I killed tonight are still here."

"Yes," I state, and we continue walking. "I can feel every soul within my domain."

Her breath hitches. "Fantastic."

"They likely won't hurt you," I assure her, and her gaze snaps to mine.

"That's not what concerns me."

"You feel guilty," I note. "Don't. Regret is pointless. You can't change the past."

"Is that what you tell yourself?" she asks. "To justify everything you've done."

I shrug. "I don't have to justify anything. That's a mortal's burden."

She rolls her eyes and matches my pace. "If people find out how awful you are, they won't worship you."

"Why not?" I ask. "Mortals are just as bad.."

"You were supposed to be above sin."

I chuckle darkly. "Is that the fairytale you were taught? Where did you think sin came from?"

Her gaze drifts to meet mine and I hesitate when I notice tears glossing over them. "Then what's the point of being a good person?"

"Society could not exist without the concept," I say, and glance sideways at Calista, her body slathered with sprays of dried blood. Her hair catches in a gust of wind, and hues of golden brown woven with deep chestnut strands shine under the red moon. My shadows uncurl around my bones, desperate to touch her again.

"Why are you looking at me?" she asks.

"I'm not."

"Sure," she says, her magic calming with each beat of our conversation. "I mean, I understand. You've not been able to touch anyone alive before. At least not without them immediately dying."

My lips part, but I bite back my words. What the fuck am I supposed to say to that? When she calls out my vulnerabilities so brashly and uses them against me.

I place several more inches between us, and she smirks in victory. My fingers curl into fists, the magic vibrating into my palm.

Calista heaves out a breath, carefully treading over the root-stricken ground, unaware of the bones buried underneath the thin layer of dirt. "How many people are left?"

"Eight, including your sister and the traitor."

Calista brushes away a fallen leaf, then glances sideways at me. "You didn't count me?"

"I already told you. You were not chosen, even if you forcibly entered the island," I spit, anger guiding my tone.

"You gave me the idea."

I grit my teeth. "Yes, I watched you kill that girl," I say, wiping the snarky smile from her lips. "It was a beautiful display, although the townspeople didn't think so. They were shouting words such as 'monster' and 'evil'."

"Maybe I am," she challenges me, and I almost smile. "I'm willing to do whatever it takes to save Ari and Drake."

"You care not for your soul?" I counter, my vision carving out the darkness, until I see the entrance of the abandoned building.

"No," she whispers. "I know I'm already destined for the Darklands. At least then I'll be able to repay you for all your so-called *mercies*."

"I rule the Darklands," I hiss as Drake's form comes into view, his head in his palms. "My Phovi will drag you the seventh cave before you have time to find me."

"We'll see," she snaps, defiance crossing her perfect blue stare, and magic sparks to life inside of me. I must admit to myself that there is likely no other adversary than her who could destroy me.

Just her being alive angers me. I can only imagine what it would feel like to have her hunting me, desperate to annihilate me, having her always near me, on the edge of the darkness.

A shadow uncurls from my fingers, then glides around her throat. "Just remember who you're talking to. I may not be able to kill you, but do not forget I can hurt those you love."

She halts, then spins to face me. "You need me."

"For now."

We hold our breath in unison, rage swallowing my air until I tear my eyes from her. Finally, she looks at the house and steps away from me.

"Drake," she whispers as we exit through the tree line.

He stands, his glare latching onto mine the second he spots us, his muscles tense. Tattoos swirl against his olive-skin, and I grin as I watch a depiction unfold of him, tearing out my heart. I would love nothing more than to see him try.

Calista walks to him, then hesitantly brings her hand to his. "I've been looking for you everywhere since you ran off."

I glower when her fingers make contact with his skin, then move up beside her. "I ran into someone."

Drake tilts his head, then lowers his voice to a whisper. "What the fuck is he doing here?"

"It's complicated, but we need his help," she says, her breaths uneven. As if I'd ever aid the boy or the sister. I am only here to stop her from getting killed, possibly bringing the prophecy to fruition, and finding the person who stole the bodies of my siblings.

Drake brushes the witch aside, and her eyes widen.

Then he turns his attention to me, his posture shaping defensively. "We don't need you here."

"Careful with your words," I warn.

"Don't," Calista tells him.

He turns to face her, and after a moment of looking into her eyes, he sighs. "I don't want him near you."

"I don't either," she admits, as if I'm not even standing here.

I focus on Calista as she watches untie his cloak, then throws it over his shoulder.

"We have killed people because of this tournament," he states. "*His* tournament." He pauses, then points at me.

Calista touches his arms, redirecting his attention back to her, and his shoulders relax. I could so easily kill him, and my fingers flex at the thought.

"I know," she says, her voice charged with a panicked, desperate hope. "But we can end this now."

I focus on the boy, anger roiling in my bones. "You dare talk down to me," I spit and close the few feet between us. He gulps under my shadow as I glare down at him. "I am your *god*."

Shadows erupt from my core, and Cali's fingers land on my arm as the ribbons of darkness coil around Drake's torso.

"Please," Calista begs, and a low growl vibrates in my chest. "He won't say anything else," she promises, but my shadows squeeze tighter until the traitor's bloodshot eyes flow with tears.

I bring him to the edge of unconsciousness, then release him, dropping him to the ground.

He holds his stomach, doubling overs before bringing his stare to meet mine.

We both know I'm not letting him off this island.

TWENTY-SEVEN

Calista

I suck in a deep breath, pushing my torso straighter against the ancient, smooth stone, and shift my attention to the light snores on the other side of the room.

My gaze trickles over the pile of old bedding and drapes on the ground, contoured around Drake's body. Behind him, Arabella's eyelashes flicker as she dreams, and I can only hope they are not filled with flashbacks of what happened last night.

Her blood-soaked cloak covers her, as she lies on a makeshift bed, made from wooden furniture turned on its side.

The floorboards creak under my heavy boots. Slowly, I walk, careful not to make too much noise. Drake rolls onto his side, his light snores rolling relief through me. He has barely said a word to me since I returned with Azkiel, and Ari only woke for a few minutes to drink some rainwater, before falling back to sleep.

Despite promising to wake Drake two hours ago, so he could take over and be on watch, I couldn't bring myself to do it. Sleep eludes me anyway, my mind racing over the events of the evening.

Ari is the prophesied one. I've never been so sure of anything, and I keep the secret to myself. She's always been loyal to the gods—especially Essentria. My sister will never accept they're monsters, just like the God of Death. She might even be persuaded to awaken them if it means saving Drake and me. I'm certain she'll bargain for our survival with them.

My eyes drift over her soft features as she sleeps, and I wonder if she has dreamed of Essentria, too. Death's truth about the gods using Astraea's magic to speak with me sets me on edge. Because someone else on this island is also aiding them, and the question is who else the gods have spoken to.

That, or Azkiel is lying to me. Cyna's sight magic pulls inside of me, as if it is sentient, sensing my thoughts, begging for me to search deeper.

I walk into the adjoining room of the abandoned house. Rain patters against the walls as morning light filters through the window.

I cross the threshold, finding Death slouched over an armchair, his piercing eyes never wavering when he looks at me. Shadows cloak his silver tunic, swirling like snakes over his chest.

One of his legs is propped against the wall, his arm draped over his knee. "I told you to sleep."

I stand by the doorway, locked in a silent confrontation, both of us refusing to look away first. "You won't protect them," I say, gesturing to the room adjoining this one.

"So you've come to me for company?" he asks, a lazy smirk settles over his lips.

I unsheathe my dagger, and his eyes track the blade as I slide down a wall, until I'm sitting on the dusty floorboards. "I wanted to ask you something."

Above me, the rhythmic pitter-patter calms my dark thoughts. I clear my throat, the anticipation in his intense stare sending a shiver down my spine. Everything about Death evokes a rage that threatens to burn me alive. However, I can't deny that he is the only one that can help me in my predicament. "What will you do if I am not the prophesied one and you find them on this island?"

He shifts his position, his body subtly angling toward me. His hands, tainted with dark magic, rest on his thighs, and he clenches his fingers against his skin when he looks at me. "I will take them off this island, then kill them."

The blade shimmers as the pale blue of the morning light filters through the window. "Why would they have to die?" I probe, gentler than before, hoping he divulges something he shouldn't. Although, as I assess his guarded expression, I know he won't loosen his tongue as easily as before. No matter how much I bait him.

"Nyxara created the prophecy," he explains, pausing after each statement, as if he's examining his words. "She will draw them back here."

"How does she have power still? If she's asleep?"

His eyes drift to the weathered wooden beams supporting the ceiling, and the crimson splatters painting on the walls, telling a long-forgotten story that happened here. "Their magic is sentient. It lives within every witch and gives them some influence. I imagine they've gotten creative with their dreams and magic in the past century and a half."

My eyes narrow. "How come they have lured no one here before? To free them?"

He doesn't respond, and stretches his arms out, his hands behind his neck. My gaze falls to the lines of his defined muscles, and those huge fucking biceps.

What am I doing?

"Tell me," I order, then soften my tone. "If I am to help you, then I need to know everything. Look, if I am who you're looking for, then that's a good thing for you. I don't want to die."

"Let me take you off this island, then."

I shake my head. "I won't leave Ari and Drake. You know that. Besides, you don't know who took the gods' bodies."

He sighs out a breath, giving away nothing in his stoic expression. The morning light dances with his shadows, wisping around his chiseled features. Every slice of darkness that moves around him could easily choke the life out of another.

I recall when they strangled me until I tamed them. He must despise being forced to ally with someone who has some power over him. I bet he's never known what that's like. No wonder he hates me.

Every time our eyes meet, magic surges through me. Ever since Ari brought me back, my powers have been haywire. My lids close briefly as I strain them back into my core before looking at Azkiel again.

His gravelly voice resonates in my ears. "Your magic is darkening. If you don't control it, it'll consume you."

"It's heightened. I don't know why."

I curl then uncurl my fingers, finally landing them on my legs, drawing his gaze to my thighs. He shifts position again, his chest heaving, then looks away, but his shadows give him away when one of them snakes outward, seemingly eager to caress me.

His nostrils flare as he reins it back into his body. Silence lingers for a few moments, and then he says, "We will go to the temple."

"Why?"

"It is my temple, and my siblings' bodies may be there. I refuse to sit here, waiting."

"Then why did you agree to come here?"

He gives me an incredulous, arrogant stare. "I figured you needed to rest. Which is why I told you to sleep."

"I'm fine."

He leans forward, his fingers crowned around his knees. "You're exhausted." His stare drifts over me, as if he's undressing me with his eyes. "I won't let anyone hurt your fucking sister and friend, if that's what it takes for you to rest."

I push the blade into the floorboard. "I don't trust your word."

He cranes his neck back, shaking his head as he does. "Go to fucking sleep and stop arguing. You are no use to me exhausted." He pulls his cloak hanging over the back of his chair, then throws it at me. I catch it, breathing in his musky, soft, woody scent. "I can manage a few sacrifices."

"You said you won't interfere with The Harvest."

His stare darkens. "Should anyone come here, I will order them to leave. I don't have to kill anyone."

"What if they fight you?" I ask and he laughs, probably finding the notion is preposterous. "Fine," I whisper, struggling to keep my eyes open. "Just for an hour."

He nods and I drape his cloak over me, nestling into the pockets of warmth, his scent hugging me. My thoughts turn to Ari as I close my eyes, resting against the wall.

My poor sister. When she awakes, she will have to face what she did. The far-off look and trance-like movements from last night still haunt me—she wasn't processing a damned thing.

Her innocence was the price to pay for saving my life. This is Death's fault. I grit my teeth but swallow any harsh remark that bites its way up my throat. He may be our only way out of here, and I know better than most how to play the long game. I've done it with my mother for years, holding back what I really felt, losing battle after battle so I could eventually win the war and get out of that house.

None of the matters now, though. The rain is a lulling symphony, and as the room blurs, my eyes softly close. My magic buzzing alongside my heart, creating a steady, heavy sensation in my body. I pull the cloak up and over my chin, opening my eyes briefly when I find Death staring out of the window, sadness etched into every flicker of expression. For the first time since I've met him, he appears as just a man, and not a god.

My eyelids are heavy as I hazily look at the window again, watching each raindrop slide down the grimy glass. My lashes flutter, blocking out the gentle morning light until my head is lolling against the curved stone.

I can barely catch my breath when an abyss swallows me whole, and I am falling.

I clutch my throat as I fall endlessly, my body weightless, my heart thumping so fast I fear it may erupt through my ribcage.

"Help," I cry dryly, but my plea is muffled by the void of blackness. I reach out, kicking my legs against the empty space.

I land with a heavy thud, and the air whooshes from my lungs. Struggling to take a breath in, I lay under the dove-gray sky, winded, staring at the colors moving between the clouds, like rolling waves but in the sky.

My chest screams in protest when I finally gasp a lungful of air. I groan as I turn onto my side. The tall grass withered.

A heaving cough steals my next breath, aching my struggling lungs. I slap my hand over my mouth and nose. Particles of ash drift to the back of my throat, the potent, charred taste doubling me over into a coughing fit.

Reaching for the torn skirt of my dress, I clasp a handful of silver silk. I run my fingers over the small, black crystals embroidered into the fabric, flowing over the contours of my body. As I glide my fingers up the floor-length gown, I reach the boned corset, the material shimmering as if the material was cut from the night sky. I turn my head, then lift my arms, examining the tulle cape, touching the high collar and diamond inset in the center. The cloudy, gray sky illuminates the glistening buttons running down the length of both arms. I extended my hands, examining the silver band, complete with a small, dark skull engraved into it—similar to Azkiel's.

What in the Darklands? I have never seen a dress like this to even imagine it in a dream.

Unless this isn't my dream.

I scan my surroundings, brows furrowed as I stare out over the smoky-pinched meadow. "Essentria," I whisper, my lungs accumulating to the ash-captured world.

The hairs on the back of my neck stand erect when I realize I am standing in the same dream as last night, except the trees surrounding it have been reduced to piles of ash, scattered in the breeze, and everything is dead.

Lifting the skirts of my dress, the netted train dragging over the withered grass, I walk barefoot through the meadow. Everything about this place feels like I have been here before. The horizon of dark waters beyond the forest is so eerily familiar.

Is this Tenenocti? It looks so similar, yet so different, as if something has drained the island of life. I pause, holding my hands over my abdomen, my stomach churning.

Something isn't right.

Goosebumps prick over my arms. I blink slowly, taking in the monotone world. Remembrance flickers in my mind again, and a curtain lifts in my mind. I swallow hard as decay magic spills from my heart, through my veins, seeping into every limb. My eyes bulge as I extend my hands, watching the dark gray covering my skin.

My lips part as I clutch the sides of my head. I clamp my eyes shut as visions flash through my mind. Azkiel's face haunts my thoughts—those silver eyes crowned with concern—then Astraea, who is even more vibrant than her portrait in the church, with her long, dusky blue hair. Every inch of her shimmers, as if she is made from stardust.

Then, Cyna's green, pointed eyes, reflecting my sins back to me, instill guilt into my heart. "Stop!" I yell as the puzzle pieces of the vision, or memories, cascade upon me.

Wake up. *Wake up.*

"Murder becomes you," Cyna's low, steady voice booms. "Essentria was wrong. You always belonged to Death."

Death? As in Azkiel? Why the fuck is the God of Judgment here?

My eyes fling open, and I whip my head around, the decay magic thrumming stronger than ever, so much that I fear I can't contain it. Guilt shreds every survival instinct into ribbons until it is all I can think about.

I clench my teeth so hard I'm surprised they don't shatter, and with trembling arms and a quaking chest, I spot Cyna standing in my peripheral vision.

I spin to face him, a sob heaving from my sore throat. I open my mouth, but the words are smothered by the overwhelming grief, pushing through any desire to ignore it, to bury it.

"You do not belong in this world, Calista," Cyna states, and I glare at him, every instinct in my body screaming at me to run as he strides forward, the grass crunching beneath his leather boots. His dark tunic is brought to life by the emeralds sewn around the corner, and his groomed, dark beard runs into his short, slicked-back hair.

"What do you mean?" A lump forms in my throat, and I try to swallow hard to remove it. Every breath is a labor, and I drop to my knees.

He crouches, his fingers curling around the knees of his black breeches. "You must accept your fate. Too many lives have been lost shielding you from it."

A thousand thoughts scatter through my mind. I steady my breathing, despite the guilt cutting into my mind like smothering smoke. "Who's lives? What fate?" I question, growing desperate for answers.

He leans closer, the smell of pine and polish emanating from his clothes. His moss-green eyes swirl, as if they contain an entire universe, and I am entranced. "You are a murderer."

"Yes," I reply, then slowly rise, finding strength despite the residual guilt shaking my bones. Cyna's mocking smile evokes contempt. "Why are you in my dream? What do you want with my sister?"

NIGHT OF DEATH AND FLOWERS

He tilts his head, then stands, towering over me. "It seems you're smarter than my brother. No wonder he is so taken with you."

My eyes widen. "You are mistaken. He hates me."

He doesn't look convinced. "Do you trust Death?"

I lick my lips, hesitant for a moment. "I trust him more than you," I admit, the hairs on the back of my neck standing on end. "Although you are *all* monsters."

His discerning stare travels down to my fingers. "No, it is *you* who are the monster," he spits, grimacing, and a low growl reverberates in his chest. I hold my breath as he grabs my arm, his fingernails cutting into my skin. I stare into his eyes, the green mixing with veins of red and gold. "For your sins, you will be dragged to the darkest reaches of the Darklands."

"You will never fucking awaken," I shout, and push his arm back, surprised that I have enough strength to wrestle myself free.

"Yes, we will and soon." His fingers uncurl, and he growls again. "Those you love will feel the cost of your darkness."

"No, you're trying to scare me. It won't work. I will not let you hurt my sister."

He steps back, challenge threading his eyes. "It has already begun. Death cannot keep you from us forever."

I jump when he lunges at me, stumbling backward. I grasp nothing but air as I fall again, the ground opening up into an abyss beneath me.

My eyes snap open as I'm jolted awake, gulping in a heavy breath as Cyna disappears from my mind, and the darkness dragging me deeper releases its hold on me.

"No!" I gasp, breathless, sitting upright.

"What's wrong?" Candlelight flickers over Ari's face as she slides into view. "You were having a nightmare," she announces, and that is a fucking understatement. Cautiously, she glides an old piece of fabric over my forehead, wiping away the beads of sweat.

I push her hand away, then brush my hair out of my face. "What time is it? Where is Azkiel?"

"He stepped outside a half hour ago. He refused to talk to us," she explains, and my muscles tense. I whip my head around to the window, and the impeding night outside. "But there is something else," she whispers, pulling me out of the hundreds of thoughts racing through my mind. "The gods spoke to me in my dreams." Her eyes widen under the orange hue of the candlelight, the madness in them still sparkling.

My heart stammers, rolling a wave of numbness from my head to the tip of my toes. "What?"

"They say they will return soon," she explains, a desperate hope etching her tone.

"No, Ari. You cannot listen to them."

"I must. They can save us all."

"They're monsters. Death says—"

"He is a liar," she snaps, then lowers her voice again. "They told me he would lie to us. Cali, he wants us to believe the other gods are evil. He trapped them here."

"I know, but it was for good reason," I say and stare at my sister, hugging the crimson, silk robes around her tiny, breakable body. "What else did they tell you?"

She smiles, pretending all our problems have been solved, but this is far worse than I could have imagined. "Nothing, except I should prepare myself."

I grab her forearms and she flinches. My wild eyes mirrored in her violet irises as I ask, "Did they say how?"

"No, why? What do you know?"

"Nothing," I lie, knowing she would sacrifice herself to keep us safe. I need to get her off this damned island before the gods can lure her to whoever is helping them, or Azkiel finds out who she is. I rub my fingers over my temples. Good gods. What the fuck are we doing to do?

Cyna's words float back to me. *Death cannot keep you from us forever.*

"Where is Drake?"

"He's gone to find water."

"With Death?" I ask, my jaw slacking. "No, no, no." I race past her, then down to the door, finding Azkiel standing in the night as if he belongs to it, with Drake nowhere to be seen.

TWENTY-EIGHT

Azkiel

Challenge pulsates through me as I listen to my mortal admonish me from the doorway of the house.

"Where's Drake? If you've hurt him, I swear to—"

"God?" I ask and bring my thumb to my lip, tilting my head as my amused smile grows wider.

"I mean it!" she shouts, and I take a step closer, her magic pulsating as a shadow threatens to escape her fingers.

Ah. She has them, too. The *possibilities.*

"I see you're back to your poisonous self," I say. "I was concerned when you were slightly less spiteful earlier."

"Bastard!" She looks around, then calls the boy's name into the rain-filled night. "Drake!"

"Calm yourself, Poison. The traitor walked into the forest an hour ago. Something about finding food and water. He's still alive. I can feel his broody energy from here."

Her eyes grow to almost twice their size. "He's out there alone?"

I close the distance between us, my lashes flickering when I notice her breath hitch. "Think about this way," I say, gliding a finger down her cheek, my stomach fluttering when she doesn't stop me. "If he dies, then you won't have to feel guilty about killing him so your sister can win. It will be out of your hands."

She hesitates, only for a second, then bats my hand away. Her finger jabs into my chest and she hisses through clenched teeth, "Just because you have never loved, it doesn't mean love does not exist. If he dies, I will blame you."

"Why?"

"You put him in here!"

"He is a traitor. You both are. What did you expect me to do? Let him off with a slap on the wrist."

She lifts her chin, her elbow brushing against the V of my lower abdomen. "It was my idea."

"I don't think so," I say and tuck a finger under her chin. "Even so, I cannot kill you, but I can punish him. Just admit it, Poison, it will be a relief if he's dead. You know they can't both survive."

She holds me in her gaze, her breaths uneven as she balls a fist. "What way did Drake go?"

I tsk. "If you go to find him, you leave your sister here, alone, and at the mercy of the other sacrifices." I lower my voice to a whisper, then glance around at the trees, bushes, and long vines of thorns. "They're everywhere, just waiting for their opportunity."

"I assume you're not going to help," she states, correctly, her lip twitching.

"I'd rather watch it all unfold. It's far more interesting."

She huffs out a breath, her cheeks reddening. "So, you'll watch us suffer, just because you're starved for entertainment." Her icy stare doesn't leave mine. "Although that's not all you're starved for."

She angles her body closer, unaware of my shadows caressing around her figure, heightening against her pulsing magic.

My fingers wrap around the back of her neck as she gulps in a deep breath, and I wrench her closer, leaning down until her lips are just inches from mine. "If you think you can use how I can touch you against me again. You are wrong. I'm past that."

The lie falls so easily from my tongue, and I watch as she bites her lip, the smell of her confusing my senses.

"Liar," she whispers.

I drink her in, my lips parting as my cock hardens in my pants. Shadows dance up the sides of her hips, holding her in place.

With every glide of her fingers over my chest, my shadows purr under her touch. Her lips are so achingly close.

"I hate you," she breathes, her voice wavering.

A low roar rumbles in my chest as the curve of her chin dips against mine.

I growl back, "I despise you too, Poison."

Her fingernails cut through the fabric of my tunic, scraping against my bare chest. A deep groan emanates from my lips, and my eyelids half-closed.

Cyna's magic seeps into me, tightening around my brain like a band as Calista's eyes darken into inky pools. Her grip on me tightens, her body squirming against mine, and it takes every ounce of will for me not to taste her, just once.

She's so fucking close.

My stomach is a hollow space filled with fluttering as tendrils of green magic reach into me, searching through my memories. Glints of gray from the Ash War, the darkness of death, and the muted colors of the Darklands carousel in my mind.

With every flicker of memory, they slip away. Then, a vision sparks—merely a glimpse.

An image of my temple on Tenenocti Island from one hundred and fifty years ago.

I hold on to the memory, the aura of the vision framed in crimson. This must have been the last time my siblings and I were in the same room together. I watch as Cyna restrains me along with Volan, and Essentria walks to an altar holding two women, one of whom is dead. Essentria's hands carve into the living woman, tearing apart her ribcage.

Cyna's laugh tinkers into my mind, and Astraea wraps her arms around me.

My fingers twitch to push Calista away, but an unexpected connection holds me to her, something so primal and dark, yet comforting.

No.

I fist her hair, then pull her backward, slipping out her hold. "How dare you use my *brother's* magic on me!"

"I had to know if you were telling the truth."

I pause briefly, then slowly lick my dry lips, recalling the details of the memory. How did she access my mind like that? I've spent decades trying to recall my memories. Yet, when I touch her, I can feel them drifting back to me, the clues of my muddied past and why everything ended the way it did.

"I felt your pain," she whispers.

"Don't," I warn, then glide my fingers down to the back of her neck, running the tips over goosebumps pricked over her skin.

"Who were the two dead women?"

"Sacrifices, I think."

I can barely catch my breath when she says, "You don't remember."

I shake my head, reliving the memory. My brothers were holding me back. I must have been trying to stop the ritual, to stop whatever curse Essentria wanted to enact. Likely on me.

"Nyxara stole my memories, but when I touch you," I say, running my shadows over her. "I see glimpses."

"Essentria killed one of them."

"Do you believe me now, Poison?"

"Yes," she whispers, her nails digging into my arms, and sparks fly through my skin.

"If you use Cyna's magic against me again," I warn, spitting his name like venom. "I will hurt you."

She holds her breath, then glances down at the bulge in my pants, dragging her teeth over her bottom lip, noticing the effect she has on me.

"Cali?" The traitor's voice breaks the spell, and my shadows retreat from her. "What are you doing?"

"Nothing," she blurts out, placing several feet between us.

I cast a glance at the boy, my lips curving into a smile, as I watch him practically vibrate with rage. "Go inside, traitor. We're in the middle of something."

His jaw slacks, gazing at Cali.

She shakes her head, glaring at me while curling and uncurling her fingers. "We are not in the middle of *anything*," she hisses, her cheeks flushing pink, then turns to Drake. "I was looking for you."

"That's not what it looked like," he mumbles as my shadows poise to attack. "Never mind. It's not like I can do anything about it."

"You're right. Now *go inside*," I command.

"Don't leave," Cali states. "We're done here."

He tsks. "I'll leave you to it. Clearly, his vile magic has tainted your brain."

"What? Drake!" Calista calls as he pushes past us. She tries to follow him, but I grab her wrist before she can reach the door, then curl her back into my embrace.

Her back lands against my torso, and I lower my whisper to her earlobe. "I should kill him for that comment." I run my hands around her waist, surprised when she sinks into my arms.

"He's right," she says.

"Your magic is beautiful," I purr, shockwaves throbbing through my length as her chest heaves. My fingers trickle over the front of her dress, tracing lower, until I hit my mark. "Do you feel that?" I ask, dragging the shadows from her core before they slip out of her fingers, caressing me. "You're more powerful than you realize."

Her head flops back against my chest, her neck exposed, and I bring my lips to them, scraping my teeth over her delicate skin. Lust consumes me as she backs into me, the scent of her arousal driving me to the edge of madness.

"Stop," she says as my lips travel lower, tasting her sweat against my tongue. Her body stiffens, her shadows forming a dance of illusory swirls around us. "I hate you."

"You said that already," I murmur against her throat.

NIGHT OF DEATH AND FLOWERS

She gasps for air; her shadows a flurry of glittering darkness as mine ribbon from my hands, fusing with hers.

"I'm not powerful," she divulges, vulnerability cracking in her voice. "I was useless against Edwardo. I've been a fucking liability, and your magic depleted the moment I needed it to kill Rourne."

"That was me. My siblings took their powers back, and it weakened me temporarily."

Her shadows quake, burrowing deeper as she loses confidence in our power. "Nonetheless," she says. "I was useless against Edwardo, even with my powers."

I whip my head around as footsteps shuffle from within the trees. Someone's watching us. I close my eyes, sensing their racing hearts and their magic—*my magic*.

"Someone's here," I whisper as two figures emerge. They halt upon seeing me, and Calista backs toward the house, her instinct to protect her loved ones igniting.

They stare from the tree line, sharing hushed whispers when they see me. Their panicked gulps widen my grin. "Come out," I order, and the older boy pushes the girl in front of him. *Coward*.

"We, uh, did not know you were here, God of Death," she says, her stare passing from me to Calista, confliction wrinkling her soft, tanned features.

"I will not stop you," I say, my voice booming. "Go ahead."

The girl hesitates and the boy steps up beside her. "W—we don't—I mean, you are, and well we are," she splutters, unable to finish a fucking thought.

"Finish them," I command, and the pair straighten their posture. "Or you do not deserve my power."

Calista glares at me, slack jawed.

I step back as they approach the house, and I lean against a tree, my eyes alight as Calista's magic bubbles over, searing hot in her veins. Her energy tornadoes my powers from here, still fused together.

I catch one last glance before she turns to Briar, her shadows poised like vipers.

Good girl. Now let's see what you can do.

TWENTY-NINE

Calista

What the fuck was I thinking, letting Death get so close? Allowing him to run his fingers over me…

I hold my breath at the thought, anger seething into my veins like liquid fire. My thighs clench against my desire, humiliation spreading through me.

I shoot him a venomous glare as he casually leans against a tree, as if our lives aren't in danger. So much for not letting me die here.

Shadows ripple in and out of me as Briar and Cordelia get closer. I stand firm, blocking the path to the house.

"Is this some kind of trick?" The wind whips at my face as Briar steps forward. "You killed the girl in the boat," he states, then glances back at Azkiel, gulping. "You hold an ethereal power."

A loud caw sounds from the branches above, and a flash or iridescent, ebony feathers flap toward us. Neither of them notices when my crow lands on the vine-strangled path behind them.

I clear my throat, decay magic sliding into my fingertips. "Why don't you come closer and find out?"

"We're good here," he says, and Cordelia nods, her huntress eyes narrowing on me. "Where are you friends? Too scared to come out?"

Azkiel chortles from behind them, and I clench my teeth so hard I'm surprised they don't shatter.

I jolt when a hand lands on my arm, and I turn my head to see Drake, his breaths heavy. He looks at Azkiel, then whispers, "I told you not to trust him."

"Maybe focus on *them*," I hiss, turning in time to see shadows whip from Briar's body in ribbons that slash through the air before winding around Drake's body.

He screams under the constriction, his body writhing. "No!"

My magic uncoils from my core, and with each slice of darkness erupting from my hands in an uncontrollable net, the path beneath us vibrates.

My vision darkens as the ropes of night wrap around Cordelia, dragging her closer. I ready my fingers, when Arabella's footsteps sound behind me.

Thorn takes flight, his wings batting the surrounding air, then lands on a fallen dresser to the left of the entrance.

My heart hammers as I turn to make sure Ari's okay, and I'm forced through the front door and into the foyer of the abandoned house by Cordelia. I lunge at her before she can speak, reaching for the ends of her dark hair and forcing her body to crouch over.

My magic pulses through my fingers as the locks crumble to ash, but my powers do not reach her skin. She jumps back as I twist my body, unsheathing the dagger, then launching the blade toward her abdomen.

She's nimble, fast, and evades my attempt to get closer.

I almost drop the blade when I watch her eyes darken into a deep crimson. Magic leaks from her sockets in blood, dancing into the air in tendrils of smoke. I gasp when the magic reaches my forehead, seeping into my skin.

"Cali!" Ari's panicked tone reaches me through a swarm of nightmares, building into a crescendo.

Drake's heavy grunts sound outside. My eyes clamp shut, but a blinding light pierces my lids as I assume Drake has conjured an illusion to counteract Briar's shadows.

"Stop," I shout as my deepest fears are unearthed, pulled mercilessly from a buried part of myself. Visions of Arabella falling to a pile of ash screech into every thought—my sister, dead, at my hand.

The decay magic guides Cordelia's power, the darkness enveloping my soul, craving more power. Bloodlust singes each thought, as if it was a part of who I am—a destroyer of everything good.

It starts with a heaviness settling in my head, pounding in my temples. Isolda's mental resistance magic pulls at Cordelia's, like an elastic band that may snap at any moment.

Ari's footsteps pound past me as my eyes fling open, the visions fizzing into nothing.

Cordelia's lips part, her crimson eyes bulging. Her arms drop to her sides, a slight shake to her head as she stares at me. "How…"

I have never been so grateful for Volan's power.

A shadow is cast over the moonlight, as Ari forces her way past Cordelia.

I stumble backwards, falling back against the cold bricks with a thud, as a massive root bursts through the doorway and window. I barely cover my eyes as glass shatters around the small entranceway. A hiss escapes my lips as tiny shards shred my bare arms and chest.

Cordelia shakes her head as Ari steps into the room. "We were told you're nothing but a healer."

"I *was*," she states, then raises her trembling fingers, her gaze locking onto the vines uncurling from the large, brown root taking up half the space. She twists her fingers, manipulating the plant like a skilled puppeteer.

Blood seeps from Cordelia's eyes, twirling in the air toward Ari. Her fear induction magic caresses the vines, close to touching my sister's face, when it halts.

Drake falls backward through the door as Cordelia drops to her knees, mouth parting. My eyes widen as I drop my stare to Cordelia's abdomen, and the large, thorny vine sticking out of it.

A second vine whips toward her, wrapping around her throat, then a third burrows into her chest. Her scream rattles the room, and Thorn squawks, his wings flapping, panicked as he flies to me, then perches somewhere beside me. Hot, wet blood splatters over my face, gown, and the floorboards.

The thorns from the vines latch onto the skin before the vine is released, tearing chunks of flesh with it.

My hand claps over my mouth as I witness Ari's darkening eyes and the tears that accompany each action. "Oh, gods," she exclaims, the color leaving my sister's face. "I should save her. I should—"

"Don't," I command, my fingers reaching Cordelia's arm before the light flickers from her eyes. The moment my fingers graze Cordelia's skin, her bones crumble, her body crumples into a large, sifting pile of ash.

A gust of wind catches it, sweeping her remains over the ground, the rest of her slowly falling through the cracks in the floorboards. Ari stares at her blood covered hands. "I killed her."

"No," I say, breathlessly. "*I* did."

I run toward Drake and Briar, but halt when we're plunged into a prison of darkness.

I fumble through the shadows, absorbing any light. Thorn's squawk races my heart, as a second shrill, pained sound leaves his beak.

Drake yells, and Ari shrieks. My eyes widen, panic rolling through me in waves as I'm immobile, unable to know what direction to go in. A pungent tower of pollen erupts into the room, followed by a burst of choking and spluttering coughs.

Someone's hand finds my arm, tugging me back into the wall. A mixture of fear and desire tightens around my core, as the shadowy sickness of magic twists and curls, ready to break out of me.

Waving my arms, I swipe at the fog of dark gray and black, coughing as the pollen clogs my airways.

Briar's shadows consume, the pollen suffocating as we are trapped, attempting to claw our way out of the room. The house shudders around us, the foundations trembling under the building pressure of powers.

"Keep down," Ari shouts, her voice cracked in place as she splutters again. I hide my nose and mouth under the fabric of my dress, then kick away from the wall.

Just as the darkness fades, and a creeping clarity overcomes the blindness we were submitted to, Briar's shadows warp into shapes—some becoming bats, others ravens. All of them swarm at us.

A small, orange flower draws my attention to my right, and recognition floods my mind. Nocturnum Somnus, known for inducing a comatose-like state in those who ingest copious amounts.

Sitting up, my eyes widen as these flowers are now spread all around us, saturating the house with pollen. The tickle at the back of my nose increases, and I sneeze.

"Ari, stop," I splutter as the room spins around me and a trance-like euphoria captures me.

It must be her. If she continues, we will all fall into a temporary slumber.

My mind whirls as I try to steady myself, breathing only into the fabric of my dress. Then a howl pierces the air, and the shadow ravens fizzle into nothing.

I struggle to my feet, crawling until I find Briar, slumped by the door, shadows pouring from his hands.

I'm over him, my body pressed against his as I scramble for this throat, decay leaking from my fingers and into his neck.

A scream rips through his lips, tears welling up in his eyes, knowing he's lost. Flesh hangs from his bones as they cave inward, then each limb dissolves in on itself until his body is nothing but ash.

The shadows dissipate along with the pollen, some settling on the floorboards in a sticky yellow. Ari drops to the ground, her head smacking against the dresser in a heart-stopping thud. Drake falls to his knees, shallow gasps swirling through his parted lips, and I spot Thorn, his wings twitching as he lies on his back.

"Get out," I splutter, breathing into the fabric of my dress. Ari crawls out the door first, followed by Drake, who collapse on the path.

The night air fills my lungs as I fall out behind them, then cough until my lungs feel as if they may implode.

Ari rubs the side of her head. "What happened?"

"The pollen," I splutter. "Nocturnum Somnus, it can induce a comatose state. Fortunately, the pollen's effects are temporary. Is everyone okay?"

My heart leaps when I see Thorn, his bluish-gray wings splattered in crimson. I stumble to my feet, then run to his side, placing my hand against his body. He twists his neck to look at me, but he's weak, barely moving.

My sister may have nature inducement magic, but it is far more deadly when she doesn't know what plants she's using. I must teach her when she wins.

The idea of home lingers as I pull Thorn into my arms. It's like a childish dream now. I can't return, not after I made the deal with Death. Even if Ari wins, Drake won't.

Azkiel's footsteps sound as he leaves the building. When did he enter? I crane my neck to look at him, as he towers over me, hand extended.

"You!" I growl and take his hand. As soon as I'm standing, I slam my fists into his chest repeatedly, my fists taking a battering from his hard muscles. He took advantage of me earlier, just like everyone else, and now he mocks me. "You fucking bastard. I am never fucking help you, you—"

"Monster?" he offers, unmoved by my fists. "Asshole?"

This time, my fist connects with his jaw. "Both!"

He wipes the blood with his thumb, dragging it down his chin with an unhinged grin. "Now you know how powerful your magic is." He looks as if he's enjoying himself far too much, and I go to hit him again, but he stops my punch with an effortless block of his hand. "No one died."

"They did!" I point at Cordelia and Briar.

"Good. Don't you want your sister to win?"

I shake my hand, looking at Ari and Drake. "They can barely stand."

He shrugs. "Isn't that one a healer?"

My jaw clenches. "She is too weak to heal right now."

Ari coughs, then rolls onto her side before whispering, "The river is close. You can make a potion, right, Cali?"

"Looks like I have no choice." I turn to face Death. "You're not coming with us. Our deal is over."

THIRTY

Calista

We leave for the river alone. Ari hangs her arms over me and Drake, walking in between us. I carry Thorn in my other arm, then look back at Azkiel for the last time, nausea rolling in waves as the residual adrenaline runs through my body.

Gods, I am so fucking embarrassed. I never want to see him again. I'm getting Ari away from this damn forest, even if it means dragging her to the caverns while I hunt down the rest of the sacrifices myself.

Sacrifices. The word stings my mind. How quickly I have forgotten what I stand for. It wasn't Briar's or Cordelia's fault. They were products of the elders and, by extension, Death.

I focus ahead as we stumble toward the babbling river. The first rays of dawn peek through the interwoven branches, casting enchanting shadows over the rippling water. A soft mist clings to the air, and the subtle fragrance of rain and decaying foliage permeates the area.

I carefully lower Thorn on the embankment, and he quickly perches himself upright. I tilt my head, examining his injuries. He has a minor cut to his wing, but not other noticeable damage. Gently, I press around his body, watching for signs of pain, but he doesn't jolt.

At least the shadows didn't constrict him too hard, and there are no broken bones. His weakness is likely from fending off the shadow ravens born from Briar's magic. "I'll fix your wing," I promise, then stand.

"I'll keep watch," Drake states coldly, barely saying a word since what happened.

"Drake..."

NIGHT OF DEATH AND FLOWERS

He walks toward the old, worn-out bridge, then lands his hand on the tatters of rope.

"Fine," I mumble under my breath.

Ari runs her hands over her arms, fending off the brisk gusts of wind. Her arms are littered with small cuts, matching my own. I head towards the river in search of the vine-stricken, root-covered ground the plants we need usually grow, but my attention is drawn to a cluster of Death's Bells by the water.

The hunched, long stems expand from pointed, purple leaves. Each stem holds a layer of dusky purple flowers that appear like tiny bells, releasing a subtle, musky, floral scent.

If I combine these flowers—infamous for its curative properties—and find some Sanare Medicis root, I can crush them together to form a healing paste. However, the root grows in the depths of riverbanks, and that means dipping my hands into the waters.

I draw nearer to the edge and gaze into the river, a dark mirror that reflects the hauntingly beautiful trees and bare branches intertwining overhead that create a contorted ribcage encasing the area.

 The calm surface ripples as spectral hands of the vengeful spirits that lurk beneath break the waters, then retreat. Within the depths of darkness, a tapestry of faces floats just under the surface, looking at me with their fish-eaten eyes, and mouths agape into a silent scream.

I imagine them, those who have died in shipwrecks or drowned during a Harvest, dragged under the Black Sea, lungs bursting, their souls forever lost to Death's domain.

I jump when I glance to my side, noticing Ari leaning over the edge, her body quaking with sobs as she desperately tries to rinse the blood from her hands and arms.

"Get away from there." I race to her side, my knees landing on the damp soil of the riverbank. "This river runs from the Black Sea. The waters are brimming with the dead," I say and pull her back, but she wrestles my hold, then stares at her hands.

Drake whips his head to look at us from the bridge, but I quickly nod before he leaves his post to see what the stir is about. The bridge offers the best visibility into the forest and to the other side of the river, giving him a good vantage point should anyone try to sneak up on us.

Ari sighs, then whispers, "Edwardo's power is darker than I expected, even though we're in the same coven," she admits, then squeezes her eyes shut. "He used nature manipulation magic offensively, likely since he first inherited it."

Decay magic sizzles into my fingertips, reacting to her heartache as she slowly loses herself to the dark magic. "I know the feeling." I hide my hands, then rock backwards, sitting on the back of my legs.

"Father will come," she says, her voice laced with a tired hope. Slowly, she rises to her feet, then tears the red silk robes from her body, revealing her pink dress underneath. The robes land in the river in a ripple of crimson, as she discards the blood-stained clothes to the night. "If not them, then the gods."

I shake my head. "You dream of them still?"

"Yes," she whispers, but doesn't elaborate.

"What do they tell you?"

"Nothing of importance," she states, although I don't believe her. There's no chance of her opening up, not when she's barely processing all of what's happened. My heart gallops as I watch her eyes darken.

"Tell me, Ari."

"They just keep saying to prepare."

I grind my teeth. "You cannot listen to them. I used my Sight magic on Azkiel. He's telling the truth. They're evil, and they want you dead."

She shakes her head. "Azkiel manipulated you, forcing you to see what he wanted you to see. You've grown too fond of him."

"Sight magic doesn't work like that, and I can assure you, I have not grown fond of him."

Her worried eyes find mine. "Drake told me you two were almost kissing outside the house."

"That will never happen again. It's the magic," I explain, the powers thrumming into a deep rumble. "Lay down for a moment," I offer as she rocks backward. "I'll be done soon."

"You can't work like this. Your arms are covered in cuts."

"I'm fine. Really."

She raises her brows. "You're not, and it's not just the cuts. This magic takes a toll." She glances out over the riverbed, then takes a few steps back, finding a clear spot under a tree only a few feet from me. "I wonder how Father managed it. I hold only two powers, yet I feel as if I am going to explode."

I lower my voice to a whisper. "We both hold an ethereal power from the gods. I think they somehow enhance the other powers inside of us. It's why the magic we've siphoned from the fallen affects us so much. It must be."

"Perhaps." She gazes off, lost in thought, then rests her head on her arm. "I'll lie down just for a minute."

"Drake's keeping watch," I assure her, and she closes her eyes.

Once I've done a quick sweep of the area, I kneel beside the river, my fingers buried in the thick mud in search of the root.

NIGHT OF DEATH AND FLOWERS

I delve further into the mud and water; the tips of my hair floating against the surface as I ensure the rest of me stays on dry ground.

I huff a breath, sweat beading my brows as I hit a rock. If only I can dislodge this damned stone.

Pain radiates through my hand as something sharp jabs under my nail. I curse under my breath, pulling away, then kick the ground as if it is purposely thwarting my plans. I resume my search with new vigor, my arms aching as the wind gushes against me, sweeping over the slices in the sleeves of my dress, stinging the wounds beneath.

Finally, I pull out the roots of the plant, then tug them onto the bank. It takes several minutes to ground them into a paste along with the Death's Bell flowers in a stone bowl we brought from the house.

I groan when the thick paste turns purple, instead of the paler beige needed.

The morning lightens a shade, and the silhouettes of the trees and shadows of ravens on their branches surround me. Small creatures watch me beyond the babbling waters as I kneel against the mossy mattress.

Something moves in my periphery, and my eyes dart to the underbrush just as a black tail with blue markings disappears into a hollow log. A hiss sounds behind me, followed by a rustle of dead leaves while a shadow viper slithers closer.

I turn my head slowly, my heart pounding as adrenaline courses through me. The snake's eyes lock on me, and I look at Ari. She's still sleeping. Oh, gods. Out of all the things I may die from, it cannot be this.

The small, deadly creature rises on its long body, standing a foot tall, poised to attack. I brace myself to run, hoping I might get away before it strikes. But, before I can stand, the creature inches closer, and I freeze.

Spotting movement out of the corner of my eye, my gaze snaps to the forest where I glimpse white robes and a blond braid. As the viper launches at me, realization dawns on me that someone must be controlling the creature.

My scream is quickly silenced as I am pulled under.

The murky depths envelop me as the dead hands curl around my neck and arms, constrained by the fingers of the Black Sea's spirits.

Time stretches painfully as I wrestle against the dead, every movement draining the last reserves of my energy. My body releases a surge of shadows that twist and turn through the water, ensnaring the spirits and binding their limbs. But there are too many.

NIGHT OF DEATH AND FLOWERS

The spirits writhe around me, their frigid, rotting hands grip my arms and legs, dragging me deeper until my lips part. I kick my legs, my shadows a dizzying mess when I hit the riverbed. Bubbles leave my mouth as my lungs ache under the pressure, my eyes bulging.

I barely notice when the dead release me, and I float upward. My eyes close against the permeating darkness of the dark river, memories of my loved ones spin in my mind: discovering our first book of spells with Ari when I was nine, stolen from Father's library, playing in the meadow with Cecilia and Eliana, then hiding behind trees as we played hide and seek, and the afternoons of walking through the woods with Drake, talking for hours.

Arms constrict my waist and water whooshes around my torso as I'm pulled out the water.

Feeling returns to my fingers and toes, and I cough until I'm spluttering and wheezing, adrenaline coursing through my veins.

I peel my eyelids back to reveal Azkiel's face. Wet, silver strands slather against his forehead, water drops dripping from his parted lips. "Breathe, Poison," he urges through the haze in my mind from the lack of air.

Dregs of air slide into my throat as I struggle in a breath, my lungs feeling as if they're going to burst. Azkiel's hold on me tightens as he sweeps an arm under my limp legs, the other firm around my back. Scooping me up, he walks us out of the river. My back lands gently against the cold ground, and I turn onto my side, water spilling from my freezing lips.

Of course Death looks so worried. He can't have me dying on this island when he thinks I'm the prophesied one.

Azkiel growls under his breath as he looks around. "An elder was here."

Drake is at my side in a heartbeat, careful not to touch me as Azkiel slathers the paste I made over my arms, but it won't do much since it's not finished.

"Cali, can you hear us?"

"Yes," I splutter, then sit up, looking around, my fingers clutching the fabric of my dress. "You said an elder was... Where's Ari?" I ask, when I notice she's not lying where I left her.

"It was Dephina," Drake explains, clamping his eyes shut. "She was in the trees, and then she took Ari."

"What?" I shout, and crawl onto all fours, coughing again until my throat is coarse. "Why didn't you stop her?"

His expression crumples. "You fell in the river, and they were already gone. You could have died." The sun glints in his eyes, and I'm reminded of the boy I have been friends with since I was a child. "Then Death came."

Azkiel isn't listening, his eyes scanning the trees, an ancient blackness stealing the silver from his irises. "Where's Thorn?"

"He flew away," Drake answers.

I fold onto my knees, my head in my palms. "We must save Ari. They're going to sacrifice her. If Dephina is here, then—"

Azkiel's tone teeters on dangerous when he booms, "What do you mean *she* will be sacrificed?"

I close my eyes. *Fuck.* If I tell Death he'll try to kill her later after getting her off Tenenocti, but the gods may kill her *now*. Dephina must have been the one to move the bodies.

"Ari's the prophesied one," I blurt, and take Drake's arm to steady myself as I stand upright. "She always was, and you picked her at The Choosing, just like the other gods wanted."

THIRTY-ONE

Azkiel

The air feels different by the time we arrive back at the house, as if the island is charged with a new current of bloodlust.

Calista blocks my path before I can veer into the forest without her, arms crossed over the swells of her breasts outlined under the wet fabric slicked to her body. Droplets cascade from a few tendrils of hair curled around her forehead. "We're going with you."

"You will only slow me down," I reply, circling around her, but her hand lands on my arm.

"She is my sister. I need to find her."

I hear the traitor's footsteps behind me, then silencing a short distance away. I can't wait to watch the useless boy die. If I hadn't stalked them to the river, then Calista would be dead.

So many words build in my mind when I look at her, holding onto me with fierce determination. "I said no."

Her nostrils flare, and she licks the river from her lips. "You cannot hurt her. We can find another way to stop the prophecy. Not all fates are written in stone! They can be changed."

She sounds like me, a week ago. Yet, every time I believe I've out-maneuvered Nyxara, another revelation unfolds. All paths end with their awakening, except for death. It is the only thing that is permanent.

"How do you know it's your sister?" I ask, a question I should have asked at the river, but the bloom of anger swelling in my chest stole all rational thought. If it's true, then it doesn't explain why she exists—a woman with my decay magic.

Calista lifts her chin, then runs her hands down to her hips, my eyes following the trail. "Ari has Essentria's ethereal magic."

"How do I know you are not lying?" I lean closer, then hiss, "With that venomous tongue of yours."

The sound of her teeth grinding gruel in my ears. "You don't, but are you willing to take that chance?"

I bite my tongue, then grab her wrist. "Have it your way. You're staying with me until I know which sister to kill."

The boy races to her side, like the good lap dog he is. "Let her go."

"Speak again, and I'll tear your tongue out."

"Drake, back off," Calista snaps, harsher than expected, quenching the murderous thirst toward the traitor. "I want to go so shut up and come with us or stay here."

"You're taking his side?"

"He is a god!" Calista shouts. "An asshole, yes, but he can actually save her."

She's chastising *him*? Shock roots me to the spot, and I release my grip on her, then clear my throat. "I'm going to the temple."

"Alone?" Calista asks slowly, disappointment etching in her face.

"Keep up," I say and walk into the forest ahead of her. "Or I'll leave you behind."

I pause by a tall, narrow graywar tree, the scent of lavender perfume lingering over the bark, the same smell left in the trees after she snatched the sister right under my nose.

I've watched mortals die in the most imaginative of ways over centuries, but Dephina's will be spectacular. They must have headed to my temple. There are altars there from when those who inhabited this island performed human sacrifices.

"Why did we sto—"

"Quiet," I command, then close my eyes. First, I must make sure.

The island is a blur as I sift through animals on Tenenocti, scrying into their minds, temporarily melding with them. I observe the wilds of the forest through the perspective of a viper, silently maneuvering through the foliage in search of its next meal. My mind links with the creature, then another, but the viewpoint is too limited.

My magic surges, flying me high into the sky as my consciousness connects with a crow. I witness the sprawling labyrinth of tangled vines and towering foliage, concealing the remnants of a society long gone. In the distance, I spot one of the sacrifices walking into a building on the east of the island, far from us. However, it is not the sister.

After several minutes of circling, I command my powers back to the island, and my mind melds with a spider, skittering across intricate, rain-stricken webs spun between ancient ruins. Weathered by the passing of time, crumbling stone structures stand tall, reminiscent of a time I can barely remember, but that remains entrenched in heartache and regret.

After searching, glimpsing visions of the inside of the temple in search of Arabella or the elders, I retreat and open my eyes, back in my body.

"What was that?" the boy asks, remaining quiet until now. His hand remains on the dagger on his belt, as if it'd do any good.

"Animal scrying," Calista answers before I can. If I wasn't so focused, so angry, I'd praise her observational skills. She turns to me. "Did you find them?"

"No."

"Did you check the temple?"

"Only a few rooms. The perspectives of animals are limited," I explain.

"Well, try again, and this time focus on the rooms she could hide in."

"It doesn't work like that," I bite out. "Do you have any idea how long it would take me to find her through the eyes of a spider? Days, Poison. The temple has many rooms. There is still a strong chance they're there."

Cali huffs at the condescension in my tone and brings her hand to her throat, grazing a finger over her clavicle. "Let us not waste more time, then."

A wave of panic ripples around us, but Calista is oblivious. Footsteps pound in my ears, and I whip my head to the left.

"Someone is running in our direction."

Darkness seeps into my hands, my power vibrating through my body as I prepare for the chase. As the girl comes into view, her brown eyes widen when she sees us.

Calista's touch jolts electricity through me, as her fingers entwine around my wrist. "It's Elenore," she states. "Whatever you are considering doing, don't."

The girl runs to Calista, tears streaming down her face, twigs and skeletal leaves sticking out of her curls. I breathe in the scent of blood, and my eyes trickle to the girl's stomach, and the dark crimson seeping through her robes.

The girl looks me up and down, and my nostrils flare at her tears. "Help me," she pleads, then crumples to the ground.

The boy reaches the girl, then drops to his knees beside her. She lies on the ground, grasping at her stomach.

"Who hurt you?" I boom. "Was it an elder? Tell me!"

The traitor covers the girl with his arms, as if to shield her from me.

Rage splits through every pore as I glare at him, wondering if I could gauge his eyes from his face before my touch turned him to ash. My sudden interest must have been apparent on my face, because he quickly averts his eyes.

Calista frowns. "Leave her alone. She's dying!"

"That's what people do, Poison." I force my way to their side. "Who stabbed you, girl?"

"Alaric," she cries, and I groan under my breath. Her eyes roll around as her lids close, a cold sweat forming against her forehead.

"Leave her," I command, but they lift her robes, then tear her dress beneath it, revealing her bloodied abdomen.

"I'm not going anywhere. She lives close to our house. I'm not going to leave her to die alone."

I glance down, exhaling slowly as I assess the sacrifice's blanched face. She's lost too much blood. "You can't save her."

Something changes in Calista's eyes before she gazes down at the girl. "I'm going to help you."

The last moments of a mortal's life are the most private and intrusive of times, where one can glimpse a mortal's true self. But Calista doesn't seem to care. Instead, she runs a hand over the girl's forehead, slicking away the sweat, and pushing back some stray strands bouncing over the sacrifice's eyes.

"It's okay," Cali says with a softness I've not heard before. "You're going to be okay. The pain will go away soon."

I watch as the girl concedes to death, her muscles relaxing as decay magic seeps into her bones, ash consuming her until she is gone.

"She was barely eighteen," she says, her voice croaky, bloodshot eyes narrowed on me. "A child!"

I shake my head. "She reminded you of your sister, that is all," I say, recalling their similar, soft features. "We cannot waste time."

"This," she states, her shaky tone increasing an octave, as she points at the sacrifice's body, "is the reality of your disgusting tournament."

"Your sister's death will be your reality unless you pull yourself together."

"You let us almost die back there." She shakes her head, then pushes past me. "You put my sister on this island, and you have still failed."

"I helped you! I showed you that you are not powerless."

She scoffs. "Is that what that was? Because you sure seemed to enjoy the show."

"Think me the villain," I say. "I do not care."

"Good, because that makes two of us."

THIRTY-TWO

Calista

We cut our way through thickets of vines and bramble and follow Death into the forest. My boots crunch over pieces of bone, either from an animal or a person.

We walk over the uneven, mossy mattress, to the bridge over the river. Then, he leads into another slice of forest.

NIGHT OF DEATH AND FLOWERS

I should feel guilty for shouting at Drake, but it's so hard to do so when he didn't go after Ari. He knows me well enough to know I would never want him to choose my life over my sister's.

Then there's Azkiel, who made me feel something for a moment. It was just lust, nothing more, but he used that to lure me close. I withhold the urge to sink my dagger into his chest, only because he's my best chance at finding Ari.

Drake's whisper carries into my ear. "I'm sorry. Truly. I didn't think Death would save you, and I couldn't let you die."

An eerie silence settles over the trees as we carve our path toward Azkiel's temple. "We will talk later."

As I cast my eyes around the maze of trees, a sense of doom washes over me. In the distance, waves crash from the river separating the island and us.

Every aching, tired bone in my body was no match for the adrenaline coursing through my veins, pushing me to keep going despite the heaviness of my recently acquired magic. Unlike the decay magic, my newfound powers rebel inside of me, refusing to submit to its new owner.

Eleanore. Isolda. Cordelia. Briar. Rourne. I list their names together for the first time, then add in Edwardo, and whoever else was killed by Edwardo. The townspeople sing songs of the fallen of each Harvest, the elders wearing the names as a badge of honor.

I imagine Ari's name, or Drake's included in sonnets or odes, and my heart stammers.

"We'll find her," Drake whispers, as if he can feel my panic. I've felt so distant from him since arriving here—the island of fucking terrors.

I hold on to the hope that Ari is alive. Surely, if she died, Azkiel would have felt it. He told me he could sense the dead, and this is his domain. While he doesn't fully believe she is the chosen one, he won't take the chance of her dying. I should have gotten her away before The Choosing. We could all be on a ship right now to another land, even one filled with non-magical humans who want to kill us. We could have hidden, or even gone to the mountain courts in Dahryst.

I'm responsible for Ari. We were closer when we were younger, and we would sneak into our mother's room to pretend we made potions with her imported perfumes. Mother would get so mad, but her anger was worth it. Those memories keep the darkness of my magic at bay.

I turn hastily, following Death as he makes a sharp turn into yet more forest.

I seldom pray, but now, having confirmed that what I knew was true—that the gods are evil—I am suddenly aware of how comforting prayer was in the difficult moments. Because whenever I was alone and afraid, there was something soothing about asking a higher power for strength. Even after I stopped believing they were good, I wasn't certain, and that glimmer of hope that I was wrong gave me a reason to keep fighting.

As I play a tug of war with my conscience, a twig hits me in the face as I attempt to push through a narrow overgrowth. An unexpected laugh escapes my lips, and Drake's eyes widen. Azkiel pauses for half a second before continuing to walk, and I slap my hand over my mouth. Why the fuck did I laugh? There is nothing humorous about this at all, yet the irony and amusement of it all plasters a smile over my lips.

Great, I've lost my fucking mind.

Azkiel's voice slices through the silence, his tone as smooth as the shadows clinging to him. "You're dehydrated," he states, explaining my sudden outburst.

My brows furrow, and I'm suddenly very aware of how dry my mouth is. I dart my tongue between my cracking lips, then attempt to swallow, but only the tiniest bit of saliva coats my throat. "I'll find water soon."

Drake only shoots me an incredulous look as we keep walking, his eyes sweeping over Azkiel's cloak clinging to me. My calves burn by the time we finally reach the temple, transcendent amongst groves of thick vegetation.

Drake halts next to me, his jaw slacked as we take in the towering, stone pillars reaching through the trees, strangled by parasitic plants.

I recognize two of the rare species from my books—Tempest root, sprawling over the uneven, cracked steps leading up to the entrance, and Nightmor, orange berries attached to thickets of brambles covering a stone effigy of Azkiel.

Moss covers the tan stonework, glimmering under the fading light of the moon. Vines strangle the pillars, but the majestic, fragmentary stone remains are only enhanced by nature reclaiming the structure. With every step toward the double brass doors, my heart pounds and breath hitches.

Azkiel side-eyes me, and I shut my jaw quickly, then huff out a breath as my eyes travel the various statues of him, and I quickly discern that one is made entirely of gold. I roll my eyes up, then shake my head.

I let out a tense breath as we climb the steps, praying Ari is inside. I place my hand against the door, sliding my fingers over the greenish-gray metal, engraved with inscriptions in the old language.

"Uncover one's face upon entering," Azkiel reads, the permanent smile on his features feeding my desire to punch him in the face again. "For here we enter the residence of the great Azkiel."

I grimace, then push the door inward before he can read anymore of the tributes to him. The metal grinds in my ears, as the doors scrape fragments of stone across the ground. A musty odor hits the back of my throat, and I cough against the dryness of the air.

Light filters through what is left of the roof, illuminating a cracked statue of Azkiel. I always thought they made him look taller than he is at around six-feet-ten, but as he towers over us, it's obvious that they are very accurate depictions of the cruel, handsome god.

My throat burns when I try to clear it as the air sinks into every crevice of my lungs, making me cough again. I venture deeper, listening to the distant crash of waves against the cliffs and rocks, which signals we must be closer to the edge of the island than I thought.

Azkiel shakes his head. "They're not here."

"What do we do now?" I ask, desperation clawing at the edges of my mind.

His gaze rolls over me, the intensity burning into my shadows. After a minute, he nods to himself, but doesn't share whatever he deciphered. "We stop here for the night."

"Why? We have to keep looking."

"We wait," he reiterates. "They can only perform the sacrifice here."

Drake grimaces at his back, and I sigh, dread threading every thought. "What is that?" I ask as a large chamber room comes into view, the walls crumbling into a pile around what is left of a wooden door.

Azkiel's footsteps echo as he slowly walks over the ancient, stone ground toward the entrance. Carefully, he swings the deteriorating door, then glances back at us. "The Preparation Chamber."

I tilt my head as a light reflects from a shattered mirror. Drake steps closer, his arm brushing against mine. Death's gaze snaps to the lack of distance between us, then back to my face.

"For sacrifices," I deduce, my heel hitting a rock.

Normally, such things wouldn't bother me. I've always had a fascination with death, but physically being here, sensing the violent energy around me, has my mind swirling. I touch my forehead, the skin searing hot against the back of my hand.

Azkiel's brows knit together, his eyes taking shape under the light of the moon. What's wrong?"

My powers curl out from my core, swirling like a tornado in my lungs. A breath escapes me, and I close my eyes to ground

NIGHT OF DEATH AND FLOWERS

myself. But the darkness, the lack of water, and the dry air overwhelm my senses. "Nothing. We'll stay. If you say this is where they will try to perform the sacrifice, then I'm not leaving."

THIRTY-THREE

Calista

I peer into the darkness, wondering what's taking the elders so long. Surely, they should have brought Ari here by now.

I shuffle my position on a jagged stretch of temple wall, hidden behind thickets of brambles and vines.

A part of me wonders if my father is involved. He's not the most moral of men, but he loves his daughter. Surely he wouldn't allow this.

NIGHT OF DEATH AND FLOWERS

The more death I witness, the closer I feel to finding comfort in the darkness. It's harder to find empathy, and I can't help but wonder if the powers in my veins are taking over. In a way, I understand Azkiel's apathy toward death. He's likely witnessed hundreds upon thousands of people die. I've come so close to the permanence of death a few times since being here that the lure of it has become a melody, calling me.

Drake's footsteps come to a halt behind me, and I flinch, as if he might somehow hear my thoughts.

His labored breaths sound in my ears as he climbs over the wall, then positions himself next to me. "Hey Wildflower," he whispers, and I almost smile. I watch as he places his hands on his knees, then lets out a long sigh. "Now that we have a moment away from *him*, I have to ask—"

"What you saw that night was nothing," I say before he can finish the sentence, because I refuse to relive the shame of knowing how close I let him get.

He turns his darkening stare toward the forest. "I just worry about you."

"I worry about *you*. You shouldn't be here. Azkiel won't hurt me, but he will kill you."

"I'm not running away, and I'm keeping my distance from him." He fumbles his fingers, then says, "Death has taken an interest in you. Be careful."

I swallow thickly. "Only because I'm the first person he's been able to touch."

"You say that as if it is a small thing. Imagine never being able to feel another person for centuries, then to get a taste of it…"

"Regardless, he hates me," I whisper, my stare trained on the trees, searching for any movement in the shadows. "He picked you to punish me. He watched me almost die under Cordelia and Briar's attacks and did nothing to help, and then strangled me with his shadows."

"Was that what he was doing when I saw you wrapped in his arms?"

I shuffle my position, then look at Drake. "Drop it," I warn.

"Azkiel saved you from the river."

I roll my eyes up, then sigh. "Because he thinks I'm the prophesied one."

Drake shakes his head. "You didn't see him on that riverbank. He could have gone after them, but he saved you instead."

"Saving me was to his benefit," I retort.

He bites his lip, then slumps his shoulders. "It's just seeing you with him, flaunting him in front of me like that."

"Seriously?" Rage unravels in my center, and I grip the wall. "I already told you what you saw was nothing, and even if it was, what does it matter?"

"Of course it matters!" he blusters, his green eyes alight under the moonlight. "To see you cozying up with God of Death, knowing he is evil… It makes me sick."

"I'm being fairly nice with him, for Ari's sake. If you don't like it, then you should just leave. You obviously don't trust my judgment."

"So, you're choosing Azkiel over me."

"This isn't about him!" I shout, then quickly lower my voice when I remember we're hiding. "Stop being so jealous."

"I am not… it is not about that. He's a fucking maniac."

The temperature drops a few degrees as a storm brews overhead, dark clouds shrouding any moonlight. Wind whips around my ears, freezing my clothes to my skin as a drizzle of rain falls over us. I glance up, then say, "We can't be at each other's throats. Not with Ari missing. But if you stay, then stop judging me because I can't take it."

"I am not judging you."

"You are! You hate my magic."

His eye twitches, nostrils flaring, and my heart sinks as a sweep of disgust washes over his face, even if only briefly.

"See?" I reiterate.

Drake drags his sleeve over his face, wiping away the water droplets, then runs his hand through his tousled, dark hair. "I don't hate you. I could *never*. It's him." He points at the temple, where Azkiel is sleeping. "*He* did something to you. I don't know how, but he fucked up your magic. It's making you act… unhinged."

"Perhaps I am," I admit aloud for the first time.

"I know this isn't really you talking."

I don't respond, mostly because I'm afraid I'll break any tethers of our friendship.

He jumps down from the wall, then grabs a leaf. "Here."

He brings it to my lips, as if I can't do it myself, then slowly tips the water into my mouth, but I take the leaf for him before I drink my fill.

The air thickens, winds splicing icy gusts between us, the hammering of the rain permeating the fresh mud into the air. Anger claws in my chest, threatening to tear me apart, but I won't abandon our friendship over one conversation.

"We could die out here," Drake blurts. "Look, I know you have plans, but they may not end in the way you think they will." He pauses, drawing closer. "I have to do this, if only once."

My breath catches as he leans in, shock rooting me as he brings his mouth to mine. I've wanted this for so long, but when his lips move against mine, nothing happens, and only disgust rolls through me.

I pull back, and Drake winces, rejection threading his stare as he closes his mouth, then steps back. "That was the wrong time," he admits and regains his composure. "You've had a long night."

"Drake—" I say, but he cuts me off before I can explain.

"Go get some sleep. I'll keep watch until Death takes over." He climbs back onto the wall. "We can forget this ever happened."

I enter the sacrifice room, finding Azkiel staring at a bunch of symbols etched into the ancient, stone walls.

I'm about to leave upon spotting him when his voice echoes around us, stopping me in my tracks. "Don't go."

Spinning around to face him, my attention is immediately drawn to his exposed, chiseled abdomen, and the defined V-line disappearing into his pants. He shoves his hands in his pockets, his expression unreadable as he turns to me. "You're wet."

"It's raining," I say breathily, gesturing to the small puddle draining to the corner of the room, as rain lashes through the open crack in the roof.

"Come here."

I swallow thickly. "No."

He sighs, then crosses the room to me.

"Do you want to be warm?" he asks when I recoil from his touch. "Hold still."

"What are you doing?" I push back, but his shadows creep over my body before I can stop them.

I glance down, my heart racing as I watch his shadows transform the fabric of my dress into a star-spun gown. The dark gray ombres from the bodice hanging below my shoulders, down to my lace sleeves and silver skirt.

I run my hands over the thin layers of fabric, wondering what manipulation he's using now in doing me this small kindness. Although, it feels good to finally be out of that dress, so caked in blood, mud, and sweat. I've never seen that magic done up close before. "Am I able to do that?" I ask, my shadows rippling around my fingers.

"With practice," he intones.

"I feel a little overdressed for a murder tournament," I state, not wanting to admit it is the nicest thing I have ever worn. It's too nice, for me. "It'd look better on Ari, when we find her. You can make her one instead, considering she is the prophesied one."

"It was made for you." He inches closer, and I crane my neck to look up at him, when he whispers. "You are devastating, Calista."

I step out from his shadow. "I—I am going to find somewhere to sleep." *Away from you*, I think the last part.

"We must talk."

I cast my eyes to the ceiling, trying to find an ounce of patience. Having to be cordial with him is so fucking difficult. I hate that I need him. I sigh, then force a small, grim smile—For Ari. "Okay, go ahead."

He paces, then walks to a different wall, this one covered in a collection of drawings. "I've been thinking about your ability to resurface some of my memories. We're going up against the gods and elders blind." He points at one faded drawing. "See this? I don't recall it being here, which means it was made after my memories were stolen."

I sweep in front of him and glide my fingers over the temple wall, over a painting depicting a girl with her heart removed.

His voice is a velvety ribbon of darkness as he commands, "Use Cyna's magic. Access my memories."

I turn to face him, my back cold against the stone. "Last time you hated that."

Azkiel presses me against the wall, then lifts my chin with his thumb. "I'm not asking, Poison."

"For Ari," I say, then place my hands on his chest, splaying my fingers over his heart. Tendrils of Sight magic leak into him, guiding and transporting me as the bare skin of my back rubs against the wall behind me, over the image carved into stone.

The room transforms, with intricately decorated vases and candles lining the length of the walls. A musty, floral scent permeates the area, and I notice the stone altar, decrepit and cracked just moments ago, now polished, and embellished with various fauna and foliage. Painted symbols from crushed berries decorate the sides, and red silk covers the three stone steps leading up to it.

But before I can hold on to the memory, it falls away. "I can't."

He presses harder, his fingertips brushing the curve of my jaw. I can feel him tensing, restraint pulling at every part of him. "Yes, you can. Try again."

I close my eyes, focusing as he strokes his thumb around my throat, a low growl emitting from his throat.

The claws of my Sight magic sink into him, and he holds me in place as I delve deeper. Unlike last time, however, the memories are longer, the emotions melding with my own until I can't breathe.

I watch Azkiel through the centuries, with every living thing he tried to touch turning to ash in his hands. His rejection is my own, when he is cast into the mortal world by his family, to wander between life and death. With every thump of his heart, I'm transported into his sadness, gazing as he becomes hardened, vicariously watching the world move on without him while he's forever alone.

I find a memory, ingrained so deep beneath the scars of his heart I wonder how long it's been buried. His lips long for another's, his soul torn when he knows he can never feel her lips again.

Again?

I'm thrust out of him before I can go deeper.

"Enough," he barks, his voice waning. He stumbles back, catching himself against the side of the altar.

He balls his fist over his chest, his eyes squeezing shut, and I realize I hurt him. I should be glad. I always wanted this. But when I look at him, I only feel sad.

"Don't pity me, Poison," he says breathlessly.

"I don't," I whisper.

"Good." He stands straight, then wipes the sweat from his brows. "It will weaken you."

"You think it's a weakness?" I ask, my brows furrowing when his expression crumples. "Or do you not believe you deserve it?"

"Do I?" he asks incredulously.

"No."

"Good. I'd hate to see you soften after you've promised me such pain."

I take a hesitant step forward. "Perhaps pain is easier to accept for people like us."

Our eyes clash across the room, and before I can say anything else, he turns and walks out.

THIRTY-FOUR

Calista

"You're awake," Drake says when he walks into the chamber. He hands me a goblet and I peer inside. My tongue darts between my dry lips the moment I see the orange inside, thicker than water, but not as heavy as honey. "What is it?"

"Cimicifuga Serrulata Extract."

I hesitate, lifting it slowly to my lips, then breathe in the cloying scent. The heavy liquid coats my tongue and throat, and as I drain the last few drops, I'm desperate for more. The hydrating and nourishing properties of Cimicifuga Serrulata Extract take little time to replenish my energy. I place the goblet down, then wipe my lips. "Still no sign of Ari?"

He shakes his head, then leans in and whispers, "This is a dead end. They're not coming. We should leave."

"No. Azkiel said the sacrifice must take place here."

His tone deepens with every desperate word. "What if he's lying just to keep you here, safe and away from them? We must go. He'll follow once he realizes you're gone. He still thinks you're the prophesied one and can awaken the gods."

My brows knit together when the words leave Drake's mouth for the first time. He has not pushed me to elaborate about the prophecy or the gods since everything happened. Although, I suppose he doesn't care. Not with us almost dying every other day. "Why are you so intent on leaving?" I ask. "We're safer here. Do you want to keep fighting and killing?"

"How many do you suppose are left?"

I shrug. "Eleanore, Rourne, Isolda, Briar, Cordelia and Edwardo are dead. We know Edwardo killed someone, and with you and Ari, that makes three remaining."

"Or fewer," he counters. "Alaric stabbed Eleanore. Who knows who else he's killed?"

NIGHT OF DEATH AND FLOWERS

I grip the stone ledge of the cracked altar. "Drake," I say slowly, mulling over my sister's speech about the gods and her dream. "What if Ari went willingly?"

His eyes widen by a fraction, his breath halting. "No," he says, averting his gaze from mine. "I don't think so."

I swallow hard against a lump forming in my throat, and the room somehow seems colder. Death's footsteps shuffle from the back of the chamber, his boots rolling over tiny rocks. Drake whips his head around, then glances at me.

I nod slowly. "It's my shift."

"I'll do it," Drake offers, lifting his index finger in the air before I can object. "I don't mind. I have nothing better to do."

My lips part as I watch him leave. Something tugs at the back of my mind, but I can't quite put my finger on what. Not that I have time to think, when Azkiel is already walking toward me, shirtless, and wearing a stoicism that I can't tell what kind of mood he is in.

I expect him to stop in front of me, but he passes me, his eyes assessing the painted images slathered over stone. His deep voice resonates around me. "You did well last night. We should try again."

My gaze tracks his movements as he walks over and then pulls himself onto the altar. He leans forward, his hands on his knees as he sits where people were once sacrificed.

"Are you a sadist?" I ask, the flick of his stare laced in warning. "I hurt you last night."

He drags his fingers through his silver strands, tousling his hair in a way that I wonder what I would be like to run my hands through it. "I can handle pain, Poison."

Tentatively, I lift myself until I'm sitting next to him, curiosity guiding my words. "When I was inside your mind, I saw you in the Darklands, and how lonely you were." I pause, then look down at my mud-caked boots. "Your family cast you out."

"I had to carry out my duties there and in the mortal worlds."

I shake my head, recalling the sting of rejection framing his memories. I know the feeling well. "Did you see them?"

"Occasionally our paths would cross."

I chew the inside of my cheek. "What about Astraea? I saw your bond with her."

"She betrayed me, too. I just don't remember how." He pauses, then leans closer, his long legs reaching the first stone step from the altar.

"Nonetheless, you must miss her," I say and as he stares at me, his pupils dilating, I see the broken man behind the god.

"Sometimes."

"You love her, like how I love Ari," I say, glimpsing a rare vulnerability on his face, one I can use so he will spare my sister after we find her.

"Are you trying to play on my emotions?" he asks. "Don't bother. I've been separated from my siblings for one hundred and fifty years. Any love I had, including for Astraea, is long gone."

I tsk under my breath, and a low growl sounds in his throat. "*Sure*."

"I am not interested in discussing my family." His tone is stern, but the edge of anger has dissipated since last night. "Only in returning the memories one of them took from me. We don't have long."

"I agree. Ari still hasn't shown up. The elders must know we're here."

His fingers crumple the fabric of his pants as he holds his knees, and my stare trickles to his muscles. "They will come." His fingers glide over the stone between us. "This temple is set upon centuries of bloodshed. It is here where the women were sacrificed to bind my siblings to the island. They can only undo the magic on this altar. Your sister is alive. I can sense her and the one other sacrifice besides the boy."

I blink twice, a jolt thrumming through my chest. "One? It's almost over," I whisper aloud, to no one in particular.

"Where will you go when it's over?" he asks, and my stomach knots. I hadn't thought much about that. The blood oath is still intact, and if I can save Ari, I will still have to leave Dahryst.

"Another land," I say. "Or I'll stay here."

"What if I allowed you to go home?" he baits, and I hold my breath for a moment. Would he really let me return? Or is this a test?

"I'd still leave Ennismore," I reply. "I'll go to the mountain courts."

His muscles tense, and his fingers grip the edge of the altar.

Our fingers brush as I shift position, and he lifts my wrist, turning them to see the scars left by my mother. "It seems we are both without a home."

The tips of his fingers glide over the half-moon scars and faded bruises, then up my arm, his eyes tracking every touch. The light filtering into the room glides through his silver hair, each one glistening as if it is made from stardust. My mouth dries as I turn my gaze from him, but I keep getting drawn back, gravitating to him. I hate it. I hate him. So why does my magic pulse at the thought and my shadows purr in my bones?

He almost smiles, reminding me that while he may be a god, he is still a man—one starved of any affection or love.

Magic unexpectedly seeps into my hands, darkening them, drawing his stare at my fingers.

"Your powers are heightened here," he states.

"Yes."

"How did you come to be, Calista?" he asks, and I blink twice when I hear my name on his lips again. "If you are not the one fated to destroy me."

The powers burrow deeper. "Bad luck?"

The corner of his lip curves upward. "You said that once before."

"You remembered."

"Your words are not easily forgotten." Azkiel slowly stands, his shadow casting away all the light. "I won't let you lose control."

I inhale sharply, then curl my fingers against the magic beating within them. "I can handle it. All I care about is finding Ari and stopping you from killing her after you get her off this island."

Goosebumps prick over my exposed skin, as he lifts his dark stare, and shadows ripple around his body. "I don't need to kill her, only to remove her from this island."

Is that mercy? "Why the change of heart?"

My gaze trails his defined muscles as he stands to full height, and my heart thuds when his gaze softens. "The decision is beneficial to me," he states, although I cannot see how. "She will go with you to the mountain courts."

"Let me get this right. You're going to let us both leave with our lives?"

"Depending on your sister's willingness to aid the prophecy."

I shake my head. "She doesn't want to die."

"Good. Now, help me find the memories Nyxara took, or I may not be able to help her," he says. "Before I change my mind."

Drake crosses my mind, but I save that plea for later. Not that I should have to ask him for anything. He imprisoned his siblings in Tenenocti after all, so this is his fault. Still, I can't help but wonder if I would have done the same in his position.

My fingers flex as I brace myself to delve into the buried parts of his psyche, but touching him feels far more intimate than before. So much that I hesitate before landing my hands on his chest. "Thank you."

He stills, his muscles rigid, his breath catching. He clenches up around me upon hearing the words.

I move to pull back, but his firm hands land on my hips, holding me in place.

NIGHT OF DEATH AND FLOWERS

I don't realize he's not breathing until he lets out a long, heavy exhale, and his chest moves.

His fingertips press deeper into my back, guiding me forward to close any gap between us. I oblige, his touch tingling electric over my exposed skin, and as he brings his head lower, his lids close as he holds onto me, every touch desperate.

His heart pounds in my ear, thumping harder against his ribcage, then picks up speed, matching my own as he squeezes tighter.

Breathing in his smoke-tinged evergreen scent, laced with ocean spray, I run my hands slowly over the bulges and curves of his back. My lips glide over his collarbone, as all sense of time and space fall away. My magic hums, purring as we hold each other, and I close my eyes, familiarity tingling through my bones.

A memory flashes between us of Tenenocti Island, and I jolt in Death's embrace. I travel my eyes to meet his, and I am frozen, his eyes alight with the longing of a man who has spent a lifetime parched, now savoring his first drop of water.

His hold on me tightens, and I close my eyes as the vision unfolds. I hold my breath as the world around me changes, the temple's white bricks glittering under the afternoon sun, and the Graywar trees surrounding it in full bloom, blue leaves covering their long, twisty branches.

The God of Will stands with Azkiel, and as I draw nearer, Volan raises his deep voice. He's even more muscular than his brother, his dark hair tied back, the long braid hanging down his back, which is covered in painted symbols.

"You make us look weak," Volan shouts at Death, who stands his ground. "Our powers are sacred."

"Love is not a weakness. You do not know how it has felt, not being able to touch anyone," Death hisses and my anxiety spikes as they grow closer, both poised to fight.

"Essentria was right to cast you out," Volan spits, his fists balled at his side. "You allow your heart to rule your brain."

"At least I have one."

"Insult me again!" Volan challenges.

"I would," Death retorts, his eyes darkening, "but you still won't understand it, you fucking cave dweller."

The vision fades, and I'm slammed back into reality with such force that Azkiel has to hold me up. I glance up at him, watching as a silent tear falls down his cheek.

"Love is not a *weakness*," I repeat, my voice barely above a whisper. "He was yelling about your powers. Why?"

"I do not recall that argument," he admits, then steps back, his hands landing on the altar as he steadies himself. "I remember nothing from that year, only after, when I landed back in

Ennismore. They were already buried, and all I had was a note I wrote myself to never let them awaken."

Azkiel lingers over me, his scent captured in my robes, his touch remaining on my body. My magic purrs, my fingers trembling, and I shake my head to scatter the thoughts and refocus on the present.

I sigh as Death's hurt rolls through me as if it is my own. "At least you won."

He blinks twice, then lifts his eyes to meet mine. "Won what?"

"Your argument against that *cave dweller*."

His lips curve, and the first genuine laugh escapes his lips, a sound so perfect I'm surprised it came from him.

THIRTY-FIVE

Azkiel

It's been two days without a sign from the elders or the sister.

I walk out of the sacrificial chamber, grimacing when I notice the traitor sleeping between a stone pew and a statue, covered by the torn remnants of his robes. In him, I sense Astraea's magic, so pure and beautiful that it pains me knowing some of it belongs with him.

Killing him will be so easy. The desire to do so crawls into my veins. All I would have to do is lean over and lay my fingers on his skin. It would also remove the guilt Calista will inevitably face when she has to choose her sister over him.

No. I need my witch in her right mind for when the elders come, and they will.

My palms twitch when I think about hunting them down. But that's exactly what they want—us, away from the temple so they can carry out the sacrifice. I was a fool for not seeing it sooner, when I could sense Essentria's creation magic in Calista's sister, but I put it down to Arabella inheriting two of my sister's powers.

The longer the elders hold the girl, the more I know Calista is not the prophesied one. That does still not explain why she holds my magic—power I can sense from here as it thrums out of control.

Rain lashes around me, creating puddles in the mud. The sun sets over the island, painting the sky in a deep orange.

I find her, sitting on the wall, hidden behind thickets of brambles, a dagger in her hand. Her eyes clash with mine when she spots me.

We've barely said a word to each other since she last pulled my buried memories from my mind, intruding into the darkest parts of myself. She's so beautifully dark, filled with so much love and anger all melded into one, and I wonder how she can be real.

I hand her my cloak, and her eyes drag over my rain-slicked clothes, sticking to my body. I hold my breath for a moment, and she averts her gaze, then whispers, "Thanks."

It's such an overused word by mortals, yet when it falls from her lips, my heart unexpectedly swells. How does she manage it? To be ostracized by her family and society, yet somehow the flicker of life in her eyes burns far brighter than anyone I've ever known.

Such a beautiful contradiction.

"They still haven't come," she says, and eases her way off the wall. "Drake's right. We should look for them."

"They will come. We are winning right now."

Her shoulders slump. "It doesn't feel like it."

"You should go inside," I say. "I'll take over."

Her knuckles whiten as she tightens her grip on the dagger. "I'm good here. At least I'm doing something that may actually help, instead of being in there, with only my thoughts."

I nod in agreement. "When I was in the Darklands, I spent a lot of time alone, *thinking*," I explain and pull the hood of my cloak over her head. "Sometimes to the point of insanity." I sandwich her icy fingers in my palms and look down at her. "When it would become too much, I'd close my eyes and listen to every sound, trying to decipher what each one was. I found it cathartic."

"Isn't it all tortured screams and crying in the Darklands?" she asks, and I almost smile.

"Occasionally," I state. "Mostly, I can hear the haunting melody from the forest, and the winds dragging leaves across the grounds."

My breath hitches when she curls her fingers around mine, the orange hues from the sun slathering her skin in a beautiful glow. Her body presses against mine, her heart hammering when she looks at me with those softening eyes.

I'm dying to kiss her. Just once.

She closes her eyes, taking in the heavy pattering of the rain, but it only lasts a minute before she opens them again. "I can't breathe sometimes, knowing Ari's out there somewhere."

"She is alive," I say, choosing my words carefully, because I cannot promise that she is unharmed. "When she returns, I will get you both out of here."

"And Drake?"

The muscle in my jaw feathers when I think about him. "He is a traitor."

"So am I. We did the same thing."

I pause, not knowing what to say. "What would you have me do, Calista? The Harvest can only have one winner."

"Break the rules."

I smirk as she grows closer, her hands running over me in an obvious manipulation. Against all my instincts, I push her away. "You'll have to try harder than that."

"I know you have a heart under there," she says, bringing her hands to my chest, my heart racing under her splaying fingers.

I lean down, bringing my lips to her ear, "I told you before, Poison. Don't make the mistake of thinking I am good."

"I don't think that," she points out. "None of us are innocent, but I believe that behind the monster lies just a man who is deeply hurt."

My eyelids flicker, her touch suddenly so uncomfortable that I would tear off my skin to be away from her. I step away, my jaw clenching in warning when she attempts to get close again. "You do not know me."

"You're afraid." Her words shoot through me like an arrow.

"I've never been afraid," I warn, but she invades my space again, shadows tearing from her fingers, evoking my own.

"Liar," she hisses.

"What about you, Poison?" I ask, and her eyes darken. "What are you scared of?"

"You," she admits, then lifts her dagger between us, and I lean into the blade. "Is that what you want to hear?"

"Are you trying to seduce me?" I ask and drag my thumb over her plump, red-rose lips. "So I will free your friend from his oath?"

Her chest rises and falls as her breaths grow uneven. "Is it working?"

I draw nearer until her lips are only an inch from mine. My hand slides around the back of her neck, and I hold her still, my gaze piercing into hers. "Don't tease me if you don't plan on doing anything about it," I whisper hoarsely, my resolve crumbling with a brush of our lips. She tiptoes, her eyes closing. "Because I will not hold back."

"Then don't." She licks her lips, her fingers waltzing to my thighs, and I struggle in a breath as she lifts my shirt, her icy tips contacting my skin.

Her shadows dance around us, heightening my own powers. Does she even know what's happening to her? Her magic is out of control.

Goosebumps prick over my arms when I hear footsteps dragging through the wet leaves. I almost missed it, over the sound of my thumping heart.

"Quiet," I whisper, the focus returning to her eyes.

My lips part as the sister walks out from the trees. They're finally here.

THIRTY-SIX

Calista

The world falls away when I see Arabella running toward us.

My eyes swiftly sweep over her, checking for any damage. Relief settles into my bones as I see no visible signs of injury. "Ari!"

"I found you," she blurts, choking on a sob as she falls into my open arms. "Oh, Cali. It was awful."

Tears slide down my cheeks as I hold her so tight I wonder if she can breathe. "Where are the elders?"

"Dephina's in the caverns. I escaped," she whispers, wiping her tears with the back of her hand as she withdraws. "Where did you get this?" She asks, admiring the lacy dress Death created for me.

My gaze flicks up to Azkiel, who is observing us intently.

"That's not important." I pull her at arm's length, my hands planted on her shoulders. "What happened?"

Her eyes trickle to Death, her bottom lip wobbling slightly. After a few seconds, the quiver in her lip steadies. "Dephina took me to the caves."

"Who else was there?"

"Just us," she says, although I am not convinced, and Death doesn't seem swayed either.

"She said the gods want to sacrifice me." She glares into my soul. "That if I die, they will bring me back to life."

A knot tightens in my stomach. "I will not let that happen."

Azkiel steps up behind us. "Essentria can't revive you, not after a sacrifice," he tells her. "You know that, don't you, Arabella?"

She nods but cannot hide the anger quivering her bottom lip when she looks at Death. "Yes."

"Where's Thorn?" I ask.

"I don't know," she says, and the hope that he followed her fades away.

I shake my head. "I'm sure he's settled in a tree somewhere. His visits are always brief."

She shoots me a look and swallows thickly. Then her gaze drifts past me, focused on something behind me. Or someone, I notice when I hear a soft sigh. I turn my head, finding Drake standing outside of the temple's entrance.

How long has he been there?

Ari runs to him, and Drake pulls her into his embrace. She gasps for her breath as he squeezes her tight, his muscles rippling as his arms hold her in place. "You fucking scared us," he says, but draws back, sweeping the same assessing stare over her that I had. "You must be thirsty. There's rainwater inside."

Her hand lands on her lower stomach, palming her navel. "I'm hungry more than thirsty."

"I have some food I foraged yesterday," Drake replies, then guides her into the temple.

I trail a finger over my throat, then thumb the side of my neck when Death catches my eye.

"Do you believe her?" he asks once they've disappeared into the temple. "Why shouldn't I?" I question, because I don't want to cement his beliefs.

"Let's get inside," he says.

My mouth is dry, and the urge to glide my fingers over my lips is extreme. Instinctively, I step closer, and into his aura, then bite my lip.

I don't look at Azkiel as we make our way through the crumbling building, reaching steps taking us to the intact lower rooms, underground, but I can feel his stare boring into me.

This is ridiculous. It's as if my mind has turned to putty. I was meant to be the one seducing *him*, using him, so he'd free Drake and Ari. But as we walk, and I glance sideways at his lips, my breath hitching at the intensity carving his chiseled features. My heart races and I find myself looking for an excuse to touch him again. Because he knows how it feels—to be alone, an outcast, and even now when he glances at me, a silent exchange flows between us.

Do I *like* him?

"Cali." Drake's voice slices through my thoughts.

I blink twice, noticing we have reached the bottom of the steps. "Do you want to sort through it all?"

I nod quickly, checking through the pile of berries Drake collected yesterday, from outside the temple. I scowl at the berries, sorting them into three piles: delicious and edible, just edible, and poisonous.

Ari whistles from the corner of the room, and when our eyes lock, there's something telling in them, yet I cannot make out what she is trying to say with her stare.

Azkiel comes up beside me, the Skhola on his index finger sliding down a nudge as he touches the poisonous berries, turning them into ash. I gasp slightly as his arm brushes against mine, and he leans over, his breath soft against the top of my ear. "In case anyone accidentally mistakes them for food."

I gaze at Ari as she slices foraged mushrooms with a dagger once used for animal sacrifice. Dark circles encircle her eyes, her face blanched. "Ari. Come here."

She walks over to me, and I take her hands in my mind. "What's wrong?"

"We're getting out of here."

I force a reassuring smile and nod. Drake regards me through bloodshot eyes from across the room. "Thank gods," he says with a sigh of relief.

"When?" she asks, impatience teetering on the edge of her tone.

"Tonight, but first," I say, sensing her waning magic, "let me heal you."

Her eyes widen. "How?"

"Eleanore," I say with a croak, the spark of her gold magic swimming in my core. "She was already dying."

Her chest lifts then falls as her breaths uneven. "I'm malnourished and tired. Healing magic won't help."

"Okay, we'll eat first, then you can rest just for a couple of hours."

"I don't need rest," she argues, and I arch a brow when she yawns. "Okay, but *only* for two hours. I want to get as far away from this temple as possible."

"Of course. Azkiel is going to break the blood oath tying you to the Harvest so we can get out of here."

She lowers her voice to a soft whisper and tugs me to the side. "Do you trust him?"

I wrestle with my answer for a moment. "Our leaving is what he wants."

Her eyes run over my dress. "Did he make this for you?" I nod and she grimaces. "Have you…" she leans closer to my ear, "grown close to him?"

"No!" The lie curls around my tongue, like a tendril of silence—because admitting the truth is far worse.

She nods. "Good. I'd hate to see you fall deeper into darkness." Knowing threads her eyes, and she turns and walks back to Drake before I can ask her more about what happened.

Azkiel lights a torch from the wall, bathing us in shadows of flickering flames, and we form some kind of meal—mushrooms, with berries and plant leaves.

I grimace when I bring the clay plate to my nose, but my stomach grumbles in protest, and I quickly shovel down the food. When I look up, both Azkiel and Drake are glaring at each other.

Until Azkiel, he was the only one I ever thought about kissing. There were other boys, for years, ones I kissed and allowed them to touch me—distractions from the boredom of living in Ennismore. But not once had any of them consumed my thoughts. Not like Drake, and definitely not like the God of Death.

I shove my plate aside, then stand. I can't be thinking about Azkiel's fucking chest, or those lips, or those damned thighs. It's my magic. *It must be.* Its heightened state is making me feel things toward him that I know I shouldn't.

Ari's blonde brows lift. "Are you getting sick, Cali? You seem flustered."

"I'm fine," I lie, then touch my fevered forehead, but she doesn't look convinced. "I just need to lie down."

Azkiel stands, his lips forming a hard line. He casts his eyes over all of us, pausing over Ari, then landing on me. "I will take the first watch," he informs.

The wrinkle between my brows deepens as he leaves, torch in hand. We follow him, not back up the stairs, but into an adjoining room instead. He places his torch in a bracket on the wall, and my eyes trailing the flickering flames from the sconce, spilling light over the wide bedchamber.

Arabella walks up beside me, then grabs my hand as her violet gaze assesses the room. "I'm going to sleep. You should too, so we can get out of here."

I pull my hand away from hers when decay magic stings into my fingers without warning. "I will. I just need to do something first."

I breathe in the musty, yet lightly perfumed odor of the room, as if the incense burned here over a century ago still somehow lingers.

My mind spins as the reality of my sister's return sinks in, accompanied by the desperation to leave this island. But the magic in my body stirs, building to a pressure that's almost intolerable.

I press my palm against an ache in my temples, then run back out into the rain. The food did little to ease my hunger. My fingers are charred by the time I see Azkiel again. His eyes focus on the forest, wearing a quizzical look.

"Something's wrong," I say, coming up behind him. Ever since Ari returned, her magic has somehow heightened mine. I clamp my eyes shut, and when I open them again, Death is staring down at me with such intensity my breath stammers.

"You need to let it out, Poison." His fingers intertwine with mine.

"How?" "I can absorb your magic," he explains. "You're practically vibrating with it."

"So I would be powerless?" I ask, unconvinced.

"No, just depleted. I can't remove your magic, but I can weaken you until we figure out what's going on." He looks around, then beckons me into the trees so the temple is still in sight.

We reach a clearing. Beyond the trees, a glimpse of sea disappears into the starry horizon, the black waters reflecting the bright, full moon. Heavy drops soak through my dress until I'm shivering. "I'm not sure about this."

My powers quake, building to a crescendo as he lifts my hands onto his chest, and I scrape my fingernails into the fabric of his navy blue tunic.

"I cannot risk you accidentally killing your sister," he says, and my stomach dips at the thought.

Azkiel's velvety tone caresses the edges of my magic, heavy with command. "Calista, release yourself."

THIRTY-SEVEN

Calista

My powers meld with his, combining in a rhythmic thrum, starting in my thighs, then lifting through my stomach. As a bloom of heat swells in my chest, a moan topples on my tongue when my mouth opens, the magic swallowing me until it tips me to the edge of reason.

    The release is a stab of anger sizzled with satisfaction as his shadows slip around my body, unknotting the tension in my coiled muscles. My eyes roll into the back of my head as he pulls the dark powers from me, shred by shred, tearing it into pieces until there's little left.

He grunts but remains unmoving against each blast, absorbing every ripple of power. When I look at him, darkness sinks into his chest as shockwaves of decay magic escape through my hands.

"Good girl," he whispers as the last of my shadows curl around him in tendrils, sliding around his throat. I bite my lip, the words diffusing warmth into my chest.

Restraint bands in his eyes as he releases his hands from mine, but I close my fingers around him.

His shadows are wild as he drags his thumb across my cheek. A glittering ribbon of darkness ripples as it extends from his fingers, then slides around the contours of my body.

My heart pounds, then skips a beat, leaving me in a temporary numbness as my mind empties of thought.

I shouldn't trust him, but the eyes are the window to the soul, and when our gazes collide, all I see is a man starved of touch, genuine affection, of kisses… and love.

My lips part as I still, my pulse thudding as a tangible force draws us together. The bond between us is explosive, and beyond any reason.

NIGHT OF DEATH AND FLOWERS

The darkness in his eyes consumes the silver until his irises are the color of night. Lengths of silver hair, tousled, are wild around his face, and I hold my breath, aching to run my fingers through them.

A tense silence hangs between us as I inch closer to him, enveloping his essence and drinking in the musky, delicious scent of him. My restraint falls away as I sink deeper into his hungry stare.

I lift my eyes to his cruel, handsome face. "I'm tired of trying to hate you."

My breath halts as his fingers grip the back of my neck, forcing me closer. "I'm sick of you consuming my thoughts," he retorts, restraint thick in his tone, as if he may snap at any moment.

Heat flares in my veins as his words sink in, fluttering my stomach into butterflies.

I consume his thoughts?

His lips drift to mine, and I tiptoe, grasping him tighter, my shadows exploding as a feeling ignites through me—a desire that burns out of control.

Our lips crash together, his fingers sinking into my skin with starving desperation. My hands explore the expanse of his chest, then travel to his biceps as he deepens the kiss and takes command of my sanity.

Azkiel wages war against my mouth, demanding my tongue battle with his. My core clenches painfully, desperate and aching.

He moans as his hips gyrate against me, and I swallow his soft, guttural sounds. His wet tongue strokes against mine, and I immediately lose myself in thoughts of him devouring other places on my body.

His hands carve the curve of my chin, his fingers pressing against my tender throat with possessive need. I cling to him, every stroke of my tongue demanding, as if I am the one who has been starved of touch until now.

Shadows quake around him, vibrating against my limbs as a slow, pent-up ache builds between my legs. He breaks the kiss, and my eyes flutter open as we're consumed by a tornado of shadows encompassing us in glittering blackness.

"*Calista.*" He says my name like a prayer against my skin. He traces his fingers in a fiery path from my throat, down my back, then over the fabric of my dress.

My back arches to his touch, his lips frantic against me once again as he devours me with such intensity, it feels as if I may die.

He holds one hand over the curve of my back, then slips the other lower. My breath hitches as he hikes the skirt of my dress up, his fingers caressing the inside of my thighs. He lets out a tense, shaky exhale and my thighs fall apart under his touch.

I press myself against his thick cock bulging under his pants. "Lower," I plead in a quivering breath, as he traces the contours of my inner thighs.

His fingertips tease over my flushed and swollen opening. His eyelids flutter to a close, his lips falling apart as he meets the slickness building.

I gasp as his shadows shred my dress into ribbons with each needy whip.

His palm presses against the rest of my sensitive expanse, as he circles two fingers over my throbbing clit in a deliberate, building rhythm. Tingles shoot through my chest, palpitating my heart.

His fingers pulse dark magic with each glide, leaving me dangling on the precipice of oblivion. I moan into his chest, and my fingers dig into his waist.

I bite my bottom lip as heat emanates from his hands as he pulls away. A spiral of shadow spreads my folds, then thrusts into me until I am filled with his darkness.

Rising moans hum in my throat as he brings me to the edge. Shadows snake over my body in threads, devouring every inch of exposed skin, then coil over my breasts. I barely gasp when the inky ribbons pinch my nipples, coaxing a whimper from me.

I chase the high as his shadow engorges inside of me, the others working my breasts in a symphony of pleasurable touches until I reach a crescendo of undiluted bliss and the pressure mounts to unbearable heights. "*Please*, don't stop," I whisper as he slows.

He smirks down at me. "You beg so pretty, Poison."

I ache for release as surges of intoxicating pleasure sear through my veins, my hips matching every one of his shadow's brutal thrusts.

"Come for me, Calista."

His words shove me over the cliff of ecstasy.

My stomach knots as my climax sizzles from the tips of my toes to the apex of my thighs, and I'm biting his shoulder, barely able to quench the quaking moan.

Tension unknots as he winds me into an ecstasy that fogs my mind. He quickens the pace of his fingers, circling my clit as he tugs the last shreds of my orgasm from me until my eyes roll into the back of my head.

His hands palm the curve of my ass, as I anchor my arms around his neck. He lifts me with ease, and I wrap my legs around his hips. My mind spins momentarily as the blood rushes back into my brain from the sudden vertical shift.

The air rushes from my lungs as my back meets the solid trunk of an ash war tree. Shocks of pleasure ripple through my stomach as his solid, cock presses up against me.

Shadows tendril down his pants, tearing them from him, revealing his toned thighs and defined muscles, down to two V-lines at the bottom of his abdomen.

He's so fucking handsome.

"Tell me you're mine," he says against my skin, as he presses kisses against my neck in between words. "Even if you don't mean it."

Sadness aches in my chest as my heart jolts at the thought. As he divulges the vigor of his possessive need. "I'm yours," I whisper, because at this moment, at least, I am.

His mouth meets the swell of my breast, his tongue blazing heat over my peaked nipple. I grip his hair tightly in my fist as he breathes hot air against my skin, then gently sucks.

Every move is desperate. Each guttural grunt and feverish touch heightening me to a pleasure I didn't think was possible.

A fiery sensation creeps through my chest, each tug of his teeth against my nipple pricking sparks through my body.

My legs hook tighter around his hips, guiding him closer, and he moves his mouth back to mine, consuming me with a kiss.

Our mouths separate as I press a hand against his chest. My lips part when I look at him with hooded eyes, a carnal need sharpening his features. My thighs clench as desire continues to burn me alive. I need him inside of me *now*.

I glance down at the gap between us as he thrusts his hips back, and I gasp upon seeing the pre-cum coating the head of his thick cock, long, blue veins throbbing around the shaft.

I drag my tongue over my lips, and my eyes widen as his taut length twitches, so engorged I wonder how I will be able to take all of him.

Pre-cum drips from the head as he eases inside of me, pushing himself deeper inch by inch, and my eyes flutter close as he emits a guttural groan, filling me entirely.

His gaze locks onto mine, the restraint in his eyes snapping as he pounds me against the tree trunk.

My toes curl as he holds me up by the curve of my ass with one hand while the other is tangled in my hair. A shuddering breath escapes him as icy gusts of winds whip between us.

His fingers dig into my flesh hard enough to leave bruises as he takes me harder and deeper, holding my gaze. A low moan slides from my throat, and he groans in response. Every movement is greedy, enveloping me tighter with shadows as if he wants to consume every elicit of pleasure in my bones until I'm left aching.

"You feel so good around me," he moans as he thrusts his hips rhythmically, and I slide an inch up the tree. His groans send me higher than I've ever been. I bite down on his shoulder, the bitter taste of copper flooding my tastebuds, as he lifts me away from the tree, both of his large hands grasping my ass. My breasts rub again against Azkiel's chest as he holds me tightly against him, then lowers me onto the vine-stricken ground.

I tilt my hips once we're lying flat, tilting my legs to give him better access. His fingers cup my thighs, then lift my ass, sinking deeper until the flesh of his groin is hard pressed against mine.

I moan in tune with his powerful strokes. Flames lick through me as my orgasm builds swiftly to a pinnacle.

"Calista." He grunts my name between thrusts as the pleasure threatens to drown me, dragging me deeper and drenching me in sweet darkness.

He buries his face in the hair tangled around my neck as a vibration ripples from the head of his cock, shooting shockwaves into me. My body jolts violently when the vibrations travel to my clit. His primal roar rocks through us as he comes undone, spilling into my tight heat until my quivering thighs are dripping with his release.

The sounds of our bodies slapping together fill the air as he groans, then holds still, his muscles tightening. My release shreds through my mind as the ground beneath us shakes. He rocks the final pulses from me as I chase the last dregs of my earth-shattering orgasm. Short, husky grunts leave his half open mouth and his eyes close to slits.

Slowly, he pulls out of me, leaving a trail of glistening cum on the ground. My heart stutters as the emptiness in his place leaves me hollow.

THIRTY-EIGHT

Calista

Every muscle in my body relaxes as I lie over him under the canopy. He catches his breath, the sweat glistening over his toned body, then reaches across and grabs a cloak, so dark it could have been cut from the night sky. The fabric glides over my body as he pulls it over me.

Our heavy breaths exchange as I look up at him, the curve of my chin gliding against his chest. He presses his lips to my forehead, a kiss so gentle it startles me. "How do you exist?"

"Bad luck?" I tease, recalling our first meeting.

"Terrible," he says, with a lazy, satisfied smile. I roll onto my side, lifting my chin to look into my eyes. "How will I let you go, Poison?" he asks, drawing close until our lips meet again.

Our lips move in sync, and I refuse to think about what happens after this. "Don't," I whisper against our kiss.

He breaks away, his lips curving as he drags his thumb over my lips. "I don't want to." His fingers pinch my chin, as if he's examining my expression. After a few seconds under his penetrating gaze, he groans, his lids closing briefly. "You ruin me, Calista."

He drinks me in with those ethereal, star-swept eyes, and I feel as if I cannot breathe. His grip tightens around me, and I am not afraid of anything, except his heart. I find my voice, unexpectedly small at the back of my throat. "I know this can't last."

"Everything must end, my love, especially when we don't want it to."

My heart almost fucking stops, and I try to catch my breath. My *love*.

That's when I see it for the first time, the true essence of him—those silver and black eyes filled with endings, his heart thumping as if it is a clock, ticking away the hours of all lives.

His eyes devour my body, spills of darkness leaking from his fingers until they cover my body, until the shadows settle into a soft fabric of blue. Diamonds glitter in a line down both sleeves, and across my waist, as if he plucked the stars for my dress.

Death's shadows spin into a flurry, forming a matching cloak with silver lining and a hood before settling. I lift my fingers to my neck, grazing them against my collarbone as Azkiel stands, then walks, stopping inches in front of me.

"I need to learn how to do that," I say, breaking the tension. "We should wake Ari."

I tilt my head up to glance at him, and he leans down, his knuckles gliding down my arm. His mouth opens in argument, but he pauses, heaving a sigh. "We will take a boat back to Ennismore."

"What about Drake?"

He doesn't look at me. "Take him."

I don't respond, in case he changes his mind. Instead, I watch as the sky paints in shades of indigo behind him, the last dregs of the moon highlighting the toned curves of his bulging muscles.

Shadows ribbon from his fingers, then seep into his legs and torso, his magic creating a tunic, pants, and boots.

His words echo in my mind as we walk back to the temple, and I hold on to them like a dark, dangerous jewel I should not covet. Before we arrive, a thought crosses my mind. "You still call me Poison."

"Yes."

"Why?"

He turns and faces me, halting me in my tracks. "Because," he says throatily, stealing my next breath, "Your words are like venom to my soul. I am completely captivated and devastated with every sentence you throw my way. So, yes, you are my poison, and I can think of no better way to die."

I swallow hard, then hold my breath in my lungs, not knowing what to say. My heart balloons when I look at him, the high of feeling him buried inside of me, fogging my mind.

I cannot explain our connection. So why do I feel like a fly, unaware it was in the spider's web until it was captured? His power already expands in my body. Perhaps being his domain enhances the magic, continually, like an endless well. How many times can he pull it from me before I can't cope?

"Your powers are growing again," he states.

"It only happened since I've been here. I could control them when I was Ennismore," I say, curling my hands into fists as if it may restrain my powers.

His brows knit together, but he takes off before I work out what he's thinking.

I shake my head, pulling myself out of his trance as we reach the beautiful, ivy constricted pillars of the temple. I follow Death inside, his steps echoing as we head down to the hunter's room.

Ari and Drake come into view, locked in hurried, intelligible conversation. They stop whispering when they see us, and Ari gasps. "Where were you?" She looks at Azkiel, then grits her teeth.

"The forest," I say. "We were checking the area."

Drake's tone drips with venom. "Was that all you were doing?"

"Yes!" I grab my dagger from the table they had used to cut the berries and mushrooms, then place it in the holder strapped to my thigh. "Let's go. You too, Drake."

He shakes his head. "I can't leave." His glare snaps to Azkiel, and I put my hands up.

"He's breaking the blood oath," I explain, and he scoffs, glancing between me and Azkiel, holding back the countless things I know he wants to say.

"Thank her," Death commands before Drake can leave the room. "Now."

Drake halts, his tense breath coming out in a rattle. "Shouldn't I be thanking *you*?"

"Stop," I say. "That's unnecessary."

"It is," Azkiel counters and my stomach dips. Fuck. Now they definitely know what happened.

Drake turns, the bulb in his throat bobbing, his eyes crowning wrinkled anger, tears glossing his green irises. "Thank you, for whatever you *did* to *persuade* him."

Shadows erupt from Death before I can throw myself between them. "You promised to let him go," I say, and Azkiel hesitates when he looks at me.

Reluctantly, his shadows retreat. He peers around me, to Drake. "You are lucky, traitor."

Ari nods, a far-off look in her eyes. "We all are," she counters, always the peacekeeper, although I can sense her disdain when she stops beside me. "We should leave before Dephina comes for me."

It's dark by the time we reach the edge of the forest to the Black Sea.

We pause by a clearing, and Ari gathers a bundle of Nocturnum Somnus—the same plant that almost put us into a comatose state when Cordelia and Briar attacked.

"Careful," I tell Ari as she stashes the poisonous plant away between some leaves. "That's not for eating."

"I know," Ari says before pocketing the root and flowers of the plant. "It's just, if Dephina makes another appearance, I want to protect myself."

"No one will hurt you while you're with me."

My heart skips a beat as Azkiel emerges from the darkness, his lustful eyes finding mine across the clearing.

Drake looks from him to me, then shakes his head, sighing. Ari follows Azkiel deeper into the depths of the forest, and I breathe in the woody scent, closing my eyes.

When my eyelids flutter open, I find Azkiel's eyes focused on me and a prickly sensation climbs through me, and my lips press tight at the memory of him buried inside of me.

My cheeks flush, and Death's lips part to speak, but Drake clears his throat, stepping beside me. "Nice dress."

"I've been waiting for you to say something," I say, ensuring Azkiel continues walking so he doesn't attack Drake again.

"Am I right in my thoughts?" Drake asks.

My face burns and Drake's green gaze tracks my facial expression, then spots the marks from Azkiel's nails embedded in my wrist.

He grabs my hand, then drops it while Ari and Azkiel walk ahead. "Tell me you didn't," he hisses in a whisper, then shakes his head, disappointment filling his rugged features. Unlike me, he stinks of blood, while I smell like the wilds, mixed with a musky scent, like… Azkiel.

"I can't," I admit, lifting my chin.

Drake's dark brows draw together, his lips down-turned as he looks me up and down.

"What the fuck is wrong with you? He's a murderer. He put us on this island."

Ari pauses ahead, her brows rising as we all come to a halt.

"He did, but he is also getting us out," I shout, putting out my arm when Death draws closer. "Stop! I can handle this." I turn my gaze to Drake. "If you hate Azkiel for his actions, then you should despise me, too. I killed Isolda just so I could get here. I've done worse and will continue to, to protect the people I love."

He jabs a finger in Death's direction. "You're becoming darker by the day, and it's drawing you to him."

Azkiel halts, then turns, his shadow casting a tower over Drake. Twigs crunch under his boots when he reaches us, and I rub my temples as a low growl leaves his voice. "Be very careful of your next words, boy."

Drake scoffs. "I'm not afraid of you."

Death's demeanor shifts into the ancient darkness I'd seen before. Red crosses his stare, a dangerous flicker of fire that—if not extinguished—will burn Drake. "You should be."

I barely throw myself between them in time as Azkiel's hands reach for Drake's throat. Death's fingers meet my neck instead, grabbing his hand before he can kill him. "Enough. I don't need your help!"

Ari grabs my arm. "Why don't we stop for a little?" she tells Drake. "So we can calm down. I—I'm not feeling well, anyway."

"What's wrong?" I ask.

Ari's soft touch roots me to the spot. "I feel weak. I need a minute." Ari sucks in a deep breath, then places a hand against the trunk of a graywar tree, leaning over.

"We're so close to shore. I can carry you."

She turns her bloodshot, wild eyes to me. "No. I just need a drink. I'll go get some rainwater."

She shoots Drake a look. "I'm thirsty, too."

Conflicted, I settle under the contorted tree. Clouds merge overhead, rain slowly pattering from a drizzle into heavy thuds through the interwoven branches above.

She turns, turning her back to me as she fumbles under a tree, gathering water with Drake.

I avert my gaze from them and turn to Death, the tension palpable as he refuses to look away, drinking me in with his moonlit eyes. After a few minutes, Ari slides next to me with a large leaf shaped into a bowl that holds rainwater. "I got you some, too."

"I'm good, really."

She arches her brow. "You are parched. Now drink."

I roll my eyes, then smile. Ari's eyes widen as she watches me drink it, then places it in front of Azkiel. He hesitates briefly, but upon seeing my urging smile, he accepts it. "Thank you, Arabella."

My heart balloons as he says her name gently, then drinks the water.

The hurt from Drake and my feelings for Azkiel is a cocktail of confusion.

"I'm going to sit for a few minutes," Ari says.

I nod as we lower ourselves against tree trunks, and Drake settles against a long one close by, avoiding making eye contact.

I curl up closer to my sister, leaning in, while keeping my eyes fixed upon Death, who is sitting across the other side of the clearing.

"Are you sure you're okay?" I ask. "I really don't mind carrying you."

"No," she says shakily after a brief pause. She fumbles her fingers—hands usually adorned with delicate rings and manicured nails, now crusted with mud. "Do you really care for him?" she whispers. "Azkiel, I mean? I see the way he looks at you."

My stomach knots as I cast my eyes from her to Death. He leans back against a tree, his legs apart, knees in the air. His fingers meet in the middle as he turns the Skhola ring around his finger.

I purposely turn my attention back to Ari, my arm pressing into hers, and she leans her head sideways on my shoulder. "You must think me foolish."

"No, I don't blame *you*." She lets out a long sigh, her wide eyes slowly closing. I roll my eyes up, nodding in agreement, then gently drape an arm around her shoulders, running my fingers through her silky, blonde locks.

"You've always protected me." She wraps her arms around her stomach, searching for pockets of warmth among the thin fabric of her dress.

I half-smile. "I will always protect you."

"I know, but I must do this," she whispers, and I look over at Death as his lids close. A wave of exhaustion washes over me, tempting me with the enchanting allure of sleep, as if invisible ribbons of magic are binding me in place. A haze settles over my mind, as I struggle to keep my eyes open.

What is happening?

I try to speak, but haziness pulls my words from leaving my lips. Poison. She's fucking poisoned us. The effects simmer into me. Into Death as well, although it will hold him for far less time than I.

Ari shoots me one last watery smile when she stands, her eyes sliding toward Azkiel, then back to me. "Astraea will take care of him," she says. "I'm sorry, Cali. But I'm doing this for us."

I try to open my mouth when she leaves with Drake, but I'm already being pulled deeper into a hazy darkness until I pass out.

THIRTY-NINE

Azkiel

My sister plagues my dreams. Her haunting essence is a constant companion as I fall through the layers of my subconscious in my sleep, unable to wake.

Astraea's presence, once calming, is infused with malignance. Invisible coils of betrayal constrict me, holding me in my dream as it transforms.

I'm standing in a field of long, gray grass littered with skulls, both animal and human.

Familiarity etches the world surrounding me, the memory an accurate portrayal of the Ash War. Dead trees, adorned with bones, knot their branches toward the blue and purple, starry sky.

I close my eyes, sensing my sister behind me, her sadness so deep it may drown me. "Brother."

"Sister," I reply, my tone deeper, and calmer than expected, as I turn to face Astraea for the first time in over a century and a half. "I see you've finally visited me, instead of hiding behind Cyna."

Her orb-like eyes lock with mine, once filled with comfort and love when she looked at me, now crowned in contempt. "I wasn't ready to face you, after what you did."

I hold my breath as I take in her familiar appearance. Her dusky-blue waves cascade down to her waist, tattoos—similar to my own—adorning her skin, and a frown etched on her soft features.

"What is it I did?" Every cavity of my soul aches when I see her, when I hear her voice, and I'm suddenly aware of how lonely I was in her absence.

Her thin face contorts in anguish, and the ethereal-like colors in her eyes seep into a profound darkness that surpasses my own. "You used mine and Volan's bodies to keep Essentria, Cyna, and Nyxara trapped here. You cursed us all."

"If that is true, then why did Nyxara take my memories?"

"So you wouldn't return."

"She underestimated me."

"I knew you would return," she says. The longer I stare, the more colors I notice swirling in the depths of her eyes. Blues, purples, and silvers weave her irises, capturing her ethereal magic as she continues to build the surrounding dream.

"How?"

"Because the mortal is here. You're drawn to her."

"Calista?"

"Yes."

"Why does she have my power?"

Her delicate, silver sandals glide over the long, gray grass. She stops in front of me, her presence demanding eye contact. "I do not need to tell you. Instead, I will help you remember."

Her fingers lift to my ears, and I flinch as she slowly lowers her hands around the crown of my head. I've waited so long for this, but now that the time has come, a part of me holds onto the amnesia.

Astraea tilts her head, her dusky-blue curls sliding over her shoulder. She glances up, then closes her eyes, blue shimmering and glittering over her skin as her magic engulfs her being, then tendrils around me.

The memories reveal themselves in our dreamscape, as the surroundings shift and change, warping through time.

My heart skips one beat, then another, pain slicing through every inch of me as I recall the events that led to trapping my family.

A woman appears in the vision, the one from the sacrificial chamber. I gaze into the eyes of a mortal woman, and my love for her floods back to me. "Calista."

She stares at me, through another's eyes, but I recognize her soul, although there are subtle similarities—from her crooked smile, to the challenging glint in her blue eyes, and the way she purses her lips when she's angry.

Her dark hair, woven within a crown made of leaves and thorns, shimmers under the setting sun as we stand by the temple on Tenenocti, the surrounding houses in their former glory.

I shake my head as the throbbing in my skull increases, a pressure threatening to erupt. The memory continues to unfold, and I close my eyes, envisioning the scene with a newfound clarity.

Essentria sits by the fire, her long fingers, covered with rings forged from plants and vines. Her thick, dark curls are decorated with poisonous purple and yellow flowers, her plump, peach lips pulled into a hard line as she watches us from the sidelines.

NIGHT OF DEATH AND FLOWERS

The scenes cascade into one another, like an ocean of waves, painting the story in a montage: How Calista and Arabella were Essentria's favorites. We could not have children of our own, but when my sister laid her eyes upon the two sisters, her pupils dilated, and I noticed the motherly care laced in her irises, woven in every softening expression as she taught the pair how to enhance their magic. Both, healers, gifted with her ethereal magic: Creation.

Only my sister wasn't the only one enamored with Calista.

She was so filled with vigor that watching her live, dance, and laugh reminded me of how beautiful being in the mortal world could be. I couldn't help but live vicariously through her. I never imagined she would feel the same toward me. But the connection was undeniable.

It was torture being unable to touch her, and everything in her was so filled with life. I couldn't help myself. When I was with her, I finally found what I imagined home to feel like.

I should have left her then so as not to give in to my own selfish desires and create her in my image, but I couldn't resist. I needed her. Without her, I could not breathe.

It was Astraea who helped me harness a spell to link Calista to me, gifting her my ethereal magic alongside Essentria's. Binding us. Except my decay magic took over.

It didn't matter then, that she wanted it too, so we could be together. I was at fault because she could have known what it would do to her.

I splutter for air as I recall the decay magic heightening with each passing day, how the decay magic leaked into every crevice of Calista's soul.

I did not understand why it affected her so badly, but our powers tore her apart until she turned mad, and Tenenocti Island was decimated with shadows and decay.

We tried to contain her, dragging her and Arabella into the temple. But her sister got too close and when she stabbed her with a dagger, that was when I knew the essence of her was gone.

Goosebumps cover my skin as my deepest memory surfaces, and I am panting, unable to breathe. I stand in the temple, the recipient of Essentria's bitter scowl as she hovers over Calista on an altar, crying as Arabella lays next to her, dead.

Essentria's venomous glare latches onto mine. "This is your doing, Azkiel."

My sister carves her fingers into Calista's ribcage, crunching her bones into dust, and before I can scream for her to stop, my love's heart is in her hands.

I rush to her side, holding Calista's lifeless fingers in mine. Tears fall thick and fast. I hold my beloved's body, and I am alone, falling into an abyss of darkness.

I open my eyes, struggling to catch my breath. I stare at my hands, my nails biting into my palms.

Once Cyna imparted his final judgment, damning Calista's soul to the darkest reaches of the Darklands, to be torn apart, I knew I had to stop him. He would have me punished by destroying her. My brother would have had Calista obliterated from existence. I couldn't let that happen.

Using Calista's and Arabella's hearts, I did something I never thought I would—completing a sacrificial ritual. Their deaths bound the magic to spell my siblings into a permanent slumber that could never be undone by anyone but them.

A shudder dances into my bones. They need me. Cali needs me. I need to wake up.

I open my eyes, hot tears streaming down my cheeks as Astraea stares at me.

"Calista," I splutter and clutch my chest. "I wanted to protect her soul from Cyna."

The prophecy recites in my mind, as it has for over a century, except now I listen with newfound clarity.

A daughter of creation, doomed with death.

Of course. It was both of them.

Two witches on opposite sides of the same coin—one light, and one dark. Both with the power to awaken the gods.

"You trapped me here, when I did nothing to you," Astraea says, and I refocus back on my sister. "You chose the mortal over me, your *sister*."

"Yes," I confess.

"I always chose you!"

"I know," I say, tears sliding down my cheeks as it all settles back uncomfortably in my heart.

"Soon I will awaken."

I shake my head. "I can't allow that. I'm sorry. But I must protect Calista. She remembers nothing from her past life."

Astraea nods. "You should be glad about that. If she did, she'd likely hate you. Yet, I see she is still a murderer. The essence of your magic is still attached to her soul. You must let her go, Azkiel. For all our sakes." She pauses, her eyes widening. "We created this world, and the mortals worship us. What of those who worship you, who trust you? Will you damn everyone for one girl?"

The answer comes all too easily. "Yes."

"Then we continue to find ourselves on opposite sides of this war."

Astraea fades into a pit of darkness. She pulls on my magic, weakening me as I am forced out of my dream. My eyes fling open, and I turn onto my side, my heart pounding against my ribcage, each beat a desperate ache as adrenaline courses through my body.

Staring down at me through tear-stricken, bloodshot eyes, I find Calista standing over me.

"You wouldn't wake up," she rasps, her voice shaking.

Words evade me as I take in her beauty, her essence. Every micro movement in her wavering frown is a memory of when we had spent a life together. "What's wrong?" I ask, sitting up.

"Ari's gone. She spiked us with Nocturnum Somnus."

Fuck.

"Why aren't you saying anything?" she asks, eyes bulging.

"She's gone to the temple," I say, realizing the dream was a distraction, so Astraea could hold me in my sleep while the sister escaped. "She will be dead any moment now. They're coming for you. I must get you out of here."

She pulls her hands from mine, then paces to the other side of the forest clearing. "I'm not leaving without her."

"I won't let you go," I warn and rise to my feet, standing in front of her. The odds were always against us. Gods were never supposed to fall in love with mortals. The endings were catastrophic. Even now, as I see the darkness steadily creeping into her fingertips, with my magic consuming every inch of her, I still can't stop myself.

"Please," she croaks. "You have to help her."

"It's too late. I am sorry," I whisper, running a knuckle over her cheek. "I will keep you safe."

In the chasms of despair, she is all I have.

Calista pulls back, her eyes locked on me, then plunges her hands at my chest. Betrayal slices into me deeper than ever before when I look down, realizing she'd stabbed me with a dagger. With every beat, blood rushes the potent poison on the blade into my veins, slowly paralyzing me.

She stumbles back, leaving the dagger in my chest. I grip my fingers around the onyx hilt, then drop to my knees.

"Cali…"

FORTY

Calista

The wind whips against my face as I run, pinching my cheeks in an icy embrace. My hair is a knot as my strands are pulled back in a flurry of cold gusts. I'm barely halfway to the temple when I run through the same clearing we'd been attacked on our first night.

Pieces of Edwardo's corpse in the late stages of decay cover the ground. I slap my hand over my mouth and nose, the scent overpowering.

"I've been looking for you." A man's voice echoes from behind a tree, and I white-knuckle the dagger, then spin to face Alaric, just making out his brown eyes and tousled, dark hair. "Where's your sister?" he asks.

"I don't want to fight you." I clench the hilt of my weapon. "I *will*, but you should know I'm not a participant in The Harvest."

His eyes narrow, his cheeks smeared with dirt, blood caking his week-old, brown tunic, with no sign of the crimson robes. "Yet you took *my* kill!"

Decay magic quakes in my bones as he takes a step closer. I shift my position, lifting my dagger in warning. This can't be happening. He must be talking about Eleanore, which means he was watching us.

I shake my head as a sense of dread crawls over my skin. "Where's Dephina?" I decipher.

"How do you know she's here?"

I swallow hard, a fever sweeping over my forehead. "What did she tell you?"

He hesitates, then shrugs. "She sent me to stop you. If I take you out, I'll win."

I shake my head. "She's lying."

"I'll take my chances," he spits. Dephina must have sent him to slow me down. She knows I'll kill him. Who the fuck else have the elders been manipulating?

"Where are the other competitors?" I ask.

"I killed Cain and Marsilia," he exclaims. "Her magic showed me where you'd be tonight. Now, enough talking."

Adrenaline surges through my veins as I wrench my arm back and hurl the dagger towards his silhouette in the darkness. It slices through the air, the blade slicing into a tree trunk as he narrowly dodges it.

With lightning-fast speed, he moves through the air, landing on top of me before my brain can process how fast he fucking moved. I reach for his throat with charred fingers, but he laughs, eyes alight with the darkness of Volan's incredible strength and speed. His movements are a blur as he slams my wrist against the ground, evading my touch before I can lay a hand on him.

The forest echoes with my grunts as he thuds his fists into my ribs. I twist my torso, his fist connecting with my chest this time, a searing pain ringing through my ears.

I splutter a cough as the world spins for a moment. I lift my throbbing hand, releasing my shadows like a nest of vipers.

Our eyes lock in silent challenge. I need to get to Arabella!

I wipe the blood trickling from my lip, a primal urge to kill numbing the pain until I'm standing.

Energy surges into my fingers with a torrent of force, and I watch as my shadows knot and curl around him. Combining and harnessing the magic inside of me is easier than I thought, despite Azkiel depleting me last night.

"Die, you fucking asshole," I shout, each breath rattling my aching ribs, knowing he could have cost me my sister's life.

He spits blood as a shadow tightens around his throat, his eyes bulging scarlet. A sinister smile creeps over my mouth, knowing he's completely under my control. My darkness ensnares him, and several ribbons of shadows twist around his limbs until he's on his knees, wrestling against them. But I am far fucking stronger than he is.

My chest purrs as I embrace the magic I'd pushed away for so long. I run to him, landing my hand on his chest.

The sudden scream pierces the peaceful atmosphere, causing birds to scatter from the branches overhead.

His body disintegrates under my touch, his shape crumbling into a wispy cloud of ash. The wind whispers through the air, sweeping away any trace of his existence. The stillness in the air is palpable, occasionally disrupted by the faint sound of leaves rustling and the steady rhythm of my heartbeat.

I swallow hard, holding my ribs. My feet hit the damp soil as I race over the uneven ground, cutting through vines, and finding my way through the maze of trees. Each breath rattles my lungs as pain sears into my abdomen and chest, but I don't stop. I can't. Not even for a second. I keep running, despite my body screaming at me to stop.

I let out a shaky exhale when I reach the bridge, and the moonlight offers a reprieve from the denseness of the forest. I race harder, and rain pelts the island, seeping through my cloak and dress. Finally, the temple comes into view, under the overgrowth and poisonous plants of the island.

Please don't be dead.

Lit torches line the entrance, flickering light onto broken effigies and tall pillars. They're here.

A sense of doom follows me as I navigate the temple toward the sacrificial room.

I should have known when she wanted to stop for water and had pocketed the poisonous plant. This had been her plan all along, to lure us away from the temple. She knew I would never go unless I believed she was safe.

The slice of treachery cuts through me.

Echoes of voices sound from the sacrificial chamber, and I run inside, then stop when I see Arabella across the room. Her eyes meet mine, and I look from her, to Everist, then Dephina, and finally, Drake...

He stands next to the elders, his chest heaving when our eyes clash, and I realize how deep the betrayal runs.

Memories float back to me—how Drake never asked many questions about the gods, Ari's potential sacrifice, or prophecy, and how he kept insisting we leave the temple. His hatred for Death ran far deeper than I knew, enough that he'd betray me. His hushed conversations with Ari when they were alone.

"Drake?" I splutter. "Don't do this."

I stop walking when I see their weapons so close to my sister. Cautiously, I evaluate the dagger curled in Dephina's ring fingers. Everist's hand rests on Ari's shoulder, and bile rises in my throat when I notice she's adorned in new, crimson robes, ones meant for a sacrifice.

"You left me no choice!" Drake answers, his voice far colder than I thought possible. "I warned you of Azkiel, yet you took his side. This is the only way to stop him."

"No, it's not! You can't kill her."

"She'll be resurrected!"

"She won't!"

He turns his head, his bloodshot eyes pinning me. "Look at you, Cali. Death has you so tight in his grasp."

I glance down at my charred fingertips, a constant now the decay magic has a firm hold on my soul. "Azkiel was right. You *are* a fucking traitor," I spit. "They won't bring her back."

"Because Death said so? I trust the gods over the words of that monster."

Dephina shushes him, and Drake falls silent. I turn my focus to Dephina and Everist, their hands on my sister. I take a step closer, and Dephina raises the dagger just an inch.

Ari doesn't notice the slight act of aggression, and I quickly step back into place, next to a tall, ivory pillar. "The gods cannot be awakened," I state. "They are evil."

"No, Azkiel is the evil one," Dephina exclaims, and moves her hands so the dagger is pointed downward, over her stomach. I'm just grateful it's a little further away from Ari, who is shaking despite her attempt to appear brave.

She thinks Essentria will bring her back.

"You've brought a great imbalance to our fragile society," Everest spits.

"I did nothing," I argue, but Dephina interrupts me, her lofty tone echoing in the chamber.

"If you had just allowed your sister to come here, when Azkiel picked her, instead of trying to stop her destiny, then you wouldn't have to see this. So many people wouldn't have had to die."

They knew about this from the beginning. Nausea grips me as I stare at them.

I step forward as they walk her toward the altar. "Don't hurt her. She doesn't want to die. Right, Ari? Tell them you don't want to die!"

They halt. Her rosy lips part, and a raspy breath passes through them. "Essentria will bring me back."

"You can't trust the gods."

"They told me everything," she says, her eyes pinched with fresh tears. "I returned to complete the prophecy. Azkiel has destroyed the balance of our world. This is the only way to stop The Harvest, to restore balance, and to save you from Cyna. We made a deal."

"He does not intend to keep it!"

"Please don't shout," she begs, and I see a flash of the little girl I'd spent my life protecting, in the tremble of her lower lip, and the innocence in her eyes.

Shadows from the flames of the torches flicker against the sides of their faces, highlighting Ari's red, raw cheeks. She'd already been crying.

Her voice breaks when she whispers, "You killed me, in our past life. We were like daughters to Essentria. She loved us, and Death corrupted you."

My eyes bulge, jaw slacking as the information sinks into my mind. "What? That's not true."

"It's why you have his power, Cali," she says as she stands beside the altar. "He loved you and he gifted you his most ethereal magic, then it destroyed you."

I can't stand her looking at me like that, as if I'm the dangerous one—a threat—while the real villains stand beside her, daggers drawn. "No. They're just saying all of this to us just to get you to sacrifice yourself."

Drake clears his throat. "It's true. The gods spoke to us in our dreams."

Tears slide down my cheeks. "Don't you talk to me! I trusted you," I shout at Drake. "We have known each other our whole lives."

"I'm doing this for you!" he growls back. "Essentria will bring Ari back. I wouldn't have helped if I didn't believe it."

I turn my stony stare to him. "I hate you," I hiss and his nostrils flare, his brow twitching.

Ari turns to look at me before climbing the stone steps to the marble slab. "This is my choice," she says.

"Don't do this. I beg you, please."

"You can't stop me."

My shadows snake from my body as I race forward, desperate as they lay Ari to her death. I'll kill them all if I have to.

Before I can take six steps, a barrier of shadows forms an invisible barrier. Shockwaves force me against the pillar, echoes of pain traveling down my legs and arms. A haze of blue mist hits me next, waltzing into my nose, lulling my mind into a false sense of calm.

Everist and Dephina unleash their powers, and I wrestle their darkness as shadows bind me to a pillar. "Stop!" I scream. "Ari fucking listen! They cut out the hearts of sacrifices in this ritual. You can't be resurrected without a heart. Even you know that. Once the body is destroyed, too far gone, it's—"

"They will not cut out my heart. They will…" she glances at Dephina, then at the dagger, as if it's the first time she's thought about how she will die. "They will cut my throat."

A shiver shudders through my bones, slinking down my back and spreading goosebumps along my arms. "Don't be naive!"

I twist my body against their magic, the haze of calm stealing my strength piece by piece.

NIGHT OF DEATH AND FLOWERS

The altar is blurry through my tears, but I can still make out the stone slab adorned with beautiful flowers, just like my vision of the sacrifices who were once killed here. There is a basket waiting for a heart.

They adorn her body with petals, then mumble some words over her body. The silk of her robes cascade down the sides of the altar as she shifts position. When she refuses to turn her head to look at me, I look at Drake. "They're going to take her heart. Drake. Help her!" I beg as hopelessness claws into me.

I slam my fists against their magic, pins and needles shocking through my fingers with each hit against the pillar, going right through the black smoke. This must have been what Alaric felt. Oh, the fucking irony.

Dephina glides the dagger to Ari's throat, then hovers the pointed blade lower, stopping over her chest.

I must save her. It can't end like this. A newfound strength rushes through my body, and I remember when I tamed his shadows, but these are unlike his—they don't answer to me.

I can still save her.

Ari's voice reaches me from the table. "I'll come back. They promised. I know you don't understand it now, but I am atoning for both our sins. I'll make everything right…"

Her words are lost to my screams as the dagger is plunged into her chest. Confusion sweeps her features as she looks at Dephina, her lips parting as her brows crease for the last time.

"NO!"

Rage courses through me as I hammer against the shadows, every anguished scream lost to the adrenaline in my veins. Time stretches for an eternity, the world falling into slow motion as I watch blood spatters over them like a painting.

I blink, suddenly aware of my soul as I look through the eyes of my body, feeling detached from it. Nothing feels real. My lips part, and I'm not breathing.

This isn't happening. It must be a nightmare. I need to wake up.

Dephina carves Arabella's chest, the blade grinding against bone. They're working on her as if she is some animal brought in for slaughter.

Ari's fingers twitch over the side of the altar, and I'm aware of every tiny movement. It's too late.

I don't move, staying motionless, my mouth open.

Her name is faint in my mind, swallowed by another—dead.

My sister is dead. Everything goes silent for a soul-shattering moment.

Ari. My baby sister. No.

NIGHT OF DEATH AND FLOWERS

A blood-curdling scream leaves my mouth, the permanence of what they just did rolling into my mind. I'm so cold.

I clamp my eyes shut as if I may hold on to some semblance of the past before she was dead.

I lower my head as a howl erupts from the pits of my stomach, each breath held as I wail, unable to speak, to think.

She's gone.

I choke on another, visceral, soul-crushing wail as the pressure of the grief crumbles everything inside of me. Desperation has me reaching out for something tangible to break, to shatter in my fingers. I don't want to believe it, and when I look up through blurred eyes, I am forced to watch as they drop her red, still beating heart into the basket.

Bile rises in my throat, burning my tongue. Nausea bubbles in my stomach, sweat dripping from my forehead. Regret etches on Drake's face, and I can't wait to fucking kill him for this.

"Put it back," I shout hoarsely, my voice not sounding like my own. "Her heart! She needs her heart."

Insanity fingers my mind as Dephina places the heart on a separate, smaller altar, squeezing the chambers until blood coats the ancient stone. Dizziness consumes me as I watch her slather my sister's heart, so roughly, as if it is nothing.

Hot anger envelopes my grief when I climb my gaze to my sister's blood-drenched, heartless body.

The gods. They lied to her. Essentria lied to my sister. They never intended to bring her back. They *can't*.

I barely notice Drake apologizing as I struggle to stay upright, under the weight of a pain that cannot be alleviated, but the elder's shadows hold me in place.

I watch as Dephina squeezes her fingernails callously into Ari's heart. Swirls of gold, blue, purple, green, and red rise from the altar in illusory swirls of smoke, cloaking the heart and blood. As it slowly fades, the ground erupts with a thunderous boom. My legs slide against the marble as a loud crack penetrates my ears.

When the smoke subsides, the heart and blood are gone. Consumed by the god's magic.

"The ritual is complete," Dephina states to no one in particular. "The gods are awakening."

I glare at them, the pain is so deep that a part of me wants nothing more than to die, so I won't have to feel it. But I won't. I will sharpen my grief into a weapon against them. Including the gods. *Especially them.*

FORTY-ONE

Azkiel

Memories shatter into me with every step, the pain from the dagger still lingering by the time I reach the temple.

Trepidation threads in each step as I watch the remnants of silver magic shred into ribbons, falling around Tenenocti in a dome. My domain is gone, and my siblings are awake.

I have to get Calista out of here before they find her.

Her heartache echoes with each sob sounding from within the temple, and my eyes close for a moment.

Fuck!

I walk to the entrance and then pause mid-step when a familiar tingle waltzes down my spine. I grimace upon sensing Essentria's magic—a vibrancy, filled with life, suffocating me.

"Miss me, Az?" Her deadly, lullaby of a voice reaches me.

My jaw clenches as I turn to face my sister, standing in an ombre of brown and gold. Shimmering dust covers her arms and shoulders, the rest of her body wrapped in a dress forged from vines and dead leaves.

I push my tongue against the inside of my cheek, then laugh sardonically. "You look rested, Sister. Good sleep?"

She nods rapidly, pulling her bottom lip between her teeth. "I hear Astraea helped return your memories. Now that the prophecy is fulfilled, you can live with every painful detail." Her eyes are alight with revenge, fingers wiggling at her side as gold magic swirls around her hands. "But do you want to know a secret?"

I block the temple's entrance, ready to die if it means stopping the bitch from going inside, to Calista. "What is it?"

She waves a hand in the air casually, noting my stance. "Don't worry. I have no desire to go inside and take the girl. See, while the rest of our family is awakening in the cavern, I wanted to come and find you before they could." She steps forward, the thorn of berries and flowers around her tight, dark curls withering. My eyes narrow when I realize she's not at full power yet. None of them will be.

"Why come see me?" I ask, tilting my head. "I hope you're not here to admonish me, because I regret nothing."

"I know, Az." Her nostrils flare. "You stole her from me," she says. "The girls were mine."

Fists ball at my side. "Now one of them is dead because you lied. Arabella believed you'd resurrect her."

Her lip trembles, the movement so fleeting, but I caught it. "I had no choice. She will rejoin this world, eventually."

"Yes, but she won't remember a damn thing!" I retort. "Calista has lost her sister. You wish to punish me, yet you only hurt *them*."

"No! I hurt you *through* them," she hisses, growing closer. "It was never your magic that drove Calista mad," she says, her eyes sparkling, while my stomach knots. "You know there is no removing an ethereal magic once gifted. Why do you think she can still touch others when you cannot? Because my power still lives within her." The muscles below her brow twitch, insanity lacing every word. "She had *everything*, yet she chose you and you tainted her with your decay and rot."

"I loved her!"

"I did, too," she shouts, and arrows of gold and green shoot from her fingers. Vines rise around us, quaking the ground until they stop, forming a wall of knotted overgrowth encasing us. She rolls her shoulders, commanding her magic to settle when she looks at me, desperate to hide her rage. After a tense breath, she whispers, "It does not matter now. We are awake and will take our revenge. While they think you are the villain," she says, her laugh tinkering in my mind, and I grimace. "We will know the truth, and they'll never believe you over me, their loyal sister."

"What the fuck are you talking about?" A growl rumbles in my chest. "They know what happened."

"Fool! It was me," she divulges, then smiles sweetly as if she's not evil fucking incarnate. "A bloom of my magic still resided in her, and I used it to heighten yours, driving her to madness." Her whispers become breathy, uneven, her pupils growing so tiny. "Sending you to the Darklands was not punishment enough. I knew you were watching her slowly turn as dark as you would destroy you, and it did."

My breaths deepen, my muscles tensing until the fabric of my tunic strains. "You did that to her? When you supposedly cared for her? Loved her?"

"She picked you!"

"Love does not simply evaporate after one wrongdoing, you selfish bitch."

She walks back, her long lashes flickering as her eyes twitch. "You know nothing of my heart, but I know yours. That is why I asked Nyxara to take your memories. Our dear sister thought it was for our benefit, to aid the prophecy, but I needed you to forget so you wouldn't find her again in her next life. If I couldn't have her, then neither would you."

"You tore out her heart!" I shout.

"Yes, and now you know," she whispers, "to never take what is mine again."

I shake my head. "It was *you* who did it again. Her powers only started acting up when she was on Tenenocti."

"Hmm." She smiles. "She was close, finally. I could taste my magic in her from where I slept. Then the elders came, so easy to manipulate. And that boy, the new Harvest winner."

"Drake," I hiss.

"Yes. We accessed their dreams. After you returned and we took back our powers, it was easy." Her gold eyes narrow. "Go to her. We'll all be coming for you shortly."

"I'll tell them," I shout. "Astraea will believe me."

She scoffs a laugh, disbelief etching her features. "Now, Brother, you can't really believe that. You trapped them for a century and a half. If you see them, you won't breathe long enough to tell them. Even if you could convince them, they'd still despise you."

She dangles the truth over me, like a cat playing with her food, taunting me with every word. If it wasn't for Calista so close, and my need to get her off this island, I'd bury Essentria.

She turns her back to me, then glances over her shoulder. "Go to her, Azkiel. Good luck trying to save her. Our magic will devour Calista soon enough. You can never absorb my power from her, or all of yours. It is just a matter of time, and you will watch her slowly fade away from grief and darkness, knowing that her soul will be obliterated by Cyna the moment she falls into death. You can't protect her anymore."

"I will kill all of you," I promise, and she grins.

"Oh, I count on you trying."

With that, she flees back into the forest. The primal need to chase her down, cut her to pieces, and tear her soul apart is almost unbearable. But Calista is more important. If Essentria is right, then she'd die soon, or destroy everything.

I race into the temple, whisking past the pillars. I find Calista, on the ground, crumpled in a ball under her navy cloak. My gaze drifts to the altar, cracked down in the middle.

I race to her side, then drop to my knees. "I'm here." I lift her head in my hands, cradling her as she gazes up at me, her expression so filled with heartache that it tears me apart.

"Ari," she croaks, tears falling into her hair. "She's gone."

"I know, but we must get out of here." I swallow hard, thinking of Essentria running toward the caverns now. My siblings will come here soon to find us, and I plan to be as far away from this damn island before they can. "I need to keep you safe," I whisper, my body over hers as I hold her head in my hands, staring into her bloodshot eyes.

"Drake betrayed me." Tears slide from the corners as she gulps. "He helped them kill her. I killed Alaric, which means—"

"I know." A muscle feathers in my jaw as I add the traitor to my list of people to kill. "He's the next elder."

"I'm going to kill him."

I nod slowly. "We will, but first, we must escape before the other gods come."

"I—is it possible? To bring Ari back?" she asks, although she must know it's not possible. A flicker of hope lights in her eyes, but quickly fades when I confirm her suspicions.

"No. I saw Essentria."

She grits her teeth, and a glint of that darkness flashes over her sharp features. "What happened?"

I shake my head, anger clouding every thought. "I'll explain everything once we're away from here."

"What about Ari's soul?" She sits upright, and I roll back onto my knees. "You're the God of Death," she cries, her lips trembling with a mixture of anger and hurt. "Can't you find her?"

"My domain's destroyed. She would have likely crossed the veil already," I admit, lifting her chin as she looks at the ground. "Come on. We must move."

Slowly, she gets to her feet, then stares at me with a newfound bloodlust that roots me to my spot. Her stare darkens as the ground trembles, and she glances at the temple door. "Let them come. I'll die happy knowing I took at least one of them with me."

My heart palpitates as she talks of her death so casually. I lift her in my arms, and she wrestles against me, pounding her fists against my muscle but I only tighten my hold. I'm getting her away from here, willingly or not.

NIGHT OF DEATH AND FLOWERS

As soon as we're outside, the sky flashes with purple lightning as rain hammers around us. The entire island buzzes with magic as a roar trembles the ground, the monsters awakening from the caves. Across the forest, my siblings' powers grow in strength and the last tatters of my domain fall around us.

GLOSSARY

The Gods & Goddesses

Nyxara–The Goddess of Destiny (Knee-are-ah)
Powers: Foretelling, aura reading, and time hopping.
Ethereal power: Fate Weaving and Memory Manipulation.
An ethereal power is a power only the god or goddess can possess.
Nyxara creates the fate of those who will be born into the mortal world, giving them various paths that they can follow depending on their decisions.

Essentria–The Goddess of Creation *(Ess-en-tree-ah)*
Powers: Healing touch, nature enhancement and manipulation, and elemental magic.
Ethereal power: Creation
After fate is woven, Essentria gives physical form to the person's soul, bringing them to life within the mortal world.

Astraea–The Goddess of Dreams *(Ass-tray-ah)*
Powers: Memory and dream alteration, illusion casting, and animation.

Ethereal power: Dream Creation

During their mortal lives, Astraea gives the subconscious mind, a place where mortals can hide their fears and darker base urges, then slowly discover them throughout life, learning lessons in guidance with their fate.

Volan–The God of Will *(Vol-an)*

Powers: Extreme physical and mental strength, mental resistance, and mind persuasion.

Ethereal power: Manifestation

During their mortal lives, Volan gives the conscious mind and the ability to develop mental fortitude so the mortals can fight and survive the lessons they need to learn.

Cyna–The God of Judgment *(Sin-ah)*

Powers: Vision touch, guilt induction, truth detection.

Ethereal power: Final Judgment

Upon the moments before their death, Cyna discerns the truth of a person's soul and heart, evaluating their life and the decisions they made to choose where they will go in the afterlife, the Darklands or the Everlands (ascension).

Azkiel–The God of Death *(az-keel)*

Powers: Fear induction, light absorption, shadow manipulation

<u>Ethereal power:</u> Death's touch *(also known as decay magic)* and animal scrying.

After judgment, Azkiel takes their lives, departing the souls from the mortal world through the veil into the ether and accompanying them to their final destination.

Covens

There are **six covens**, each worshiping one of the six gods and goddesses.

Each coven was blessed by each god and goddess with diluted forms of their powers, that a witch or warlock may inherit and practice.

Every coven has up to three powers that can be siphoned from the god or goddess of their coven, except for that god's most ethereal power. Some witches and warlocks can inherit two powers, although most can only handle and practice one power.

Azkiel's Coven
Ruled by the God of Death
Possible inherited powers:
Fear induction **(rare)**

Light absorption

Shadow manipulation

Essentria's Coven

Ruled by the Goddess of Creation

Possible inherited powers:
Healing touch

Nature enhancement and manipulation

Elemental magic **(rare)**

Volan's Coven

Ruled by the God of Will

Possible inherited powers:
Extreme physical strength and speed

Mental resistance **(rare)** *(resistance against some other powers like weavers)*

Mind persuasion (compulsion).

Nyxara's Coven

Ruled by the Goddess of Destiny

Possible inherited powers:
Foretelling *(also called threaders)*

Aura reading

Time hopping **(rare)** *(also called time mages)*

Cyna's Coven

Ruled by the God of Judgment

Possible inherited powers:
Vision touch **(rare)** *(also called sight seekers)*

Guilt induction

Truth detection *(also called discerners)*

Astraea's Coven

Ruled by the Goddess of Dreams

Possible inherited powers:
Memory and dream alteration *(also called weavers)*

Illusion casting

Blood animation **(rare)**

Places

Dahryst

Dahryst is a continent governed by a theocratic government, known as the elder coven.

Dahryst is surrounded by the Black Sea on the east of the mainland, and the Pistoren Ocean on the west.

Tenenocti Island

Tenenocti Island is a thirty-three-acre island set half a mile off the northern east coast of Dahryst. Tenenocti is an island within

Death's domain, and the original town and temples were built on sacred ground.

Various tragedies have happened there, and the island is entrenched with a long, bloody history. In the present day, Tenenocti is out of bounds to the general population but is used for The Harvest tournament, as the sacred ground allows the sacrifices sent there to siphon the powers of the fallen.

Ennismore

Ennismore is a small, coastal town in Dahryst, set within the heart of Morcidea Forest which surrounds the town.

The town is one of the smallest in Dahryst by population but is a popular destination for The Harvest as it is situated the closest to the shore overlooking Tenenocti Island. The sacrifices are sent from Ennismore and The Choosing takes place in Ennismore every decade.

Morcidea Forest

Morcidea Forest is a large forest surrounding Ennismore, the Black Sea Coast, and other small villages and towns. It is home to the venomous shadow vipers, and there are occasional Phovi sightings.

The Ether:

The afterlife, a void outside of the Everlands and Darklands.

The Darklands:

A realm of darkness, filled with barren wastelands and Phovi, who use fear induction for punishment. The Darklands is ruled by the God of Death and is reserved for the darkest of souls. Souls remain in the Darklands, imprisoned by their own minds until they are ready to be reincarnated to the physical world by the Goddess of Destiny and Creation to fulfill their destiny with the opportunity to take a different path.

The Darklands has different layers depending on how damaged the soul is. The deepest layers are reserved for the evilest of people, commended there by the God of Judgment. The bottom layer, also known as the abyss, is inescapable.

The Everlands

A realm of peace in the afterlife, where the gods reside when they are in their ethereal forms. Each god has a domain in the Everlands, while Death is the only one with a domain in the physical world. This is where souls ascend once they are at their highest vibration.

Incarcuris

Institutes where suspected criminals are taken for interrogation. Also used as an insane asylum.

Creatures

Phovus–Phovi (plural)

Shifters with dark masses for bodies that appear like smoke. They can change shape and have large bat-like wings. They have yellow eyes and are nocturnal. Phovi were once witches and warlocks whose souls became so fractured that there's barely a hint of the person they once were. They are loyal servants to the God of Death and were created using Essentria's magic via Azkiel.

Shadow Vipers

Venomous snakes created by death. They can grow up to ten feet long, and have red eyes, with red and black markings on their bodies. Their venom causes paralysis to their victims.

Nightbor Spiders:

Venomous, black spiders with long legs and large bodies. They feast upon small animals and move in groups of up to thirty. They are infamous for having intricate, beautiful patterns in their webs. These creatures are native to the cold regions of Dahryst. Their venom is usually not fatal to humans, but can cause death with multiple bites.

Blackbeak Crows:

Ebony crows who are under Death's command. They have iridescent feathers and can mimic languages.

Reapers:

Cloaked, skeletal beings created by the God of Death, who guide souls departing the mortal world to their final destination in the afterlife.

Gurgers:

Gurgers are only mentioned in book one and are not shown until later in the series.

Sea monsters, with ten long tentacles with hundreds of sets of teeth. It's known for destroying ships and drowning the sailors on board. They are native to the Pistoren Ocean.

Botanicals

Nightmor. (Mortonix)

These orange berries are used in rituals to summon the dead. They can be deadly when ingested in large amounts.

Death's Bells *(Contributor—Megan Long, Superbacker)*

Death's Bells is a flowering plant with small flower heads in the shape of bells, in dark shades of purple, permeating a musky scent.

These grow in colder climates and can be found in the forests in the north and midland areas of Dahryst. The flower heads have healing properties when crushed and mixed with specific root plants.

Night Evedelain *(Contributor—Amanda Eschmeyer, Superbacker)*

Gothic looking plant with black roses. The flower can induce insanity when properly crushed. Layers of red petals, slowly turning black the closer they get to the center.

Cimicifuga Serrulata

It has small, blunt tipped leaves, which are usually dark orange. It also grows small flowers, which can be yellow and light blue. Produces an orange extract that can be drunk. *(Contributor—Bradley Bolt, Superbacker)*

Night Blossom

The plant grows like a vine and the vines themselves are black, but the leaves are green. The flower looks similar to a Lily, but it's dark purple, with silver-colored veins through the petals, and the stems are silver as well. While not rare, they are uncommon and can grow in almost any environment, excluding environments of extreme heat or cold, and they bloom only on the night of full moons. The nectar of the flower is a strong magical ingredient, while the flower itself is poisonous if ingested. *(Contributor - Amanda E. Hughes)*

Tempest Root - (Radix Tempest)

Truth serum lowers inhibitions to suggestions. Harvested by shaving the root.

Nocturnum Somnus

The odorless and tasteless flower of the plant is primarily used in tinctures for sleep aids, but when the root is ingested, it will place the user in an eternal comatose state.

Lumonice Lux

A plant used as a stimulant in some species but is extremely rare and found only on Tenenocti.

Sanare Medicis

Grows in the peat rich land surrounding the dark river in Morcidea Forest. The root and stem are ground and used as a potent healing paste.

Currency

Libren. Gold, heavy coin.
Guildre. Silver, heavy, large coin. (Five guildre to a libren).
Knog. Bronze, small coin. (Ten knogs to a guildre).

Rituals, Tournaments, and Celebrations

There are three stages for The Harvest. The first is the offering, where volunteers are to use blood magic to place their names and their offerings into a pool, which will be chosen from during the Choosing. The Choosing is a ceremony where either the God of Death, or his magic by proxy, is used to pick the name of the twelve witches who will enter The Harvest. Once chosen, the Harvest will commence three days after The Choosing, and the twelve chosen ones, henceforth called 'the sacrifices', will be sent to Tenenocti to fight to the death on the sacred ground until only one remains.

The Offering

A blood ritual, where volunteers give their blood to Death's magic, either by using coins branded with the sigils of the volunteer's coven, the coat in their blood, or by spilling their blood into another anointed object such a sacred stone basin or other object where a god may touch the blood to then choose who is chosen during the Choosing.

The Choosing

A ceremony where the God of Death chooses the twelve sacrifices for The Harvest.

The Harvest

A tournament held once every decade where twelve young people are sent to fight to the death until only one remains. The tournament is held on sacred ground, in Death's domain, where the sacrifices will be able to siphon the other witch's powers upon killing them. The winner becomes the next elder to join the small elder cover to rule over Dahryst. Elders hold powers from all six covens through this sacrificial tournament, making them powerful enough to rule.

Solon

The hot months, lasting five months, when crops flourish, and the sun stays out until the early evening.

Olen

The cold months, usually lasting five months when crops seldom grow, the frost comes, and the sun sets in the early afternoon.

Evene

The two warm months transitioning between Olen and Solon. It is the most pleasant time of the year with excellent weather.

Other

Incarns

Those imprisoned in Incarcuris.

Weavers

Ability to alter dreams and memories of others. They are from Astraea's coven, the Goddess of Dreams.

Threaders:

Witches with powerful foresight from Nyxara's coven, the Goddess of Fate.

Sight Seekers:

Witches with the ability to touch a place and see the most recent memories attached to it, but only through strong, residual emotional energy. From Volan's coven.

Discerners:

Witches with the ability to discern a truth from a lie, from Cyna's coven.

ACKNOWLEDGMENTS

Without my amazing team, this book wouldn't be out in the world. I am so thankful to:

Everyone who backed the Kickstarter for making the deluxe edition possible!

A special thank you to: Amanda E. Hughes, Bradley Bolt, Amanda Eschmeyer, Hannah, Megan Long, Reece Laabs, Brandy Hartley, Jensa Fish, Suzanne Ledford, Kim Hillmer, Janette Olvera, Katherine Shipman, Franki Berliner, Susan, Madison Garan, Sabrina Lawrence, Daphne Melanson, Andy Huezo, Shanon M. Brown, Marea Quijano, Rebekah Morrow, Brooke Grigsby, Kourtney, Elise Crowley, Nela Beutel, Brittany Woodall, Ivelisse Colón, Jennifer Rose, Lady D, Penny Riley, Flavio & Cristal Juarez Lopez, Megan Zellman, Emilie Woog, Nikole C, Taylor Marie, Amelia Pluck, Cathy McLoughlin, Emilie Garneau, and Sarah L. Linser.

Daniel, for being a wonderful father and giving me the time to finish this book. It cannot be said enough how impossible all of this would be without you by my side. I love you.

V.M, thank you for taking the time to go over the doc, not only in its earlier drafts, but in the final stages when I spiraled into more rewrites. You helped polish this book into a diamond, and I am eternally grateful for the time you put in.

My developmental editor, Renee Polkinghorn, your suggestions on enhancing the world building inspired me. I enjoyed our late-night phone-calls and am grateful you're on Australian times and were awake during my night owl hours. I am so thankful for your expertise and friendship.

My super-agent, Angie Ojeda Hazen, for all your hard work and belief in me when I kept second guessing myself and fell into a bad case of imposter syndrome. Thank you for helping me navigate the trenches of publishing and for your friendship and the laughs!

My beta team, I am so lucky to have you in my corner. For your notes and encouragement, and for those of you who also went the extra mile when I was in a bind.
Thank you, Emma Hutton, Nicole Ramirez, Aimee W., Thea, Maheen, Jaclyn Glick, Erika Bailey, Ella Staffolani, Andreea, Mariana Trejo, Fionne G., Kat Avbelj, Julie-Ann Cheverton, Stephany R., Kristen DV, and Cheryl Koch.

Christine! You know why. I love you, fated bestie. Thank you for keeping my sanity intact and just for *everything*.

Court of Jamila, for taking just a simple idea and creating the most gorgeous cover I've ever seen. Thank you for your talent and care and patience when designing.

For the contributors from Patreon and Kickstarter, who named some of the plants and creatures to be featured in the books. Thank you to the curators who contributed to these special features in this world: Amanda E. Hughes—Night Blossom, Bradley Bolt—Cimicifuga Serrulata—Amanda Eschmeyer—Night Evedelain, Megan Long—Death's Bells, Suzanne Ledford—Nocturnum Somnus, Lumonice Lux, and Sanare Medicis, Melissa Fuentez—Tempest Root, and Jennifer Rose—Phovus (Phovi).

The artists who breathed life into the characters. You are all crazy talented and I am so humbled to see all your beautiful work. Thank you @ssnow_wi, @_artjake_, @gioviia, @hmmr.art, @marybegletsova, @podgorisheva_art, and @colouranomaly.

My two boys, for being my reasons to keep writing.

You, the reader. Whether this is your first book by me, or your tenth, thank you for taking a chance on Night of Death and Flowers.

ALSO BY THE AUTHOR

Shadow Kissed Series:
Paranormal Vampire Romance, complete series.
Shadow Kissed
Midnight Crown
Darkest Heart
Ruthless Royals

Corrupt Shadows Duet:
Dark Paranormal Romance Duet cowritten with CM Hutton
Corrupt Shadows
Broken Shadows (Coming Soon)

Standalones:
Spelled by Truth and Tresses
Dark Academia Rapunzel Retelling cowritten with CM Hutton

Heart of a Witch
Vengeful, dark fantasy standalone

Spellbound
Fantasy Romance standalone

FANTASY ROMANCE
REBECCA L. GARCIA

Rebecca writes dark fantasy romance, usually with gothic elements and always with morally gray characters. Originally from England, she lives in Texas with her husband, and two sons. She loves anything with enemies to lovers, slow burn, and lots of angst.

A book collector at heart, Rebecca loves creating something beautiful for her readers' shelves. You can find her special edition box sets and book boxes on Patreon, Kickstarter and her website.

As well as her special editions, all her standard hardback editions come with art under the dust jackets and beautiful formatting.

Find out more about Rebecca and check out her books here:

Website: www.rebeccagarciabooks.com

Patreon: www.patreon.com/rebeccagarciabooks

Instagram: www.instagram.com/rebeccalgarciabook

Printed in Great Britain
by Amazon